Heinz-Dietrich Fischer

Acclaimed Press Coverage of Latin American Countries

Pulitzer Prize Panorama

edited by

Prof. Dr. Heinz-Dietrich Fischer
(Bochum)

Volume 16

LIT

Heinz-Dietrich Fischer

Acclaimed Press Coverage of Latin American Countries

Pulitzer Prize Winning Articles, Cartoons and Photos

LIT

Gefördert durch Mittel der Pressestiftung RWV, Essen

The cartoon on the cover, drawn by Pulitzer Prize Winner Edmund S. Valtman and published on August 31, 1961, in the *Hartford Times* of Connecticut, shows Fidel Castro saying to a Brazilian farmer: "What You need, Man, is a Revolution like mine!"

This book is printed on acid-free paper.

Bibliographic information published by the Deutsche Nationalbibliothek
The Deutsche Nationalbibliothek lists this publication in the Deutsche Nationalbibliografie; detailed bibliographic data are available on the Internet at http://dnb.d-nb.de.

ISBN 978-3-643-90988-6 (pb)
ISBN 978-3-643-95988-1 (PDF)

A catalogue record for this book is available from the British Library

Klosbachstr. 107
CH-8032 Zürich
Tel. +41 (0) 44-251 75 05
E-Mail: zuerich@lit-verlag.ch http://www.lit-verlag.ch
Distribution:
In the UK: Global Book Marketing, e-mail: mo@centralbooks.com
In North America: International Specialized Book Services, e-mail: orders@isbs.com
In Germany: LIT Verlag Fresnostr. 2, D-48159 Münster
Tel. +49 (0) 2 51-620 32 22, Fax +49 (0) 2 51-922 60 99, e-mail: vertrieb@lit-verlag.de
e-books are available at www.litwebshop.de

Preface

While already in 1920 Justin H. Smith's history book „The War With Mexico" earned a Pulitzer Prize, followed in 1928 by Thornton Wilder's Peru-related novel „The Bridge of San Luis Rey", it took more than fifteen years before a Pulitzer journalism award dealing with Latin America was given: It was Arnaldo Cortesi of the *New York Times* who won the 1946 prize „for distinguished correspondence during the year 1945, as exemplified by his reports from Bueno Aires, Argentina."

In American journalism history it was James Gordon Bennett of the *Charleston Courier* who, in the words of John Hohenberg, „pioneered in the publication of Latin American news in the United States." But for about a century, American correspondents were rare in Latin American countries so that news from that area often came from other sources, partially translations from Spanish-language newspapers. So even the foreign news editor of the *New York Times*, Emanuel R. Freedman, in the early 1960s during a speech before journalism graduate students confessed: „We look ... hard for specialists in Latin America."

„Among the papers that maintained foreign specialists in the home office", Hohenberg states, „were the *Miami Herald* and *Miami News* in Florida, the *St. Louis Post-Dispatch* and others. It was one way to beat the cost of a permanent foreign service. Such pressures resulted in gains in Latin American coverage in the mid-60s. Fourteen new bureaus were established by U.S. media alone in Latin America, notably in Mexico City, Rio de Janeiro, and Buenos Aires. *Reuters* joined the other three global agencies in operating a special service to Latin America."

When the Cuba crisis changed the international political situation, that country and afterwards several others moved into the focus of the media. Several of them earned Pulitzer decorations for outstanding reporting from those regions. The book at hand assembles newspaper articles, photos and cartoons dealing with specific problems of Latin American countries. The materials are reprinted with reference to the „Doctrine of Fair Use" as embodied in the United States Copyright Act of 1976. According to that doctrine, excerpts of copyrighted works may be reprinted when their use does not encompass a substantial portion of these works.

I am deeply indebted to archivists and librarians in the United States and in Germany. The Pulitzer Prize-winning articles, photos and cartoons came from the Rare Books and Manuscript Library at Columbia University, New York, while the jury reports and other background materials could be used in the Pulitzer Prize Administration Office of Columbia University's Journalism Building. Specific research could be done at the Library of Congress, Washington, D.C., the New York Public Library at Fifth Avenue and the John F. Kennedy Library at the Free University of Berlin.

Ruhr University,
Bochum, Germany
January 27, 2018

Heinz-D. Fischer

Contents

This Volume is dedicated
to the Memory of

Alberto de Gainza Paz

(1899 - 1977)

He was an Argentine journalist and political activist who served as editor of the newspaper *La Prensa*. The paper was suspended for five days in 1944, after criticizing the government's health program. Gainza Paz and five other newspaper editors were arrested in 1945, charged with conspiring against the government.

In January 1951, the Perónist government forced the newspaper to suspend publication, and in March the Congress ordered the arrest of Gainza Paz, who was already in exile in Uruguay. He returned as chief of *La Prensa* in 1956, the year after Juan Perón was deposed.

In 1970 Alberto de Gainza Paz received the Golden Pen of Freedom Award for his constant fight for press freedom in Argentina.

1927: LINDBERGH'S GOOD WILL FLIGHT TO MEXICO

Nelson Harding, *Brooklyn Daily Eagle*

In 1926, U.S. President Calvin Coolidge's administration won passage of the Air Commerce Act, placing civil aviation under the direction of the commerce department, and approved the first two commercial air routes. By that time it was aviator Charles Lindbergh who trained long-distance flights in preparation for his intended trans-atlantic flight to Paris. He had private connections with Mexico, and after his flight to Paris in May 1927 he met in Washington the new American Ambassador to Mexico who en-couraged him to visit him at his post.

The first time that Lindbergh flew over Mexican territory was in September 1927 on his way to San Diego, when he literally violated mexican air space. In December, Lindbergh made his first formal visit to the neighbor country when he flew nonstop between Washington, D.C., and Mexico City. His main intention was to improve better relations between the United States and Mexico. It was editorial cartoonist Nelson Harding of the *Brooklyn Daily Eagle* who was impressed by Lindbergh's undertaking and drew several cartoons dealing with that theme. When his drawings came to the attention of the Pulitzer Prize jurors, they stated in their report of March 20, 1928, that „all of which are artistically excellent".So they placed his work on first rank of their list and Harding earned the award.

Nelson Harding, born on October 31, 1879, in New York City, was educated at Greenwich Academy in Connecticut. For his art training, he attended the Art Students' League in New York City, the Chase School, and the New York School of Art. Before he had a chance to get started in his profession, the Spanish-American War broke out. During that war, Harding did service with the U.S. Volunteers. Between 1898 and 1908 he was a member of the New York National Guard. In 1908 Harding joined the *Brooklyn Daily Eagle* and, during the next two decades that he worked on the paper, became one of the most reprinted cartoonists in the country. In addition to his drawing he wrote short humerous paragraphs under the heading „Here and Now," which were printed on the front page of the *Eagle*. In 1927 his work was granted great recognition, for in that year Nelson Harding won the Pulitzer Cartoon award. Only one year later, in 1928, did he receive another Pulitzer Prize in that category for the cartoon „May His Shadow Never Grow Less."

„HIS OWN DUST“

Nelson Harding, December 2, 1927

Cartoon mockingly accuses the „intervention jingos“ of establishing a fear of war between the U.S. and Mexico although they have produced the atrocities themselves. The U.S. was trying to improve their relation to the neighbor state, however, Mexico stayed sceptical.

„MAY HIS SHADOW NEVER GROW LESS“

Nelson Harding, December 15, 1927

Cartoon does not refer to the famous flight across the Atlantic by Charles A. Lindbergh, as one might think. Rather it refers to his flight to Mexico which was a gesture of goodwill, in order to improve the relations between Mexico and the United States of America.

„A NEW BOUNDARY MARK“

Nelson Harding, December 18, 1927

Cartoon refers to the Mexican government with President Plutarco E. Calles, under whom executions of unfavorable men were common. The christmas tree in the middle of the border demonstrates the American wish to stay on peaceful terms with Mexico.

1928: THE PAN-AMERICAN STATES MEETING IN CUBA

Paul S. Mowrer, *Chicago Daily News*

While during the early years of the Pulitzer Prizes domestic aspects dominated the reporting categories, the years in the late 1920s required a more international orientation in American journalism. So, in 1929, a new prize group was created, called „Correspondence". The new award category was defined „for the best example of correspondence during the year, the test being clearness and terseness of style, preference being given to fair, judicious, well-balanced and well-informed interpretative writing, which shall make clear the significance of the subject covered in the correspondence or which shall promote international understanding and appreciation."

While certain reliable standards had been developed for the older Pulitzer Prize categories, a tradition had yet to be formed in the new category which was primarily created for international reporting. The three jurors of the Correspondence category of 1929 unanimously selected the first winner in this new award group and stated in their report of March 16, 1929: „The articles by Paul Scott Mowrer of the *Chicago Daily News* ... seemed ... to meet precisely the terms of the award. They cover a wide range of subject; they are expertly written; they betray real understanding of the situation involved; they tend definitely to further the international appreciation that is sought by the offer of the prize." The Board joined the jury and awarded Mowrer the Pulitzer recognition.

Paul Scott Mowrer, born on July 14, 1887, in Bloomington, Ill., grew up in Chicago and attended Hyde Park High School. After his graduation in 1905 he studied at the University of Michigan and gained his first journalistic experience on the *Chicago Daily News* in the same year. Only five years later, he was already appointed Paris foreign correspondent of that newspaper. From 1912 to 1913 he covered the first Balkan War and directed the French *Chicago Daily News* bureau from 1914 to 1918. From 1917 until the end of World War I he was permanently accredited to the French armies as an official war correspondent. Mowrer also served as director of the *Chicago Daily News* Peace Conference Bureau from November 11, 1918, through August 31,1919. Mowrer was awarded the 1929 Pulitzer Prize for his articles from the previous year. Following are several of his dispatches:

January 7, 1928: »European governments, especially those of France, Spain, Italy and Great Britain, will watch with the closest interest the great sixth pan-American conference which will begin in Havana, Cuba, Jan. 16. The idea of sending official government observers or a league of nations observer has been abandond, but unofficial observers will be present and their reports will be eagerly awaited, for it is considered that the conference may mark a turning point in world affairs.

The real issue is considered to be whether Latin America will continue to keep the balance between the Unitcd States and Europe, or whether it will tend more and more to fall under the influence of the United States. No European power wants trouble with the world‘s strongest nation on any issue. All now seem willing quietly to concede that the Caribbean and Central America are a sort of United States sphere of influence, on the tacit condition naturally that the United States will refrain from interfering with what they in turn consider their various spheres of influence in other parts of the world. But none wants to see the United States get any stronger and all would be pleased if the Latin-Americans find some effective means of resisting the spread of influence of the United States in Central and South America.

Certain European powers, notably France, Spain and Italy, seem to be doing everything they can without openly affronting the United States to safeguard and extend their own influence in these regions. Financially, with the possible exception of Great Britain, Europe is unable to compete with the United States, which has for the present a virtual monopoly in furnishing the capital needed by Latin America. Commercially, the Europeans are struggling to develop Latin-American trade and seem to be aided in it by resentment of many Latin-Americans against the United States. Spain and Italy are sending emigrants to South America. There is talk of Great Britain under a new special arrangement directing emigrants to Argentina. European emigrant steamers which used to run to New York, now run to Rio de Janeiro and Buenos Aires. The steamship services between Europe and Latin America are more developed than between the United States and Latin America.

Months before Col. Charles A. Lindbergh's flight southward plans were laid for a regular Spanish dirigible airline to South America and credits were voted for a new French airplane line across the South Atlantic. Spanish, Italian and especially French literature is widerly read in Latin America. French is the principal foreign language there. Cultivated Latin-Americans when they travel tend toward Europe rather than New York. Paris is a great Latin-American capital. More Latin-Americans gather here from more Latin-American countries than in any other city in the world.

But the chief political instruments at the disposition of Europeans for action in Latin America are considered to be the league of nations and the pan-Latin movement. A majority of the Latin-American states are members of the league. They profess to find in it a counterpoise to the influence of the United States. The idea of referring Latin-American disputes to the league has not been abandoned. France and Great Britain, out of consideration for the United States, opposed the Chilean proposal at the last assembly that the league should hereafter deal with all such disputes, but the idea met with much favor and may be revived. Great efforts are being made to persuade Argentina and Brazil to return to active league membership. The league last year sent an important mission to Brazil, Argentina and Uruguay. Alberto N. Guani of Uruguay was elected president of the September (1927) assembly. Not for nothing, three Latin-American states, one of them a virtual United States protectorate, are now members of the league council - Chile, Colombia and Cuba.

Latin American influence in Geneva is so strong that one French writer fears that the United States will influence the vote of some Latin American state like Cuba in the council, where unanimity is required. It may thus be able effectively to interfere in European affairs, while preventing, under the Monroe doctrine, European interference in American affairs. If Spain returns to Geneva one of the principal reasons will be the desire to influence the Latin American group there.

Throughout Europe the pan-American movement in its three aspects - Pan-American union, Pan-American commercial conferenc and Pan-American Labor federation - is considered largely an instrument for the extension of the hegemony of the United States and Latin America - an antagonistic league of nations. The aim of the pan-Latin movement is to establish close relationships between all of the so-called Latin countries, including those in Latin America. France tends to lead this movement, although both Spain and Italy are interested. A Latin press conference is held annually. The latest one was in Bukharest and it proposed the founding of a Latin press agency and a dual citizenship for Latin newspaper men residing in another Latin country.

There are numerous Latin-American publications in Paris, nearly all more or less hostile to the United States. Manuel Ugarte, well-known Argentine writer and also consul to Nice, frequently denounces „American imperialism" and calls upon the twenty Latin-American republics to unite for defense.«

January 14, 1928: »The attention of European statesmen is now centered on Havana, where the sixth Pan-American conference opens Monday. The issue is believed to be whether the Latin-American states will be able or not to resist the encroachments of „United States imperialism."

Officially, the great powers in Europe profess not to be interested, but virtually all are highly attentive, for the matter is conceived to be one of world equilibrium. Asia is also concerned, for Latin Americans sympathize with Asia on the race issue. Mexico, which poses as a bulwark against the United States, has opened its gates wide to Japanese immigration. So has Brazil, where, it is said, there will soon be 50,000 Japanese colonists.

France recently raised its diplomatic mission in Argentina from a ministry to an embassy. German and French newspapers give copious interviews with Foreign Minister Gallardo of Argentina, who has just sailed home after a tour of several months in Europe.

Mr. Gallardo told Europeans that Argentia will soon officially enter the league of nations, with which it has never ceased to co-operate, and that Latin America will never accept the Monroe doctrine, for it believes not in America for Americans but in America for humanity.

The Latin Press congress, one of the principal organizations of the pan-Latin movement, which is supported by France, Italy and other powers, will hold its annual meeting in Havana immediately following the Pan-American conference.

Meanwhile Louis Gunaine, a leading French authority on Latin America, has just published a book dedicated André Tardieu entitled „Latin America and American Imperialism," which is a long and very able denunciation of the so-called imperialism of the United States. The illusion of United States idealism has been destroyed, M.

Guilaine argues, by dollar diplomacy, which in Europe is harshly egoistic and in Latin America a „policy of bribe“.

Of twenty supposedly independent Latin-American reepublics five - namely Cuba, Haiti, Santo Domingo, Panama and Nicaragua - have already been reduced to debtors by the United States, says this writer. Honduras is under occupation.Salvador is threatened financially. Colombia, Ecuador, Peru, Bolivia and Chile are under Yankee financial influence. Mexico was partially dismembered and annexed long ago and is now being encircled politically, he continues.

M. Guilaine believes it to be true that the United States does not desire the actual annexation of more territory, but thinks that its sole reason is its dislike of taking in Indian or half-breed populations to complicate the color question. The aim of the United States, in his opinion, is to establish complete economic domination, eliminate European influence and keep all of Latin-America as a United States spehere of influence, intervening when and where it likes to further its own intersts. Already the United States is commercially and financially predominant in this marvelously rich Latin continent. Argentina, fearing for the future and following Mexico's example, has nationalized its natural resources and Chile is preparing to do likewise.

The United States, which is stronger than all Latin America put together, says M. Guilaine, exercises its hegemony by means of the Monroe doctrine and the Pan-American union. The Monroe doctrine, as interpreted exclusively by the United States, has been changed from its original meaning and now serves as an instrumenrt of United States imperialism; Europe may not intervene in Latin-America but the United States may. Thus he declares, Latin America is a mere United States protectorate.

Certain Cenral American countries are less independent than individual states of the union, he argues. Nicaragua is less free than Oklahoma for the federal government intervenes as it likes in one, but dares not in the other. Defaulting Latin-American states my be occupied by the United States marines, but nine southern states of the United States which defaulted on their foreign debts are not interfered with.

The Pan-American union, argues M. Guilaine, is a mere annexd of the state department in Washington. It has no political power and gives no guaranty against encroachments by the United States. The reason why the United States rejected the league of nations, according to M. Guilaine, was that the covenant was incompatible with its imperialistic aims. The reason why so many Latin-American states are half-hearted in their league membership is because the league, humoring the United States, always refuses to discuss Latin-American disputes and hence affords no security for Latin-American states. However, the Latin-Americans will continue their league memberships because they gain thereby an international prestige not otherwise available.

M. Guilaine admits that Latin America's alleged plight is largely its own fault. More than 60 per cent of the people are Indian or half-breed and more than 75 per cent are illiterate. Only Argentina, Uruguay and Chile have predominantly white populations. The Indian tribes differ greatly among themselves and thus prevent true racial unity.

Indian nationalism, which tends to glorify the Indian origins and Indian heroes, M. Guilaine says, is growing and may ultimately be the principal obstacle to Latin-American federation. Except in Argentina, Brazil and Uruguay, political anarchy is the rule, owing partly to the Spanish colonial tradition and partly to the feeling of the Indian masses against the Spanish-descended aristocracy.

In Central America, M. Guilaine asserts, certain United States companies, seeking concessions willfully foment political anarchy for their own ends, subsidizing factional leaders and inciting civil war so as to provoke United States intervention. If the people knew what was being done in their name by the commercial oligarchy they would prevent it, M. Guilaine thinks.

The test will come next week in Havana. The Pan-American Institute of International Law has prepared a code which will be submitted to the conference. The code tends to make the Monroe doctrine a regional understanding instead of a policy interpreted arbitrarily by the United States. It tends to substitute joint pan-American interventions for exclusively United States interventions, where intervention is necessary. It includes a clause assimilating foreigners' rights and obligations throughout the Americas to those which affect the citizens of the various countries, thus obliging United States citizens to accept the laws inwhatever country they may be.

If the United States refuses this code, M. Guilaine thinks the only remedy left for Latin America will be some sort of federation. The basis for this exists in the still unratified understanding between the so-called A. B. C. power (Argentina, Brazil and Chile), but before this can become effective the Tacna-Arica dispute, which poisons the political life of South America, must be settled amicably. M. Guilaine's ideas may be taken as more or less typical European thought on the eve of the Pan-American congress.«

January 21, 1928: »The possibility of closer pan-American unity resulting from the present congress in Havana seems to have given a new stimulus to the pan-European movement. While superficially Europe appears to be as discordant as ever there are nevertheless profound forces operating since the world war to transform this discord into permanent harmony.

Europeans all realize that in the last war they lost their previous world supremacy to the United States. They fear that another war would ruin them beyond recovery for all time to the profit of America and Asia. They feel the necessity of standing more or less together politically to counterbalance the tremendous power of the United States if there is to be added the potential wealth and power of Latin America.

Financially Europeans have a common interest in that they are all creditors of the United States and incapable for the present of making extensive foreign investments themselves. Economically they realize that they can hope to hold their own with the United States in the world markets only when, like the United States, they can first depend for business profits on the vast interior market, using merely the surplus for the foreign trade.

No single European country except primitive Russia now offers a sufficient interior market. But if Europe's 400,000,000 people were combined into a single protected market it would then be even greater than that of the United States and hence the tendency toward tariff agreements and industrial cartels.

It is an open secret that Dr. Emil Mayrisch of Luxemburg, president of the European steel cartel, hopes that this great trust ultimately will result in a political grouping of France, Germany, Belgium and Luxemburg. Nor is the significance of this trend lost upon competent American observers. Just as European business men see in the Pan-American union an effort to exclude European goods and capital from the American continents, so certain Americans see in the European cartel a danger to the foreign trade of the United States.

Dr. Julius Klein, head of the bureau of foreign and domestic commerce in Washington, spoke recently of the „predatory plans of the European cartels," while Col. Frederick Pope, New York engineer, considers them an indication of a „commercial Monroe doctrine for Europe." The strongest and best known are the steel and chemical cartels, but there are dozens of others ranging from artificial silk through nitrogen and phosphates to glue and electric-light bulbs. Whether their primary aim is price-fixing and pooling of technical knowledge or the allotment of markets, the effect of all these cartels is to make national tariffs between the participating countries superfluos.

Meanwhile a meeting of the central committee of the Pan-European union has just been held in Paris. This organzition openly advocates the political and economic unity of all Europe, except Russia and Great Britain. It is known to have the sympathy of such statesmen as Aristide Briand, French minister of foreign affairs, Ignaz Seipel, Austrian chancellor, and Paul Loebe, president of the German Reichstag.

Among the members of the commitee are Louis Loucheur, French statesman; M. Politis, Greek statesman, and the Austrian, Finnish und Lettish ministers to France. Its president, Count Coudenhove of Kalergi, is quoted in the Paris Matin as urging an open customs union of France and its little entente allies as a nucleus to which all other European countries could then gradually adhere. The Pan-European union strongly supports the league of nations and especially the league's efforts to lower the customs barriers and popularize compulsory arbitration. Its next congress will be held in Paris in November this year.

Indeed, the league of nations itself appears in a certain sense as an organ of pan-Europeanism. While theoretically worldwide in scope, it has always concentrated economically and finacially on European problems, while politically it has ostentatiously avoided Asiatic and American questions and devoted itself energetically to European questions.

The possibility of the world's organizing by continents has aroused the alarm of some lovers of peace. „What is the use," they say, „of unifying continents if afterward the continents merely oppose one another? This will not end war, but make bigger wars than ever." Therefore, some international thinkers have begun to urge regional political organzations within the larger framework of the league of nations, giving each continent complete political autonomy while binding all together in a general peace pact and in the same humanitarian endeavors.

Alejandro Alvarez, well-known Chilean jurist, has drafted an elaborate project in this sense. Edouard Benes, foreign minister of Czechoslovakia, is a veteran advocate of regional authority within the league. In any event, if at Havana the American republics, despite recent difficulties, seem to come to a good understanding, the pan-European sentiment may be expected to increase correspondingly almost everywhere in Europe.«

February 18, 1928: »The sixth Pan-American congress, which closes in Havana Monday, has served to demonstrate to interested European powers two important facts. One is that Latin-America by no means is united in opposition to the policies of the United States. The other is that, as far as can now be judged, the political and economic strength of the United States in the western hemisphere is and promises to be so overwhelming that the United States' hegemoney in these regions seems virtually assured.

The fundamental European point of view remains unchanged. Europe is convinced that the United States today is not only the strongest, but probably the most expansive of nations. Its vast foreign loans and foreign trade, combined with its new naval program and active interventions in Central America, seem to Europeans clear indications in this sense. The Europeans mistrust any possible further extensions of our power and would like a united Latin-America to hold something like a balance of power between the United States and Europe.

But European statesmanship is, or tries to be, realistic. The Havana sessions from this distance seem to indicate that such a thing as a united Latin-America is impossible. If some of the Latin countries like Chile, Salvador, Argentina and Mexico seem somewhat hostile to the United States, others like Brazil, Peru, Cuba and Panama appear decidedly friendly.

Moreover, United States money is essential to the development of nearly all the Latin-American countries while her political unfluence is so considerable that it seems to Europeans that even such Latin-American states as may desire to oppose her cannot successfully persist in this course.

European statesman, therefore, are resigning themselves to look upon Central America and the Caribbean region as a United States sphere of influence and to foresee in the western hemisphere a sort of pax Romana wherein the United States will play the role of ancient Rome. France, Great Britain und Holland hope to keep indefinitely to their present Caribbean possessions, but they have no illusions about being able to do so save with the consent of the United States.

So far as the Pan-American congress itself is concerned, no important concrete results are expected by the Europeans. The great political issue of intervention and the great economic question of tarrifs both seem to have been shelved. If at the last moment an inter-American pact outlawing war is voted, it is expected that it will contain reservations of some description which for all concerned will leave the situation virtually unchanged.

However, the presence in Havana during the congress of a number of leading Anerican business men and bankers, including delegations from the New York and

Chicago chambers of commerce is not passed unnoticed here and it is anticipated that the contracts thus established foreshadow an increase in our economic and financial activity in Latin America in the near future.

There is some fear that the United States may try to utilize her privileged position in Central America to exclude Eurpeans from new concessions. To any such policy Europe doubtless would attempt to oppose our own doctrine of the open door. Great Britain and Germany particularly are keen toward increasing their Latin-American trade, wherein their products compete directly with ours. France also wants more trade, but it fears competition less because its exports are mainly specialized luxuries.

The league of nations, it is believed, will continue to enjoy firm support from the majority of the Latin-American countries. The stanch league supporters are Chile, Colombia, Paraguay, Guatemala, Salvador, Uruguay, Venezuela, Bolivia, Santo Domingo, Panama, Haiti and Cuba. Argentina is expected to resume full co-operation with the league after the forth-coming elections. Brazil's return to Geneva is greatly sought. This would leave only Mexico, Peru and Ecuador and three or four smaller Central American countries absent from the league meetings.

Meanwhile, on Monday, the same day the Pan-American congress ends, representatives of sixty French, Italian, Spanish, Portuguese, Belgian, French and Swiss newspapers will sail for Havana. With delegates from Latin-American newspapers they will meet on March 4 to 15 for the seventh congress of the Latin press.

This congress is one of the pricipal manifestations of the recent pan-Latin movement which aims not only at a rapproachment of the so-called Latin countries of Europe, but also of the Latin countries of America. President Gerardo Machado of Cuba will open the conference with precisely the same setting as the Pan-American congress. An endeavor will be made to quicken the sentiment of affinities, of tradition, language and customs which it is alleged have united all the so-called Latin-Americans who have just been trying to define their political and economic situation vis-a-vis 120,000,000 Yankees and will now enter into moral harmony with 120,000,000 European Latins.

The only possible controversy foreseen in the Latin press congress refers to the poet and journalist, Dantes Bellegarde, former Haitian minister of education and former minister from Haiti to Patris, who on arriving in Havana for the Pan-American congress as correspondent of various French and Haitian newspapers, including the Action Francaise of Paris, was arrested and expelled by the Cuban authorities presumably becaųse of his active campaigns against „Yankee imperialism." Explanations may be demanded.

But even French journalists who a few weeks ago were most violent in their denunciations of „United States imperialism" seem to have been quieted now by the evidence which the Pan-American congress has presented of the disunion of Latin-America and of the economic and political power of the United States. France greatly values its cultural predominance in Latin America, but it values even more its friendship with the United States. It is not a coincidence that the French „air ambassadors," Dieudonne Costes and Joseph le Brix, after their triumphal flights over Latin America, where they were hailed as representatives of the Latin spirit, have now begun a good-will flight across the United States.«

December 15, 1928: »The league of nations' momentous action in the Bolivia-Paraguay war scare coinciding with President-Elect Hoover's trip to South America and the meeting of the pan-American arbitration conference in Washington has suddenly fixed Europe's attention upon Latin-America again for the first time since the pan-American congress in Havana adjourned nearly a year ago. Altogether the situation underlying these scattered development is given by Europe as nothing less than a long and tensely dramatic struggle for the control in the future of an entire continent.

Latin America, particularly South America, is regarded as capable over a period of years, of undergoing a tranformation of progress and properity not unlike that of North America in the last century. The United States, with its vast economic and political power, is visualized as endeavoring through pan-American institutions and extensions of the Monroe doctrine to establish a dominant influence all the way to Patagonia.

Central America, it is commonly said, has already half succumbed. Our financial domination is represented as advancing into Colombia, Venezuela, Ecuador, Peru and Bolivia. Our investments in South America alone are reported to have increased since 1912 from $174,000,000 to $2,67,000,000.

Mr. Hoover's trip is explained partly as an endeavor to complete his first-hand knowledge of all parts of the world, but mainly as an effort to earn good will with a view to further commercial and financial expansion. It is believed that he will present a plan in the near future for new shipping lines between North and South America.
As for the Latin Americans, Europe feels sure that they are suspicious and desire to resist this „Yankee expansion," but are divided among themselves, disillusioned and perplexed. They need New York gold as badly as they need European immigrants. They are disappointed nearly as much in the league of nations as in pan-Americanism and the Monroe doctrine. Of the last named, they are now said to be so distrustful that several of them are waiting before signing the Kellogg peace pact to make sure that no Monroe doctrine reservation is imposed by our senate.

Meanwhile some of them look to Europe for help, some to the United States and some counsel self-reliance alone. The most significant event of the last year is thought to be the emergence of Argentina as the outspoken champion of Latin America against the influence of the United States. Europe takes due account of Argentina's attitude of opposition at the Havana conference a year ago, of its formal statement in Geneva last spring that it refuses to recognize the Monroe doctrine, its refusal to attend the present pan-American conference in Washington, and its past and present edeavors to act as the sole mediator in the Paraguay-Bolivia boundary dispute.

Suggestions are even advanced that the United States, because of its financial interests, is quietly backing Bolivia, while the sympathies of Argentina incline toward Paraguay. Europe is solicitous not to offend the United States especially just now when it needs our help in the general reparations negotiations. At the same time it intends, if possible, to preserve what remains of its cultural, commercial and financial interests in South America. Germany is going after trade and shipping.

Spain has a whole cultural trade and shipping program called Hispano-Americanism. France is trying to keep its cultural prestige. As for Great Britain there is no other place in the world where the latent Anglo-American rivalry is more keenly perceptible, for it is mainly at Great Britain's expense that the United States has been expanding there. British and American oil interests are competitors in Venezuela and Colombia. British shipping still predominates at South American ports.

But what are President-Elect Hoover's plans? British investments still predominate in Brazil and especially in Argentina, but for how long will they do so? Some observers even believe that Great Britain's famous interpretation of the Kellogg pact was intended mainly as a counterfoil to the Monroe doctrine so that if our senate makes a Monroe reservation, the British will insist equally upon a formal reservation. If the senate omits the Monroe doctrine, the British interpretation wil be more or less dropped.

The instrument of Europe's commmon feelings in these matters has become the league of nations, of which the United States is not a member, but most of the Latin-American states are. The league began by trying to cater to the susceptibilities of the United States. On President Wilson's demand, the Monroe doctrine article was inserted in the league covenant. The league refused to consider the Tacna-Arica dispute in 1927 and the Costa Rica-Panama dispute in 1921.

But when it saw on the one hand that the United States still had no intention of joining the league, and on the other that the Latin Americans were losing interest in an organization which refused to consider their disputes, it gradually changed its tactics. It established a special Latin-American bureau. It encouraged the Latin Americans to play an important part in the meetings of the assembly and the council.

When Costa Rica finally demanded an interpretation of the Monroe article in the covenant the council replied, last September, that it does not impair either the rights or duties of any league member. Accordingly after the Paraguay-Bolivian frontier battle it had no recourse except to act for both Paraguay and Bolivia, members or the organization, although Bolivia was several years in arrears in its dues.

The Cuban, Chilean and Venezuelan members of the council seemed determined that Aristide Briand should raise the issue. The Roumanian, Nicolas Titulescu, exclaimed that the league, if it had no permanent alliance with success, has such an alliance with duty. The Cuban Aguero said that if the league fails in this case, the Latin Americans will lose their interest once for all. The hesistation of Sir Austen Chamberlain and the Japanese, Adachi, was soon overcome and the league is constituting perhaps a formidable precedent by its message over the wires.

For the league not to have responded many Europeans feel would have been to surrender the whole of South America to something like a „Yankee protectorate," for it would have implied that the United States alone had the right to work for peace there. Now, however, if the angry disputants refuse to heed the council's appeal and hostilities continue, the league will be faced with the problem of taking sanctions and what will the United States say then?

But in truth no real hostilities are anticipated, for the simple reason that it would apparently take weeks and months for the rival armies to get at each other in these vast uninhabited spaces. Although the vast Chaco region, lying at an angle between the Pilcomayo and Paraguay rivers, was awarded to Paraguay against Argentina in the mediation by President Hayes in 1879, the Bolivian claim to it seems to have remained. The region consists mainly of forests and pampas, but oil has been discoverd and the big trusts are vigilant.

Bolivia, having failed in the recent mediations to regain an outlet to the Pacific through Tacna and Arica, seems now to be seeking an outlet to the Atlantic by way of the Paraguay river and especially the little river port Coimbra. But nearly the whole of the disputed territory, being easier of access to Paraguay than to Bolivia, has been occupied by a thin line of Paraguay's military outpost.

For three years Argentina, scenting peril, has been sponsoring mediations and last year got both of the countries to promise never to use force. But the bloody clash of the two patrols on Dec. 5 and Dec. 6 reminded Europe that even South America is not exempt from some forms of extreme nationalism.

Paraguay has informed the league that it will accept any and all processes of concilation, but Bolivia, seemingly desirous of making good its old claim, demands „moral reparations" for the „aggression."

Interest here now centers in who shall mediate. Paraguay seems to object to the United States and hence to the Pan-American conference commission or even to Cuba. Bolivia similarly seems to object to Argentina or the league. Some American observers feel that a solution might be found in intervention by the so-called A B C powers - Argentina, Chile and Brazil.

Meanwhile as Paraguay and Bolivia are not only league members, but signatories of the Gondra conciliation pact framed under Pan-American auspices in 1923, some European commentators see in the present situation a test case of the whole league and pact system.«

1940: GERMAN NAZI ARE EXPELLED FROM URUGUAY

John W. White, *New York Times*

In 1941, one of the largest press-material entries the Pulitzer Prize jurors ever received from a newspaper had to be evaluated. The material - an imposing cross-section of foreign news and corresponding comments on international affairs - was the *New York Times'* entry to gain the Pulitzer award for „Meritorious Public Service". However, it was the *St. Louis Post-Dispatch* being honored in that award category. Nevertheless, the jury as well as the Board were deeply impressed by the carefully chosen and organized material, supporting the *New York Times* presentation.

In fact the material was considered that interesting and worthy, that both relevant committees took their rarely used right to honor applications beside the regular Pulitzer Prize categories by conferring „Special Awards and Citationsu". So jury and Board expressed their respect for the large impact of information in the *New York Times* entry and decided on May 1st, 1941, to give a special award to the newspaper „for the public educational value of its foreign news reports, exemplified by its scope, by excellence of writing and presentation, illustration and interpretation."

The award-winning entry consisted of articles from *New York Times* correspondents around the globe, published during 1940. By the end of that year, the newspaper's staff correspondents abroad numbered 63, and clerical staffs in the news bureaus numbered an additional 13 persons. About a dozen correspondents were based in Latin American countries. One of them, John W. White, was stationed in Buenos Aires and reported from Argentina and Uruguay. Following are some of his award-winning articles:

June 19, 1940: »Germany has now begun to exert tremendous political and economic pressure on the Uruguayan Government to halt what Berlin calls an unfriendly anti-German campaign here. The Reich has threatened to break off diplomatic relations if any Nazi leaders are deported.

The fear is being expressed in Congressional and other circles that this pressure will force the government to release the Nazi leaders who are now under arrest and to drop plans for energetic measures against Nazi organizations here.

The German Government presented a strong diplomatic protest to the Uruguayan Government on Monday. The German Minister, Otto Langmann, called in person on Dr. Alberto Guani, the Uruguayan Foreign Minister, to deliver this protest. The greatest secrecy surrounds the details of the protest, but it is known that there was a demand for the immediate cessation of „unfriendly agitation" against Germany.

It is this protest that is believed to have been the cause of the government's action in urging the Chamber ot Deputies to go into a secret session on Monday afternoon to receive the report ot its investigating committee on Nazi activities. The leader of the majority party, supporting the motion for a secret session to prevent the details of the investigation from becoming public, said that the request for a secret session had been made by the executive branch of the government, which had reasons for this action that were not in possession ot the investigating committee.

The Minister of Interior, Manuel Tiscornia, told last night's secret session of the Chamber of Deputies that Julius Dalldorf, „Little Fuehrer“ for Uruguay, had told him that if Herr Dalldorf or any other Nazi leaders were deported, the German Minister would ask for his passports and would leave the country immediately. Since Herr Dalldorf is a member of the legation staff as a press attaché, it is taken for granted in Congressional circles that this message was sent by Herr Langmann himself.

Despite the government's urgent efforts to keep the investigating committee's report from reaching the public, the Chamber, just before, adjourning at 4 o'clock this morning, voted to issue a stenographic record of the secret session to the newspapers. Today the newspapers began for the first time to publish details of the investigation.

The strong pressure exerted by the German Government is causing the Uruguayan Government to take a hesitant and vacillating attitude, which threatens a political victory for Germany. It is said in circles very close to the government that the authorities are frankly afraid to take any steps that might bring reprisals from Germany and that the continuous German victories in Europe, culminating in the French request for peace, have strengthened the fear in official circles here that Germany may win the war.

The government's hesitant and vacillating attitude has been plainly evidenced by the contradictory action's of the last few days on the part of the country's three principal Ministries, Interior, Foreign Affairs and National Defense. Until Monday, the Minister ot Interior had denied that any importance was attached to Nazi activities in Uruguay. Last night, at the secret session of the Chamber of Deputies, he admitted that he had been mistaken and presented a report from his Under-Secretary, confirming the charges made in the report of the investigating committee.

The chief of the Bureau of Investigations of the Police Department had steadily denied that the Nazi plans were of any importance. The newspapers this morning announced his arrest.

Similar bewilderment is evident on the part of the Minister of Defense. When the investigating committee showed him the document containing the plans for the military seizure of Uruguay he appointed a committee of three generals to study the plan and to report to him. The chairman of this committee was General Pedro Sicco, Chief of Staff. This committee of generals turned in a report saying that the plan was proof of an extremely serious situation.

A few hours before this report was read to the Congress last night the Minister of Defense gave an interview to the afternoon newspapers denying that there was any threat of invasion or of the occupation of the country and saying that there was no cause for alarm of any kind. But in this morning's papers the same Minister published an appeal to all Uruguayan citizens, women as well as men, to enroll with the army for voluntary military service.

There is a similar contradictory attitude in the Ministry of Foreign Affairs. The political significance at the arrival here of the United States cruiser Quincy tomorrow moning has been taken for granted not only here but throughout South America. The Uruguayan newspapers and those of several other republics have described the hurried departure of the Quincy for South Atlantic waters as evidence that the United States was ready to help the South American nations if necessary.

Dr. Guani has frequently and enthusiatically expressed the pleasure and satisfaction not only of himself but of the Uruguayan Government that the cruiser is coming at this particular time. Yet this morning the Ministry of Foreign Affairs issued a statement to all Montevideo newspapers that the voyage of the Quincy had no Pan-American political significance and was merely a routine trip.

Despite the sensational revelations of the investigating committee, the German Minister apparently feels his position sufficiently strong to permit him to present his case directly to the Uruguayan people by means of letters to the newspapers that are contrary to international law and diplomatic usage.

The investigating committee last night and Monday night presented a huge amount of documentary proof to the Chamber of Deputies that one of the principal Nazi leaders in Uruguay was Arnuf Fuhrmann, who admitted to an examining judge that the plan for the military occupation of the country was in his own handwriting. Herr Fuhrmann was also proved to be the South American director of anti-Semitic operations, the director of the Nazis' South American judicial organization, the contact between Ger-mans in Argentina and Uruguay and also the South American director for whatever armed action was to be taken.

Yet Herr Langmann published a letter in today's newspapers ridiculing the Congressional committee's investigation and stating that Herr Fuhrmann was not a German but an Argentine citizen and that he had never been a member of the Nazi party.

Simultaneously with this political pressure German business houses are assuring their customers that German trade will be normal again within six months. An American company lost a big order here last week because its German competitors offered much lower prices and guaranteed delivery in September. A local German firm has just won a big contract in public bidding and has deposited a 5,000-peso guarantee of completion of the contract within the time specified.

These facts are interpreted in diplomatic circles as evidence that the Uruguayan Government is being heavily pressed by the German Government on both political and commercial grounds.

This economic pressure is of extreme importance since Uruguay, which has lost all her good markets except the British because of the European war and the blockade. Exports have ceased moving to France, Belgium, the Netherlands, Italy, Germany, Switzerland, Czecho-Slovakia, Poland and Yugoslavia, all of which were formely important outlets for Uruguayan products.

Recently the Netherlands, Poland and Belgium were the most important of all because under the various barter and compensated clearing arrangements now in force they were the only three countries whose trade left a cash balance in Uruguay.

This balance was extremely useful in financing Uruguay's purchases, especially in Great Britain.

It is freely predicted here that Uruguay's economic situation will be very serious within three months. It is expected that Great Britain will be forced heavily to reduce purchases in Uruguay and also to curtail exports to Uruguay.

Germany and Italy, meanwhile, are threatening Uruguay with reprisals if the latter does not stay in line. They assure Uruguay that they are certain of winning the war. At the same time they are trying to forecast bright prosperity for Uruguay as soon as they reopen their markets to Uruguayan products, which, they say, will be in six months.

A prominent and well-informed Uruguayan, very close to the government, discussing this situation with your correspondent this afternoon, said: „Only powerful and immediate support from the United States can save Uruguay from a serious political defeat by Germany. Unless this support is of a political nature sufficiently strong to put into immediate effect the Pan-American solidarity agreed upon at Lima, so that Uruguay can feel safe and certain in resisting any attempted putsch, the Uruguayan Government will be forced to back down. Uruguay needs immediately and urgently markets that can absorb her exportable surpluses in order to permit the government to maintain an economic balance internally at a moment when it is called upon to make huge expenditures for national defense. The United States is our only hope, but help must come quickly."«

September 29, 1940: »Uruguay, the smallest of South America's ten republics, took steps this week to wipe out all Nazi activities within its territory, in the interest of continental defense. First it arrested and began the trial of eight Nazi leaders who technically are charged under the Uruguayan penal code with conspiracy to deliver Uruguayan territory to a foreign power. Then its vigorous new Minister of the Interior, Pedro Manini Rios, issued a decree calling upon all citizens to cooperate in hunting down organizations and individuals connected with any Nazi activity, including propaganda.

The magnitude of Uruguay's action can be realized better when it is realized that its territory of 72,000 square miles is only slightly larger than the six New England States, while its population of 2,000,000 is roughly that of Philadelphia. Uruguay has practically no navy and only 8,000 men in its army, for purposes of maintaining internal law and order. It could not, therefore, have undertaken this clean-up of Nazi organi-zations if it had not been guaranteed aid by the United States and other American countries when needed.

The most important evidence against the men now on trial is the text of a military plan to seize Uruguay, „eliminate" that portion of the population likely to prove troublesome and set up the country as an agricultural colony of the Third Reich. It was the discovery of this document, toward the end of May, which caused the United States to rush two cruisers to Montevideo.

One of the prisoners, Arnulf Fuhrmann, admits that he drew up the plan, but insists it was only a joke. The prosecution is trying to break down this defense by showing that Fuhrmann is so important in the Nazi organization that he corresponded directly with Rudolf Hess, Hitler's Deputy Leader. The prosecution will also present documents uncovered by a special Congressional investigation showing that Fuhrmann, operating as a modest provincial photographer in the unimportant little interior town of Salto, was directing international operations in South America.

The whole trend of the prosecution is found in the charge that the eight men on trial were associated in a conspiracy to make Uruguay the spearhead for a Nazi invasion of the South American continent. In official circles closely concerned with the present trial it is admitted that the government's energetic action at this time, in sharp contrast with the weak, vacillating attitude taken when the Nazi leaders were orginally arrested in June, is the direct result of the Havana Conference and the agreement between the United States and Great Britain in establishing American naval and air bases in British possessions in the western hemisphere.

Uruguay now feels, it is said, that the United States is practically allied with Great Britain and also that as a result of the Havana Conference all American nations are pledged to back up Uruguay in its campaign to remove what Uruguayans consider to be a Nazi peril against the entire continent. There has been a pronounced swing of Urguayan public opinion toward the United States since the naval base agreement with Great Britain. Several editors who formerly were anti-United States are now supporting the idea that Uruguay establishes bases for use by the forces of any American nation.

The strengthening of Pan-American ties is also having a direct effect on internal politics, which are noticeably swinging away from those leaders who leaned toward totalitarian sympathies. It is felt in well-informed political circles that democracy in Uruguay has been greatly strengthened by the recent decision of the Batlle party to cooperate with the national government for the first time since 1933, when Gabriel Terra overthrew the democratic régime and set up a dictatorship. President Alfredo Baldomir inherited the remains of this dictatorship.

Because of the refusal of the country's largest party - the Batllistas - to cooperate with him he was forced to depend on the support of minority parties, several of which were frankly sympathetic to the totalitarian régimes. The national convention of the Batlle party recently voted to participate in the next elections in union with those factions of the party which broke away from the majority which has been supporting the President.

Since President Baldomir has recently been seeking democratic solutions of his political problems it is believed likely that he will have the support of the Batlle party during the year and a half remaining in his term. The solution of Argentina's recent political crisis on democratic lines also had an immediate effect in Uruguay, where Fascist sympathizers were hoping for an Argentine solution favoring their ideology.«

December 9, 1940: »The German Government, through its Minister in Montevideo, Otto Langmann, made a formal diplomatic protest this afternoon against the action of the Uruguayan Government in permitting the British auxiliary cruiser Carnarvon

Latin American correspondents of the *New York Times* in 1940

Castle to remain in port here for seventy-two hours to repair damage sustained in a running fight with a German raider off the Brazilian coast last Thursday.

Although Herr Langmann admitted tonight that he had called on Foreign Minister Alberto Guani and filed a formal protest, neither he nor Senor Guani would discuss details of the protest or the Uruguayan on reply.

Extension of the original forty-eight hours by another twenty-four was granted after the government's commision of naval experts had made another survey of the vessel's damage and the progress of repairs this morning. The commission reported that damage to the exhaust pipes in the engine room could not be repaired within the time limit originally granted and recommended an extension.

A decree issued this afternoon, formally granting the extension, fixed the hour of departure at 6:30 P. M. tomorrow, the time being calculated from the hour the Carnarvon Castle made fast alongside a dock Saturday afternoon. The ship's officers said, however, that they would sail as soon as the repairs were completed, which they expected to be soon after noon.

The seventy-two-hour period is the same as that granted to the Admiral Graf Spee, but the Carnarvon Castle has a decided advantage over the ill-fated German pocket battleship in that there are no enemy craft waiting just below the horizon to force a new action as soon as she leaves port. Rather than permit the Graf Spee to risk an encounter, Reichsfuehrer Hitler personally ordered her scuttled just a year ago this month.

The British legation said this afternoon that conjecture as to the Carnarvon Castle's destination when she sails was futile because Captain H. M. H. Hardy himself will not know, since he will sail under sealed orders, to be opened at sea. Captain Hardy, accompanied by the British Minister, Eugen Millington-Drake, this afternoon expressed his appreciation of Uruguayan hospitality by placing a huge wreath of fresh flowers on the monument of General Artigas, liberator of Uruguay, in beautiful Independence Square.

The survey by Uruguayan naval experts has failed to reveal any evidence that the German raider is armed with guns heavier than 5.9-inch, which is the German equivalent of the British 6-inchers. Naval authorities take this as indicating that the raider is an armed merchantman rather than a converted cruiser, as rumored. But as the German guns are much more modern than the Carnarvon Castle's the German ship had a decided advantage in range as well as speed.

The Carnarvon Castle's range is 15,000 yards to the German ship's 18.000. Nevertheless the Carnarvon Castle gave chase and tried to close in for an engagement at close quarterts, as proved by the fact that most of the damage was suffered in the bow, bridge and forward part of the vessel. The Germans used fragmentation shells, made of cast iron and loaded with high explosive, which burst upon impact and spread havoc over a wide area. The shells burst into tiny splinters, giving the sailors the impression they were being shelled with shrapnel.

Shells that burst on the promenade decks cut across hard teakwood boards as a razor cuts butter. Naval circles here explained today that these shells were useless against any kind of armored ship because they have no piercing power, but are ideal for raiding commerce carriers because they spread destruction and wreck the morale of the crews, especially when they get inside the ship and burst in the engine room, hospital bay or other open spaces.

One of the Carnarvon Castle's wounded, in a grave condition from burns, was landed this afternoon and taken to a Uruguayan military hospital for treatment. If he recovers he will be interned for the duration of the war.

The Foreign Ministery is consulting Brazil and other South American governments regarding a joint attitude on the action of the Carnarvon Castle in removing twenty-two Germans from the Brazilian coastal steamer Itape and later transferring them, reportedly to the auxiliary cruiser Queen of Bermuda.

Despite all the rumors of a new naval engagement in the South-Atlantic, government wireless stations have not picked up anything to indicate that British warships have yet sighted the escaping raider. The British cruiser Enterprise was at the Falkland Islands when Thursday's battle took place and she immediately started for the scene of combat at full speed, not even slowing down to exchange salutes when she passed the Uruguayan cruiser Uruguay, which was on a training cruise with cadets near Punta del Este, just as she was when the battle of Punta del Este took place last year.

Neutral naval officers express the opinion that the German ship, if as badly damaged as the Carnarvon Castle reports, will try to get back to Germany as soon as possible and that if she is challenged by some British warship the action is likely to take place far north of last Thursday's battle scene.«

1945: THE DICTATORIAL PERÓN RÉGIME IN ARGENTINA

Arnaldo Cortesi, *New York Times*

The end of World War II brought new award perspectives. The early postwar period influenced the two Pulitzer Prize categories for Foreign Reporting thematically. In the „International Telegraphic Reporting" group Homer W. Bigart of the *New York Herald-Tribune* was awarded the prize for covverage of the final days of the war in Japan. The award in the „Correspondence" category proved that the influence of the war was waning.

Arnaldo Cortesi of the *New York Times* received the Pulitzer Prize „for distin-guished correspondence during the year 1945, as exemplified by his reports from Bueno Aires, Argentina." The jury report of April 1st, 1946, about this decision argued: „Arnaldo Cortesi's dispatches through 1945 from Argentina to the *New York Times* ... are but typical of the many he has filed from that country over the last four years, both under his own byline and anonymously under a Montevideo dateline. The material was gathered under difficulties and written often under the threat of personal attack. He overcame the former and defied the latter. Essential truth shine through each one. For clarity, background and interpretation I have not seen them surpassed," the chairman of the jury stated.

Arnaldo Cortesi was born on September 21, 1897, in Rome, Italy, as a member of a distinguished journalistic family. He attended schools in England and earned an engineering degree from the University of Manchester. Afterwards he worked for some time at a Westinghouse Electric plant near that city before turning to journalism, too. His mother was an American from Boston who worked as the first *New York Times* correspondent in Rome. At her death in 1916, she was succeeded in that post by her elder daughter, Elizabeth, who resigned upon marrying in 1922. Now Arnaldo Cortesi was appointed her successor by Adolf S. Ochs, then publisher of the *Times*, who had met the young man during a visit to Italy. Since that time, he covered the Italian capital for many years. In his dispatches from Rome he reported on the rise of Mussolini as Italy's dictator and the consolidation of the Fascist régime. Moreover he was among the first observers to see that Mussolini would join forces with Hitler.

Seventeen years after he had beecome the *New York Times* correspondent in Rome, Mussolini gave the order that Italian citizens were not allowed to represent foreign news organizations in Italy. So the *Times* transferred Cortesi to Geneva and Mexico City for short stints and sent him to Buenos Aires in 1941. In this city he was able to observe the upcoming Perón régime towards the end of World War II. When the first of his articles on this topic was published early in June, 1945, in the *New York Times* Cortesi was picked up and taken to police headquarters hours before the U . S. embassy was able to obtain his release. The day before he received the Pulitzer Prize in May, 1946, for his coverage of the Perón régime during the previous year, Cortesi had become a naturalized United States citizen. Following are several of his prize-winning articles:

June 1, 1945: »The Argentine Government had not sooner declared war on Germany and Japan and signed the final acts on the Mexico City conference than it deprived the Argentine people of what small remains of freedom they still possessed. Under the pretext that in wartime anyone who did not approve of the Government was a traitor to his country, the Government embarked on a campaign of intimidation by wholesale arrests of prominent citizens and severe measures against any newspaper that dared to raise its voice in protest. At the same time political censorship was re-established in the vain hope that news of what was going on could be kept from the outside world.

Only last night censorship mangled one of this correspondent's dispatches dealing with the statement about Argentina, made by United States Secretary of State Edward R. Stettinius Jr. in San Francisco, and with a speech delivered to the American community by United States Ambassador Spruille Braden. Of five sections into which the dispatch was divided, the first was suppressed entirely, the second was edited by the censor to disguise the fact that the first was missing, the third was edited to delete thirty-three words containing the whole point of the story, and the fifth was forwarded intact. The only section that was sent as written was one containing Foreign Minister Cesar Ameghino's plea that the Argentine Government had been unjustly criticized abroad because it had been misunderstood.

Since experience has shown that there is no hope of getting the truth past Argentine censors, this dispatch is being sent by channels other than the normal ones. Censorship was re-established by a decree dated April 28 which appeared on the Bulletin of Posts and Telegraphs on May 2. One of its articles reads: „All telegrams are accepted at the sender's risk and are subject to retentions, delays and total or partial suppression without notice to the interested parties."

This decree, which is ostensibly a wartime measure, applied to news that is not even distantly connected with the war, despite the fact that Argentina in Mexico City undertook to guarantee free acess to news." For some time correspondents were unaware that their dispatches had died in the censorship offices. Moreover, the world has been so interested in other things since the collapse of Germany that many details of the Argentine situation so far have escaped notice. The time has come to say, however, that things have happened in Buenos Aires recently that exceed anything that this correspondent can remember in his seventeen years' experience in fascist Italy.

He has seen whole sections of the city occupied by the Army in full war kit; he has seen peaceful citizens searched for arms in the streets; he has seen policemen directing traffic with revolvers in their hands.

He knows that at least one innocent man was machine-gunned while entering a subway station. He knows also that reputable citizens, like the well-known lawyer, Enrique Gil, have been arrested and that others, like the prominent business man, Jacobo Saslavasky, have been spirited away while out for an after-dinner walk; that still others, like Americo Ghioldi, editor of the Socialist newspaper, the Vanguardia, have had to choose between exile and imprisonment, and that some foreigners, like the well-known Ecuadorean cartoonist, Tony Salazer, have been deported.

When it is remembered that the above names have been given only as samples and that each stands for dozens or hundreds of similar cases, one begins to have some idea of the situation. Its gravity is confirmed by the fact that all jails in the country are full to the overflowing.

It is confirmed also by this correspondent's admittedly incomplete files which show that during the month of May alone eight newspapers were closed and seven editors and other outstanding newspaper men arrested. It is no justification to say, as the Government does, that most of the prominent men arrested revocer their freedom after some days or weeks in jail, since it is well known that some unfortunates have now been languishing in prison without trial for almost two years.

It is hardly necessary to point out that the above activities of the Argentine Government, and many others like them, are direct violations of the commitments that Argentina assumed when she signed the final acts of the Mexico City conference. She undertook to abide by the principles of the Atlantic Charter, to permit free access to news, to eliminate the remaining centers of Axis influence, to support democracy and to respect the rights of individuals, and foster justice and freedom.

Foreign Minister Dr. Cesar Arneghino promises that all these commitments will be abided by and Vice President Col. Juan Perón undermakes to hold elections at some future unspecified date but meanwhile Argentine people suffer. The stipulations about democracy cannot be considered to have been fulfilled until the stage of siege has been repealed and the Argentine people have received the opportunity to elect a government of their choice. Until this has been done it may be expected that relations between the United States and Argentina will never be cordial, however correct they may be.

This, in turn, implies many things, among the most important of which is the presumption that the United States will be in no hurry to supply machinery and other urgently needed materials and that military equipment will not be made available to the present Government or to any government that has not been freely elected by the Argentine people. If this last point were fully understood, perhaps the army's attitude toward the Farrell régime would change radically.«

September 20,1945: »In an overwhelming demonstration of popular feeling, Buenos Aires this afternoon manifested its repudiation of the Argentine military Government and shouted to the four winds its irrepressible desire for freedom and law. The „March of Constitution and of Freedom, organized on a non-party basis by the Committee of Democratic Coordination, called out what all observers declared was the largest crowd ever massed in Argentina.

For two and a half hours a tightly packed column of people marched along the wide Calle Callao, calling in no uncertain terms upon the Government to resign and to give back to Argentina her lost rights and freedoms.

Perhaps most significant of all, the song most often sung as the procession advanced, and the one that brought the loudest applause, was „God Bless America.“ Never before, by all accounts, had a demonstration such as this been staged in

Argentina. Social barriers were completely down; class distinctions were forgotten; party jealousies were buried.

Men and women of all shades of political thought, of all professions, of all callings, of all stations in life, of all ages, marched arm in arm, united only by their common desire to see an end of the military dictatorship that has ruled Argentina for more than twenty-seven months. It was a remarkable spectacle, and truly gave the impression that a revitalized Argentine democracy was on the march.

How many persons participated in today's demonstration it is difficult to say with accuracy. The forecasts of 100,000 made yesterrday were without doubt amply exceeded. Best estimates place the number of those who actually participated in the march over more than thirty blocks at 150,000. At least 50,000 more lined the sidewalks and cheered as the marchers went by. Yet another 50,000 or so gathered at the place where the final act of the demonstration took place. This makes a total of a quarter-million persons who answered the call of democracy, though it should be noted that some estimates place the figure as high as half a million or more.

The march was quite orderly and peaceful despite its strong political and anti-Government character. It advanced under a snowstorm of confetti showered upon it by persons from the windows of houses along the route and amid tremendous applause from bystanders. From the throng rose constant, deafening shouts asking for freedom and demanding the resignation of the Government.

As usual, Vice President Juan Perón was the especial target of attacks, the cries of „Death to Perón!" being almost incessant. After „God Bless America," the most popular song was one ending in „We want no dictatorships, nor military governments, either."

The paraders gathered at the Plaza del Congreso, in front of the Congress building, which can hold about 400,000 persons. At one time, the square was very nearly filled. From there, the paraders marched along Calle Callao until they reached the monument to France, thirty blocks away. The head of the column had reached the monument long before the tail had left the meeting place.

In the crowd one noted the presence of many notable Argentine figures, and especially of many who had never before taken any part in politics. There was a very large delegation of women representing the pro-Allied „Junta de la Victoria," and headed by the president of the organization, Senora Ana Rosa de Martinez Guerrero.

At one point during the march, the crowd noticed Gen. Arturo Rawson, who headed the revolution of June 4, 1943, at a window of his house. He was in uniform and spoke a few words to the crowd in reply to its insistent demands. At another window of the same house was Gen. Alberto Gilbert, who was Foreign Minister in the military Government for some time and who also spoke a few words. Both declared that they had severed all ties with the military Government because it had betrayed its original program.

Upon reaching the monument to France, the crowd listened in respectful silence while a student of Buenos Aires University read a long proclamation expressing the Argentine people's desire for freedom, peace and justice. He ended: "Return to your homes and remain alert to comply with your duties as citizens. But don't let us separate, without performing a sacred duty and awearing a solemn cath. Do you swear on your country and on your honor to comply with and fight for the Constitution, that guarantees our people freedom, progress, peace and justice?"

The reply to this was a tremendous shout of „I swear." The meeting then broke up quietly. The Government succeeded in bringing such pressure to bear upon the Buenos Aires Transport Corporation that it completely paralyzed the whole transport system. But the people simply could not be kept away from today's demononstration.

The police were very much in evidence today, and especially the dreaded mounted squadron. There was no occasion, however, for police intervention. The demonstration took place without any incidents worthy of note, and the Argentine people thus proved their ability to conduct their political meetings in orderly fashion, when the police left them alone.«

October 4, 1945: »More than 30,000 university students belonging to all of Argentina's six national univerities, have gone on a nation-wide strike, thus taking the lead in the struggle of the Argentine people to regain their freedom and their rights.

Completely disregarding efforts that now are being made to reach a compromise between the Government and university councils, the students took matters boldly into their own hands and began a movement they hope will develop into a vast campaign of civil disobedience in which all democratically minded Argentines should participate.

In Buenos Aires the faculties of law, engineering and social science, which are in separate buildings in different parts of the city, were taken over yesterday by the students, who feared that the Government might occupy and close the university, thus depriving the students of a rallying point. They were besieged by a large force of uniformed policemen who, after cutting off light and water, tried to starve them out. A similar situation exists in the University of La Plata, the capital of Buenos Aires Province, and in some universities of the interior.

Police later began withdrawing from around the universities. The Associated Press reported, quoting unofficial sources as saying the move, allowing the students and professors to leave the buildings without incident, was made in an effort to avoid possible outbreaks of violence during the night.

The students' rebellious attitude called upon them the ire of the Government, which was enraged by their defiance of its authority. Yesterday afternoon things reached such a pitch that the faculty of engineering was attacked by a group of armed men who fired about thirty shots at studens inside the building.

First reports had it that nobody was hurt, but it is learned today that two students were wounded. Burrourding the faculty building is a very large force of uniformed police, both on foot and mounted. Riot and tear gas squads are lurking in near by streets.

This afternoon the United States Embassy delivered a strong official protest to the Argentine Foreign Ministry against the difficulties that the Government was placing in the way of communications between United States correspondents and their newspapers. Shortly afterward, the cable companies were informed by postoffice authorities that a previous order reestablishing censorship on outgoing dispatches had been a mistake and that there were no restrictions on press messages. This dispatch therefore was able to go through normal channels.

The censorship had been reimposed by the Argentine Government shortly after midnight when it informed the Buenos Aires offices of The Associated Press and The United Press and The International News Service that they were forbidden under pain of unspecified „measures" to send any information abroad about the Argentine student strike. All news agencies, whether foreign or local,were warned at the same time that they must not circulate any information on that subject within Argentina. No similar communication was addressed to special correspondents of United States newspapers, but cable and wireless companies had been forbidden to transmit dispatches dealing with the university situation and the prohibition therefore applied in effect to them also.

At the same time the Government gave approximately similar warnings to the Argentine press: all editors in Buenos Aires were visited by special envoy of the press under-secretariat who instructed them to publish nothing about the university situation.«

October 10, 1945: »The Argentine military base of Campo de Mayo on the outskirts of Buenos Aires, headed by its commander, Gen. Eduardo J. Avalos, suddenly turned against Vice President Juan Perón today and obliged him to leave the Government. Shortly before 6 o'olock the Minister of the Interior, Dr. Hortensio J. Quijano, announced officially that Col. Perón had resigned all his posts in the Government, namely, the Vice Presidency and the portfolios of War Minister and of Secretary of Labor and Social Welfare.

Dr. Quijano announced at the same time that on the 12th of this month a decree would be signed calling for elections on the first Sunday in April of next year. Although early reports suggested that Colonel Perón had been arrested, it was learned later by *The Associated Press* that he had returned to his apartment, where many young Army officers visited him, passing through a heavy guard thrown around the building.

The news of Dictator Perón's resignation gave rise to explosions of joy in Buenos Aires, and these, in turn, to serious rioting. Mounted and foot police dispersed the demonstrators. When the news reached Buenos Aires that Campo de Mayo had risen against Colonel Perón, President Edelmiro Farrell immediately drove there, apparently in the hope that he could induce the officers to reverse their attitude. His arrrival shortly before midday coincided with that of all commanders of divisions and chiefs of garrisons. They had been summoned to Campo de Mayo and had traveled by air.

President Farrell was soon obliged to recognise that general feeling in the Army was irrevocably against Colonel Perón, and he himself agreed that the only possible solution was to oust Colonel Perón. Soon afterward a delegation of officers from Campo de Mayo called on Colonel Perón at the War Ministery and returned to Campo de Mayo with his resignation.

Colonel Perón's resignation is undoubtedly a great victory for the Argentine people and they rightly interpret it as such. Most persons, however, still reserve their final judgment about today's events. It is not known, for instance, whether Colonel Perón at the same time as he left the Government also abandoned his Presidential aspirations, or whether he will still have to be reckoned with in the future.

It is not known yet who will replace him or what the Government's intentios are. Many persons see negative omens in the severity with which the police acted today agains the rajoicing crowds.

Nevertheless it is unquestioned that Colonel Perón is not only out of the Government but that he was forced out by a revolt of the army against him. Even if he decides to run for the Presidency he is not regarded as a dangerous contestant if, as may be resonably expected, he will not have the backing of the Government.

Most person's fears probably would be allayed if the Government were to lift the state of siege again. That, more than anything else, would help to create a suitable atmosphere for the elections. Up to the last moment before Colonel Perón's fall restrictive measures upon the press were kept in full force, and there is no guarantee that they will be relaxed immediately.

Half an hour after having resigned Colonel Perón left the War Ministry and went to his home. Later two Army trucks arrived at the War Ministry and began removing enormous quantities of papers, files and other document. It is not known whether this was done on orders from Colonel Perón or from Campo de Mayo.

The movement against Colonol Perón started last night, when an important meeting was held at Campo de Mayo. It was observed that about 400 motor cars filled with officers and civilians went there and stayed until well after midnight. The meeting was resumed this morning and resulted first in President Farrell's fruitless intervention and finally in Colonel Perón's resignation.

These sudden developments obviously caught General Farrell unprepared. After having left Campo de Mayo, he returned to the Presidential residence, where he was joyned by all high officers of the army, navy and air force. The outcome of this meeting, however, is that President Farrell still enjoys the confidence of the Argentine armed forces and that he is to continue in the Presidency. The most likely candidate for the Vice Presidency is though to be General Avalos, who led the movement against Colonel Perón.

The rebellion against Colonel Perón had the full backing of the navy. While the army was taking its decisions in Campo de Mayo, many high naval officers met in the home of Vice Admiral Hector Vermengo Lima, chief of the naval staff, and remained in close touch with developments at Camp de Mayo. After Colonel Perón's resignation had been obtained, naval officers went to the Presidential residence and participated in the discussion on the best course to follow from now on.

The best proof of the changed attitude of the army toward the present Government, as embodied by Colonel Perón was a the treatment that Campo de Mayo accorded to Gen. Arturo Rawson and Gen. Osvaldo Martin and five other officers under arrest for heading the military plot in Cordoba on the 25th of last month. Up to today, they had been kept in cells and under strong guard. This afternoon they were in the Officers Club, having their health drunk in champagne.

Buenos Aires and, indeed, all Argentina, lived through some very uncertain and anxious hours today when everybody knew that something unusual was taking place in Campo de Mayo, but nobody knew exactly what. It was evident that extraordinary precautions were being taken. Troops at Campo de Mayo and those of the First and Second Divisions were confined to barracks. The gendarmerie and what naval forces were in the city were kept in readiness for any emergency. The police ordered every available man to report for duty. All civil air fields were occupied by the military. Great numbers of planes were seen arriving at the airbase of El Palomar, right alongside Campo de Mayo.

The news spread like a forest fire, and crowds assembled in the streets almost immediately. Demonstrations were organized spontaneously. Crowds moved through the main streets crying, „We want his head." The joy probably would have spent itself naturally after some time, but the police intferred, with altogether unnessesary severity. The crowds were infuriated by charges of the mounted police, and soon rioting began.«

October 14, 1945: »The Argentine crisis precipitated by the ejection from the Government on Tuesday of Vice President Col. Juan D. Perón underwent three dramatic developments today when President Edelmiro J. Farrell accepted the resignation of all Ministers and Secretaries of State, with the exception of the newly appointed Minister of War, Gen. Eduardo Avalos, and later grudgingly permitted the Army to place Colonel Perón under arrest. Finally, the President submitted his resignation to the military leaders.

Both these events were hailed by the Argentine people as victories, although the majority are still dissatisfied because they wish General Farrell to resign also and hand over the powers of Government to the Supreme Court.

It was learned late this evening that General Farrell had sent his resignation to the committee of generals and admirals who have taken it upon themselves to carry on the negotiations to form a new Cabinet. The acceptance of General Farrell's" resignation, however, would be·tantamount to handing over the Government to the Suprem Court, as the Constitution provides that the court shall take over when there is neither a President nor Vice President.

Campo de Mayo's garrison decided against this solution. Instead it decided to keep General Farrell's resignation in reserve for the present. The plan, in other words, is to organize a new Government under General Farrell's Presidency and then later on either accept or not accept his resignation as further developments may counsel.

What happened to Colonel Perón after his arrest is not certain. It is believed, however, that he is on board a small gunboat on the River Plate and is under strict surveillance. It is stated that one of the new government's first acts will be to bring him to trial.

At least one person was killed and nearly fifty injured Friday night as mounted police, awinging sabers and firing blank cartridges, charged thousands of Argentines in front of the Military Club in San Martin Square, *The Associated Press* reported. At least five of the wounded were policemen. After the first police charge, armed civilians sniped at mounted officers from doorways. The police abandoned tear gas and sabers for armored cars, rifles and sub-machineguns as street corners became the scene of battles.

After the resignation of General Farrell's Cabinet the political situation developed into something closely resembling chaos. Of the posts left vacant by the resigning Ministers, only the Ministry of the Navy has been filled, this post having been accepted by Vice Admiral Hector Vernengo Lima, formerly Chief of the Naval Staff. Since midday today, therefore, Argentina, in effect, has been without a Government, as the only men left in power are General Farrell and his Ministers of War and of the Navy.

The formation of a new Cabinet was delayed at first by General Farrell, who stubbornly refused even to consider the appointment of new Ministers until his great personal friend, Colonel Perón, had been released. When he finally yielded on this point it was found that none of the prominent men who were under consideration as candidates for Ministerial posts would cooperate with General Farrell.

Everyone on all sides insisted that the only acceptable solution was that the Government should be turned over to the Supreme Court. This solution, however, was vetoed by the Army garrison of Campo de Mayo, which is still the dominant factor in Argentine politics.

Tonight, the prospects for a solution of this impasse seemed somewhat brighter, and it was hoped that at least the first three or four Ministers would be appointed tomorrow. One suggestion that seems to have found favor is that a council of notables should be appointed, with the task of choosing a new cabinet. Even some persons who had at first refused to cooperate in the Government headed by President Farrell seemed disposed this evening to do so in view of the urgent necessity that some decision should be taken without delay. Possibly, however, the conversations that are still going on as this is being written may render the appointment of a council of notables unnecessary.

After a day of excitement and alarms, in which ultimatums and threats of military marches upon Buenos Aires followed one another in uninterrupted succession, three distinct points of view stood out among the Army and Navy officlers who held the solution of the Argentine crisis in their hands.

First, there was the view of General Farrell and his supporters, who are trying to save what can still be saved of the military government, and who perhaps are also attempting to protect Colonel Perón out of personal friendship.

Second, there is the military garrison of Campo de Mayo, which insisted on he resignation of the entire Cabinet but resisted any suggestion that the Government should hand over its powers to the Supreme Court.

Third, there is the committee of generals and admirals, with headquarters in the Military Club in Buenos Aires, which wished the resignation of the whole Govennment, including General Farrell, and the delivery of its powers to the Supreme Court.

This last suggestion was the one that had the support also of a large majority of the Argentine people. It was discarded early in the day, however. Campo de Mayo, with its overwhelming military force at the very gates of Buenos Aires, held the balance of power and would not even hear of it.

The efforts of the committee of generals and admirals thereupon concentrated on obtaining at least the resignation of all members of the Cabinet, and this was apparently achieved without very great difficulty, since the Campo de Mayo also favored that plan. The question of how a new Cabinet should be formed was very much more complicated because all civilians who had been approached at first refused to cooperate in a Government headed by General Farrell.

The generals' and admirals' committee, which included Gen. Orlando Peluffo, former Foreign Mininster, and Gen. Alberto Guglielmone, and Navy Minister Vernengo Lima and the commander of the river fleet Leonardo MacLean, was at work at 10 o'clock this morning.

At that time it called at the War Ministry, where it conferred with the War Minister, General Avalos, and the chief of the general army staff, Gen. Carlos von der Becke, and other leading officers.

From there they went to the Presidential residence to sound out General Farrell and his aides. Then they returned to the War Ministry and from there went to the Military Club, where they consulted with many prominent civilian figures in the political and intellectual worlds.

While these events were going on, crowds of some thousands of persons had gathered outside the Military Club and made it quite plain that the Argentine people wanted the Government to deliver its powers to the Supreme Court. There was a moment of near panic when the dreaded mounted police appeared on the scene and warned the crowd that no public demonstrations would be permitted.

The day was saved, however, by a young officer in uniform who appeared at a window of the Military Club and shouted to the commander of the mounted police that if he dared to charge on the people, all officers in the club would themselves lead the people against the police and take the consequences. The police thereupon prudently retired out of sight, allthough they remained in great force in near-by streets.

Unidentified persons had chalked or written in red paint on the front of the Military Club such phrases as „To the gallows with Perón." One wit, anticipating the early withdrawal of the military from the Government, had placed a board outside the club with the words „For Rent."

While the crowd was waiting for developments members of various democratic organizations read proclamations from the balcony of a near-by house. They all contained a three-point program; namely, first the delivery to the Supreme Court of the Government's powers; second, elections according to the old electoral law, without the modifications introduced into it by the military Government, and third, the lifting of the state of siege. There were some few incidents, as when one young man was manhandled for crying „Long live Perón!"

There was great enthusiasm when, from the windows of the Military Club, it was announced that the Cabinet had resigned. But the enthusiasm was even greater when the crowds were told some time later that Colonel Perón was under arrest. Finally a few minutes after 2 o'clock Admiral Vernengo Lima appeared at a window of the club and announced that the idea of turning over the Government to the Supreme Court had been discarded, but that the Army and Navy would see to it that Argentina soon would have a Govermnent of the people, for the people and by the people.

There were numerous protests from the crowd and shouts of „We have heard such promises from Perón." The admiral replied with dignity, „I am not Perón. I am Admiral Vernengo Lima." Admiral Vernengo Lima then announced that the whole Cabinet· had resigned, and added, that General Farrell and the Army and Navy had given .him their word that they were in sympathy with the ideas of the Argentine people and they would hold the persons responsible for the present situation, and especially Colonel Perón, accountable for their actions. This last statement was cheered to the echo.

The admiral ended by saying that the new Cabinet would be constituted by the best men in the country, and that he himself, as senior admiral, had accepted the post of Minister of the Navy. Though the final solution was not quite what the Argentine people had hoped for, they nevertheless made the best of it, and Admiral Vernengo Lima's words were on the whole not unkindly received.

Large crowds remained outside the Military Club all afternoon, awaiting news of further developments. There was no noticeable decrease of enthusiasm while the people kept singing songs and shouting the catchwords that have become fashionable during the last few months of the military régime. As the day wore on and tempers became frayed, however, the people clearly showed their resentment against the army for blocking their desire that the Government's powers should be turned over to the Supreme Court. The appearance of army officers at the windows of the club brought forth hostile cries, whereas that of naval officers was applauded.«

December 23, 1945: »Juan D. Perón was heard again last week after a silence that had lasted more or less uninterruptedly for two months. He addressed a crowd that certainly exceeded one hundred thousand and spoke in conciliatory terms, making an effort to allay the fears of Argentine democrats and to win the Catholic vote for himself.

But Perón's dulcet tones could not make the people forget that up to the eve of his latest and greatest public meeting, his gunmen had spoken in the only language they know, and that the lengthening list of their victims bears mute but eloquent testimony to the convincingness of their arguments and to the accuray of their aim.

After the outrages of Dec. 8 in the Plaza del Congreso, when Perónistas killed four persons and wounded more than thirty, Senor Perón made haste to shed crocodile tears over the victims. Such practices, he proclaimed, are undemocratic and those who indulge in them can therefore be no friends of his. But he admitted that the shooting had been started by men who had shouted ,"Death to the Jews!" and „Long live Perón!"

The democratic parties are fighting with their backs to the wall and they know it. They are fighting not only against the undeniable fascination that Senor Perón exercises

„SHADOW OVER ARGENTINA"

over some strata of the Argentine population but also against the apparatus of violence and intimidation that he built while he was in power and that is now in the hands of his trusted lieutenants.

The Secretariat of Labor and Social Welfare, the Subsecretariat of Information and Press, the federal police and most federal commiasioners in the provinces are working for Senor Perón night and day. They form a combination that is hard to beat.

Nevertheless the democratic parties are perhaps encouraged rather than downcast by the recent outbursts of violence. They argue, not unreasonably, that if Senor Perón must resort to bloodshed and brute force it means that he realizes that he cannot win by any other means.

It must not be thought, however, that Senor Perón relies exclusively on violence and on his machine. What everyone can see is that Senor Pcrón, despite his most strenuous efforts, has not yet succeeded in calling out crowds as numerous as those that gather in Buenos Aires at the first bidding of the democratic parties. But Buenos Aires is not the whole of Argentina and what is happening in the provinces and especially in the poorest and most backward provinces, is still something of a mystery even to experienced political observers.

The direct observation of crowds that attend pro-Perón meetings would indicate that his appeal is mainly to the humblest and poorest among the Argentine workers. Most of his followers seem to have been recruited among the unskilled workers, whereas the skilled workers have in the main remained true to their old leaders and their free unions, which are decidedly against Senor Perón.

There is no denying, also, that many of Senor Perón's followers believe in him implicitly and with an almost mystic faith. The opposition says that large sums of money are spent on hiring people to shout „Viva Perón" and in general to stir up factitious enthusiasm. This is undoubtedly true, but, on the other hand, nobody who has watched any pro-Perón meeting doubts that some of the persons who participate in them regard him as a demigod.

This correspondent was impressed, for instance, by several thousand persons who got soaked to the skin last month standing in the rain for four hours, without any noticeable decrease of enthusiasm, in the hope - which was finally disappointed - of hearing Senor Perón speak.

This does not mean, of course, that there is not enthusiasm also on the other side. One hundred and fifty thousand or so persons who last Saturday listened to speeches at a democratic rally in the Plaza del Congreso while revolvers were carcking all around them, proved that they also had a strong conviction for which they were ready to make sacrifices.

As compared with Senor Perón, however, the opposition parties suffer two serious drawbacks. The first is that they are divided, since the National Democrats (Conservatives) do not belong to the Democratic Union and the anti-Perón vote therefore will be split. The second is that they have not yet produced a leader as colorful and audacious as Senor Perón.«

1958: THE BRUTAL BATISTA GOVERNMENT ON CUBA

Joseph G. Martin/Philip J. Santora, *New York Daily News*

When the International Reporting jurors in their report of March 12, 1959, placed an exhibit by the *New York Daily News* on second rank, they did not say a word about the contents of the newspaper's articles submitted for the Pulitzer competition. The Board declared the entry as the winner and gave the award to two journalists of the newspaper, Joseph G. Martin and Philip J. Santora, „for their exclusive series of articles disclosing the brutality of the Batista government in Cuba“. The *News* entry consisted exclusively of their collective articles.

The two reporters began their search for the truth behind the Batista régime early in March 1958. They sought out underground contacts in Washington, Miami and New York. They spent weeks sifting fact from propaganda in Havana, Guanavo Beach and elsewhere in Cuba. During their stay in Havana they were followed by Security Intelligence Police, their rooms were searched, their telephones tapped. Atrocity pictures, more than 200 of them, were obtained from secret sources and these had to be smuggled out. Martin and Santora were forced to memorize names, addresses and telephone numbers so if they were stopped and searched, the lives of these contacts would not be forfeited. The articles evoked wide-spread interest at the time they were published although in some quarters they were believed too incredible to be true. It was the first time that the real story behind the Batista dictatorship was made known to the American people.

Joseph George Martin was born on May 9, 1915, in New York City. In the depths of the depression, he quit high school in Queens and roamed the town looking for jobs in warehouses, factories and on the docks. He never got a job as a laborer, but somebody was able to place him on the *New York Daily News* as a copyboy in 1933. Within a year he was advanced to reporter, working out of Brooklyn police headquarters and on general assignment until he entered the Army Air Force in 1943; he was discharged early in 1946. Back to work at the *News*, Martin shortly uncovered a large scale-building racket on Long Island which defrauded hundreds of ex-GIs and developed other stories that won him awards from veterans' groups. - Philip Joseph Santora, born on July 29, 1911, in New York City, was educated at Syracuse University (1929) and received a B.A. degree from New York University in 1933; then he was a graduate student at the Sorbonne, Paris. During World War II, Santora was assigned to Military Intelligence with Patton's Third Army. Before he took up newspaper work on the *New York Daily Mirror* (1936-1943, 1946-1954), Santora had a varied career: boxing instructor, clerk at Bellevue Hospital, etc. In 1954 he came to the *New York Daily News* as a special feature writer. Following now are several of their award-winning articles:

April 7, 1958: »Tortured, enslaved Cuba is teetering on the brink of the bloodiest revolution in its strife-ripped history, with most of the crocodile-shaped island's population awaiting the call to death or liberation with almost cheerful fatalism. The Cubans hope the outside world will understand. They want others to understand, for instance, that when a young girl is raped by a police chief while his grinning cops hold back the heartbroken father, the day of reckoning can include no mercy. That the police official who produced a bullet-riddled body and sneered, „There's the answer to your habeas corpus" cannot be dealt with in the ordinary legal way.

These are merely random samples of atrocities committed in the name of president Fulgencio Batista. Murder, rape, corruption in low and high places, the torture methods employed by police, the systematic plundering of a rich country, the reduction to enslavement of what was once a gay, happy people - these are merely a few of the scores Cubans must settle. Is this a one-sided picture? It might seem so. But it's the picture we-found - and we went to Cuba to get both sides of the story.

During the past six years, over 4,000 anti-Batista Cubans have met death by violence - victims of a reign of terror that ranks with Heinrich Himmler's Gestapo in Nazi Germany, the OGPU in Soviet Russia and even the Spanish Inquisition. Friends and relatives of the victims have not forgotten. They want the slate wiped clean, and if it can be wiped clean only with blood - well, that's the way they want it. „We won't even try to hold them back for the first three days," said a responsible member of the underground. „It would be like trying to hold back the ocean. They have waited a long time - and a blood bath is the only way to make a fresh start."

The present reign of terror is taking place less than 100 miles from the mainland of the greatest democracy in the world. It is being conducted with ruthless efficiency and the people of Havana - no matter what their sympathies - don't go out at night unless it's absolutely necessary. The dreaded SIM, the Security Police, patrol the streets in their olive-colored cars and uniforms and shove machine guns under the chins of citizens. They're merely asking for identity cards, but the machine guns are always present. More than any other weapon, the machine gun is the symbol of Cuban rule.

There are two types of censorship in Cuba. There is the ridiculous, arbitrary type imposed by the government. And there is the self-censorship imposed by the newsmen, both domestic and foreign, who have sold out to the Batista government. Except in rare cases, the things that filter through this palmetto curtain are thoroughly distorted. „Please tell the rest of the world what's going on here," begged a Cuban lawyer.

Our trail began with the underground in New York and led to Miami, where more than 2,000 exiles are fighting to extricate their beloved Cuba from the grasp of its oppressors. It led to Havana, where foreigners who carry typewriters and cameras are viewed with suspicion and kept under constant police surveillance.

What really goes on in Havana? At night, for one thing, strange things happen in cemeteries. A woman who went out one morning to pray at the tomb of her husband, thought the slab on the above-ground mausoleum seemed off-center. Her son investigated and found three bodies had been dropped in during the past two nights. The wife of an important banker was sent out of the country by her husband because a police official became smitten with her - and what the police want in Cuba, they take.

Rumors have spread that the Communists have been supporting Fidel Castro, military leader of the revolutionaries in Oriente Province. One report states that Russian submarines have been landing arms in the Santiago sector. The insurgents deny these reports. Even though the Communist Party last week announced its support, they say, it is neither needed nor wanted. They add that the Reds are a weak party in Cuba, without resources to buy munitions. They further point out that Batista was on the Red ballot and legalized the party out of gratitude. Since then, however, Batista has outlawed the Reds.

These is a great deal to be said for the rebel argument. The great middle class of Cuba is anti-Red and extremely powerful and respected. There is a saying that when Cuba's middle class takes a hand in politics something happens. More than that - they are completely selfless. Many of these doctors, lawyers, teachers and accountants could find employment in the U.S. if they chose to emigrate. They could bow to Batista and their fortunes would be intact and their families safe from the SIM. But to them this is unthinkable. They are Cubans and they would rather stay and fight - even at the risk of having their families annihilated. Chivatos - spies - are everywhere. The bootblack may be selling information. Taxi drivers keep their ears open. The room boys at the hotel. Waiters. For a few pesos the spies sell their neighbors to the secret police. Phones are not to be trusted even when used by non-political U.S. tourists and businessmen. Cables and mail are subject to censorship.

There are 6,000,000 people in Cuba. They are a proud race and they are being held captive by a brutal minority that rules by atrocities, murders, and plunder. Batista is reputed by the revolutionaries to have $300 million in Swiss banks. Gen. Francisco Tabernilla, head of the Cuban army, is the man behind a chain of discount houses. His son, Gen. Francisco Tabernilla Jr., by sheerest coincidence head of the Air Force, flies in electric appliances and household goods in military planes, avoids the customs inspectors and thus undersells legitimate dealers. Eusebio Mujal rules Cuba's workers with an iron hand and an elastic conscience. He's one of Cuba's most feared and hated men. He even outranks Batista as a man to be eliminated. He is slated for execution at the first opportunity.

The last six years have been a nightmare for those Cubans who do not belong to the Batista group. „The island smells of death," said a Cuban doctor, „the earth is soaked with the blood of Cuban martyrs. We cannot leave it. We must win - whether it is tomorrow or next week or next year. With Castro or with someone else." Batista would like to impose martial law, he said, but this would wreck the already badly-hit tourist trade and ruin the business at the gangster-operated casinos. Schools are closed. Children are kept off the streets. Sugar cane workers are taking lessons in sabotaging the crops - they would rather go hungry than have the profits filter into the pockets of Batista and his insatiable followers.

Batista's informers operate widely in Miami and Mexico. They spy for pay, giving the time and place of arms shipments destined for Castro's forces in the Sierra Maestra mounor for Faure Chomon's insurgents in the Sierra Escambray or for the Directorio

Revolucionario. Or for other, smaller groups. „If all of these groups could be placed under one command," said a rebel wistfully, „we could take over the government within a matter of days. Much of the army would come over to us." But there is no unified command. Nevertheless, there is help for Castro's forces. Arms are hidden everywhere in Havana. Occasionally, through torture, a captive rebel discloses the hiding place of a cache of grenades or machine guns or carbines, rifles and dynamite. But there is more where those came from. Rich men are behind the movement. Even middle-class Cubans give until it hurts.

And there is sabotage. Cuba's rich sugar cane fields, the backbone of her economy, are particularly vulnerable. The rebels distribute pamphlets showing workers how to tie phosphorous to the rats which infest the fields and thus start fires. There are the bombs that set oil storage tanks afire. Rails are ripped from the railroads that penetrate the interior of the island. Could bloodshed be avoided if Batista consented to free elections? Batista, say the rebels, would merely put up his usual straw men and knock them over and retain power. There can be no solution, they insist, while Batista is in power.

Cubans who had been hurt and puzzled by the U.S. policy of sending arms to Batista, are a bit mollified by the recent embargo on munitions shipments to the Cuban dictator. The embargo became known only when the U.S. suspended shipment two weeks ago of 1,950 Garand riffles ordered by the Cuban government in 1956. „We hope that this action will continue," said an insurgent, „and that your country will not give Batista more arms with which to fight us. We cannot fight your country and our oppressor. Give us only the chance to resolve our differences by ourselves. We Cubans emulate you Americans in every way. We try to imitate your dress, your manners. We go to watch your movies. We try to learn your language. Our homes and our lives and even our schools are patterned after yours. Don't force us to cast aside our respect and admiration for you."

Havana has a population of 1,200,000. But only in the dirty side-streets and alleys do the people venture out in numbers after dark. Because these are the people who have nothing more to lose - except their lives. And lives aren't held too dearly by those who have to beg for a living, by those who have to walk the streets selling themselves into prostitution or by the wispy women who hold infants in their arms and beg coins from the dwindling tourist population. The one thing all seem to have is boundless courage. It takes courage for an underground contact to walk through a crowded hotel lobby and telephone the room of visiting newspapermen. For he doesn't know if the elevator man has decided to sell out. Or if the telephone operator is a chivato working for the SIM.

A few weeks back, a spy in Miami sold the sons of a Cuban patriot to the secret police. The Cuban had asked the secret Batista agent for the best way of sending his sons to Cuba to take part in the fight for freedom. He was told that the boys could go by plane directly to Havana and that they would be well taken care of there. The father said he didn't want the boys to go, but that they were insisting and he could not forbid

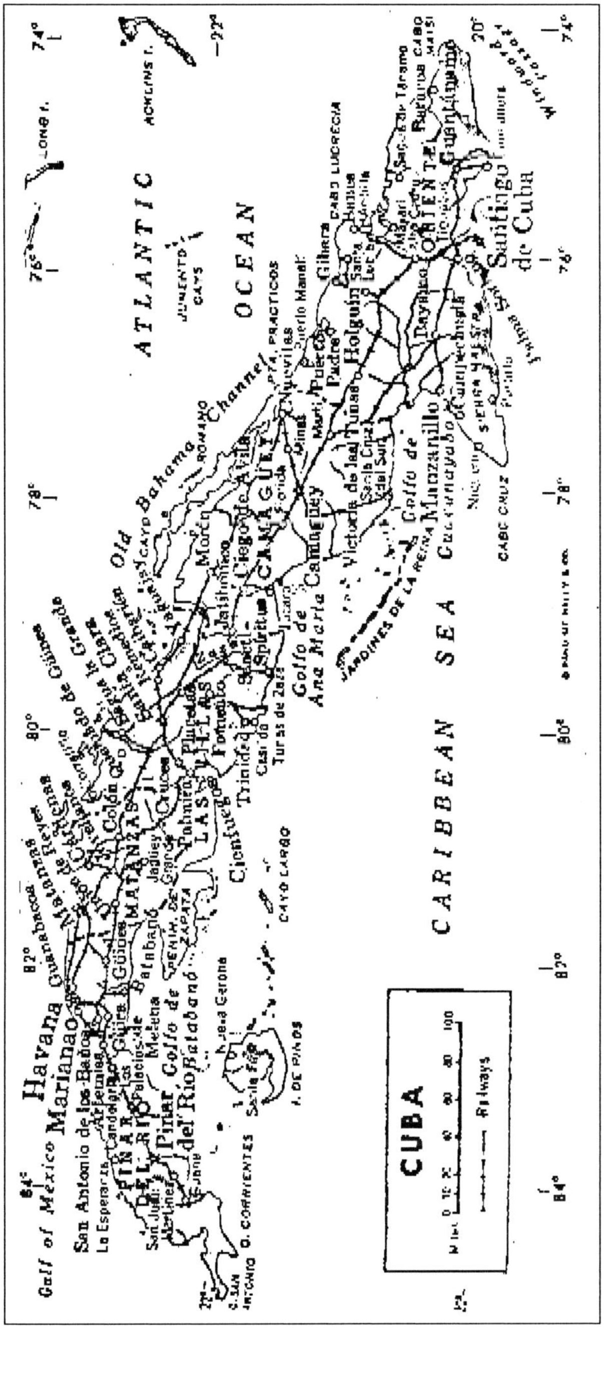
CUBA
Railways
Gulf of Mexico
Havana
Old Bahama Channel
ATLANTIC
OCEAN
CARIBBEAN
SEA
Santiago de Cuba

them. He wanted them safe. Was the agent sure this was the best way? The agent assured him that was the ticket. The contact would be made in a Havana restaurant, he said. The boys were greeted by the SIM when they landed. They were missing for several days. Then their bullet-riddled bodies were found in a Havana suburb. Back in Miami, the informer was badly beaten. He wasn't killed. „We didn't want a major crime on our hands," said a rebel. „No international incident to undo the work we're doing. But some day the deaths of those boys will be avenged." One more score to be wiped off that slate.

A general strike is the greatest weapon of the men who follow Castro and his insurgents. In every revolution in Cuba's history, the organized force of workers has been a decisive factor in the fall of the régime. The second weapon is the power held by the great middle class - the lawyers, doctors, small bankers and students. The students of Havana University - 18,000 strong - have a history of fighting tyranny that goes back over 80 years. Hundreds of these have been arrested recently. Hundreds of others have disappeared.

American gamblers and hoods who took over the casinos at the Riviera, Hilton and Capri are trying to laugh off a revolution. They insist that „Castro is a nut" and that Batista is too strong to be overthrown. They are whistling past the graveyard. It is well known that Castro and other insurgent leaders are against gambling, particularly gambling controlled by shady characters from the U.S. Castro is quoted as saying: „Gambling is the cancer that has been eating at my country; it must be cut out." „But that's a secondary item," said one of our contacts. „The régime must go. We must have free elections. We must have our real plight described to the world by journalists who can't be subsidized or bought. Just tell the true story, that's all we ask."«

April 8, 1958: »This is a grim rollcall of Fulgencio Batista's chief terrorists - killers so brutal and ruthless that even the man who helped create the monsters seems afraid of trying to control them. These are the men whose names are whispered with fear and hate, whose incredibly sadistic deeds read like pages torn from the records at Dachau. Maj. Estaban Ventura Nobo dislikes dull evenings. When one comes along, he sends his police out to pick up unfortunates who stray into one of the three police districts technically under his control - actually, he operates throughout Havana. Then he beats a selected victim into insensibility just for the kicks. Ventura's name has become a lewd epithet throughout Cuba. He is an avid student of torture, having been tutored in the fine points by Angel Borlenghi, who was minister of the interior in Argentina under ex-dictator Juan Perón.

Recently, Ventura used a Borlenghi invention - putting two electrodes on the genitals of a 16-year-old boy and shocking him into what he hoped would be a confession of „his crimes against the state." The electrodes touched and the boy was electrocuted, cutting short Ventura's fun for the day. Another Ventura gimmick is a basket made of piano wire which is fastend about the genitals. Two wires draw the basket shut, causing indescribable pain. He has been known to rip the ear off a subject when a beating with fists failed to get results.

Ventura goes under psychiatric care at intervals. But in between treatments he roams the streets of Havana with up to a dozen heavily armed bodyguards, looking for victims to assuage his thirst for torture. He loves expensive white suits and keeps one or two in each of the precincts under his command. He's also nuts about publicity and when the photographers show up, Ventura dons a fresh white suit, sprinkles a bit of cologne on his hair and pencil-thin moustache and holds a press conference. Lean, about 160 pounds, 40 years old, married and the father of two young daughters he was born in Pinar del Rio Province in the western part of Cuba. Those are the so-called vital statistics. Ventura has mistresses throughout the area of his command. He can well afford them with the money he gets from business men who either get up the monthly assessment or find themselves answering questions in the cellar of a stationhouse.

Batista turns a deaf ear to pleas - and some of these come from his top aids - to remove Ventura from his post. Even the Gerardo Abreu incident failed to away him from loyalty to the terrorist who swaggers through Havana instilling fear in the most innocent of Cubans. Gerardo Abreu's death resulted in the only indictment ever handed up against Ventura. Abreu was a 20-year-old pianist-student who was socially popular among young people in Havana. Ventura ordered him arrested on charges of terrorism - an ironic touch - and sentenced him to jail. He was released on a writ of habeas corpus. Less than a week after his release, he was again arrested by Ventura.

Immediately, there were cries for „justice“ from social and student groups. A witness gives the conclusion of the grim story: „I heard noises on the street in front of the Palace of Justice. Guards from the palace were there and they were discussing something in loud tones with other men. It was about 11 P. M. A few minutes later, I heard the chatter of a machine gun. I saw three men get into a car and drive off.“ Abreu's body was found there the next morning. No one dared approach the spot during the night. Ventura was quoted later as saying: „They wanted justice - and I gave them justice, with interest.“ The dreaded, dapper killer is also the author of the phrase, „Here's your habeas corpus.“ It was uttered when the lifeless body of a suspected terrorist was dumped at the feet of the lawyer who had obtained the writ.

Ventura was an obscure lieutenant in charge of the 5th Precinct five years ago, before he distinguished himself by working over a priest, the Rev. Ramon O'Farril, who had plotted to have President Batista ambushed on one of his infrequent visits to church. Father O'Farril was so badly beaten that he suffered fractures of two ribs, internal injuries and is permanently deaf in one ear. In Miami, the exiled priest admitted his part in the plot to have Batista assassinated. „It is high time,“ he said, „that the UN stepped into the Cuban case. They should step in if for no other reasons than the reasons of humanity. The bloodiest drama in the gory history of Latin America is now taking place in Cuba. There have been thousands of deaths - murders by the Batista régime. There are the countless tortures and humiliations. These and the exiles who have been ousted from their homeland are more than sufficient reason for international intervention in the Cuban problem. Not even the highest prelates of the Roman Catholic Church have escaped terrorist action under the Batista régime. The Cuban people are in immediate need of the help of all the Catholics of the world and also of the moral and physical support of all the upright and wholesome people of the free world."

Ventura's closes rival in the brutality sweepstakes is Capt. Julio Laurent, in charge of naval intelligence. Laurent was an unknown bush-leaguer before he murdered his first Cuban. The victim was a supporter of ex-President Carlos Prio Socarras. He was arrested in a house in the swank Vedado section, dragged out into the street where Laurent, then a lieutenant, was waiting with a submachine gun in hand. While two men held the suspected terrorist, Laurent pressed the tommygun against his body and cut him almost in half with three long bursts. Then he turned to the crowd of horrified spectators and shouted: „And anyone who accuses me will die a similar death." He was charged with murder, but no witnesses would appear against him. Along with Ventura, he was accused of the murder of a captain involved in the Cienfuegos uprising last Sept. 5. The captain, Alfredo Gonzales Brito, was brought to Havana after his arrest in Cienfuegos. In the home of the second ranking commander of the Cuban navy, he was beaten and kicked into unconsciousness. Revived, he was tortured with cigars and cigarets that burned hole over more than half of his body. The finale came when Laurent and Ventura ordered the captain and a close friend taken to a castle tower overlooking the sea. There, the two were gagged, trussed and thrown into the sea.

An incident that has caused the greatest indignation concerns a 50-year-old schoolteacher, Mrs. Esther Milanes. Mrs. Milanes was a teacher in a Catholic school and had a minor part in the underground movement. She was picked up, along with a student from Colombia, South America, by men under the command of Capt. Jose Sosa, another of the sadists who pretend to administer justice in Havana. The woman was beaten with fists and the flat feet of Sosa and his henchmen in an attempt to make her talk. They threatened to have her raped by a particularly repulsive-looking member of the precinct force. When threats and heatings failed, they took an iron bar and inserted it forcibly into her body.

Mrs. Milanes might never have been released alive had it not been for the Colombian ambassador, who went looking for the student. She and the boy were released in his custody and she was rushed to the hospital. She revealed that they tortured the boy in front of her in an attempt to break her down. Then there is Col. Manuel Uglade Carrillo, who likes to sit in the third degree room and watch prisoners being given a working over. Uglade, who was the first chief of the SIM (secret police) when Batista came into power, laughs heartily while the girsly torture goes on. The new chief of police in Havana is Pilar Garcia, who got his reputation by quelling a riot at Matanzas two years ago this month. After the uprising had been put down Garcia made „examples" of 11 rioters. He had them shot.

There is, in Santiago de Cuba, a lieutenant colonel named Jose Maria Salas Canizares who, along with his brother; gained notoriety throughout the island for violence. Canizares, 6-foot, 200-pound thug, likes to lead his men into battle with the visor of his legion-style cap turned up. Sort of a trade mark. He carries an ox goad with which he strikes people during demonstrations. When he was assigned to Santiago, he promptly ordered a blackout and then riddled a few houses with machine gun bullets so that the „people in this city will know who's boss.“ Then he went out to pick up the local leader of Castro's July 26 movement. He picked up two young men. He had an idea that one of them was the real thing but didn't know which one. So he killed them both to make sure. When the weeping widow of one remonstrated, Canizares laughed and volunteered that he and his men could take care of her sexual wants.

These are the chiefs. But the men under them can be equally brutal. In some instances, they surpass their leaders because they feel that is the way to success and recognition under Batista. Another killer was Col. Fermin Cowley, who won his spurs in Holguin, in the northern port of Oriente Province on Christmas Day, 1956. On that day, Cowley hanged 14 students, supporters of the Castro movement. One of the victims was the brother of Rep. Eugenio Cusido, who is still in office. On the day the victims were being buried, Cowley showed up and said he didn't like the way the ceremonies were being conducted. He ordered the funerals suspended. Early last year, rebels stopped a bus on the main road into Oriente. They ordered the passengers out - with their luggage - and then set fire to the bus. Cowley demanded that the passengers and driver identify the rebels. They said they couldn't. When four suspects were brought in, Cowley asked the driver to identify them. He said he couldn't because he hadn't seen their faces. Cowley hanged all four, „just in case they were all guilty.“

A year ago this month, a World War II paratrooper went to Oriente Province with 27 men. The veteran, Calixto Sanchez, was one of those suspected of having taken part in the March 1957 attack on the presidential palace in Havana. In mid-April, he was surrounded by government forces and surrendered to a lieutenant who offered him the guarantee of a formal trial. When Cowley learned of the surrender he personally machine-gunned all 28 to death. The „mad colonel“ was married seven times. He had no children, but he collected German-made toys with a sort of psychopathic intensity. His career came to an abrupt halt several weeks later when Fidel Castro sent two men out of the Sierra Maestra with orders to liquidate the colonel. Cowley - traveling confidently with a small bodyguard - showed up at a store one day to buy light bulbs. The clerk said he didn't have the type on hand and suggested Cowley return the next day. Cowley came back the following day and was shot to death by the Castro executioners waiting in ambush.

On March 24 - two weeks ago - a woman was arrested in a Havana hospital only two days after bearing a child. The charge was not made clear and she hasn't been seen since. The baby is still in the hospital. In the little town of San Juan Martinez, a local magistrate sent his sons off to the movies. The boys, Luis Saiz, 16, and Sergio Saiz, 14, got into an argument with a soldier. He shot them to death. When the funeral was held the next day, the angry towns-people had words with soldiers and police. The police opened fire and killed eight with machine-gun fire.

These are but a few of the incidents sworn to by Cubans of highest integrity but smothered by the Cuban press, which is firmly under Batista's thumb. And with such things taking place less than an hour's plane ride from Miami -less than 100 miles from United States soil - these Cubans want their democratic neighbors to know.«

April 11, 1958: »Swarthy, solidly-built Gen. Jorge Garcia Tunon is a man who - through an error in judgment - helped write one of the bloodiest chapters in Cuban history. Today, in Miami, he's a bitter, disillusioned man, reluctant to talk about it. For Gen. Tunon is the man who engineered the coup d'etat that put President Fulgencio Batista into power six bloody years ago. It is something that the general, a completely honest man living in poverty, will always have on his conscience.

„You must understand the reasoning behind the coup," he said. „Batista just 80 days before the June 1 elections of 1952, was a beaten man. He was being backed by the Partido Accion Unitaria, the PAU, or United Action Party. Less than 10% of the votes were his." Dr. Roberto Agramonte was the candidate of the Orthodox Party, or Partido del Pueblo Cubano. He had about 60% of the votes, according to a straw poll. Carlos Hevia was the choice of the Authentic Party, Partido Revolucionario Cubano. Carlos Prio Socorras was president and high-ranking army officers were unhappy with his corrupt régime.

„The army has always been strong in politics," said Gen. Tunon, „and we were concerned with the fact that those around Prio were weak, that our country needed a group of honest men in office. We had no ambitions for ourselves - or at least at that time, I believed this was so. We felt that Batista was the best man of the three. We wanted a strong man who would clean up the situation and begin a new, better period of history with liberty and order. I was a captain at the time, in charge of a company in Columbia barracks at Military City."

„We remembered that when Batista had been president eight years earlier, he had wielded real authority. We talked to him and he told us in many beautiful phrases of his love for Cuba, that he could do many things now that he could not do in the past when so much confusion had been present in his régime. He told me that he was penitent about the reforms he could not carry out in his previous term. The talk took place in the house of his mother-in-law. He told me that he had some young officers already on his side. You must understand that when people spoke of him in those days, they did so with respect. People said that the killings in the streets would be eliminated if Batista were in power - that he would bring peace to our Cuba. What an irony!"

„Originally, the plan was to make Batista prime minister. The president, at that time, was scheduled to be Alonso Pujol. He headed a military junta. But Pujol was too intelligent to be under the thumb of Batista. Pujol backed out. He not only refused to be part of the scheme but he denied he had been in on early conferences. Batista spoke of the main problems facing the new government: (1) an honest administration free as much as possible of corruption; (2) getting rid of the gangster element supported by the civilian government, and (3) to respect all the institutions of the country, such as civil guarantees, free speech, free elections, etc."

The climax of the coup was a thing out of a play. The coup was almost ruined because Batista ordered his car out of line en route to the Columbia barracks so that he could meet a friend and put on his good-luck leather jacket, one which he had worn as an army sergeant. „We prepared a plan,“ Gen. Tunon continued, „whereby 11 officers in Columbia barracks, eight in La Cabana, three in the air force and eight in the navy prepared the men under them. No one else knew of the plot. Early on the morning of March 10, four officers went to the Batista farm, Kuquine, on the outskirts of Havana. I was to bring him to the garrison, where he would take over in a bloodless coup. There were seven cars by this time - with army officers and police. I was in the first car. Batista didn't cooperate. He told us to go on ahead and he would come along later. He wasn't afraid, he was being cautious.“

„He finally consented to take his place in the motorcade. Then he did something that almost ruined our chances. When we neared the garrison his car cut out from the caravan. I ordered the rest of the cars to stop because I thought he might have changed his mind. We looked for him and found that he was changing his civilian jacket for a leather windbreaker he had worn as a sergeant. It was either superstition or ego - or a combination of both. The brown jacket was brought to him by an officer who should not have even known of our mission and moreover, an officer I did not trust. Batista even changed cars, going the rest of the way with that officer. We were supposed to be at the garrison at 2:40 A. M. sharp. The stop made us three minutes late and those three minutes almost cost us our coup, for when we arrived the officer we had expected to be in charge of the gate had gone to another part of the garrison and a new one was confronting us. An alarm could have been sounded but fortunately, the trusted officer returned and talked briefly to the sentinel and we passed through the gates. I had taken the precaution of posting the men of my own company as security guards. A driver and two men went to the home of Gen. Ruperto Cabrera, chief of the army. He lived on the post and was routed out of bed and taken to Batista's farm as hostage. Batista had given his wife a sleeping pill earlier, so that she would not awaken during the night and worry about his absence - one of the few considerate things I have ever known him to do.“

There were 4,000 men in the Columbia garrison, but so complete was the coup that not a drop of blood was shed. As each new shift reported for duty, they either joined the movement or were disarmed and put into cells. Batista called newspaper friends with the scoop. He took over completely that first day. „His old friends began appearing,“ said Gen. Tunon. „He had his claque and our group was being eased out of the picture.“ An accused embezzler, Marino' Lopez Blanco, was made secretary of the treasury. He had been trying to buy his way into the previous Prio governnment. Gen. Francisco Tabernilla, who had been kicked out by President Grau San Martin eight years earlier, was put in charge of the army. Juan Rojas, then a captain, became a general in the Batista government. The members of the junta went over to him.

Today all of the officers who took part in the coup - with the exception of Gen. Tunon are rich and powerful members of the Cuban hierarchy. „I came from an old army family,“ said Tunon, „and the men unter me liked me. I was made a brigadier general earlier because I was head of the junta. This was a popular decision with the men. I didn't realize that this didn't set well with Batista, but he reasoned that anyone who could organize one coup might be tempted to create another. I was put under constant surveillance. The men under me were· told to disregard my orders. A captain was assigned to my section to countermand any orders I might give. Then guards were put around my house - one was a gardener whom I never hired and the other a sort of handyman. I went to Batista's home to protest and ended up by resigning."

No action is too petty for Batista. Gen. Tunon was retired - and exiled to Miami - with a pension of $331 per month. Charges of conspiracy were made after he left the country and the pension was declared forfeIt. What does Gen. Tunon think of Batista? „I think that he cannot remain in power too much longer," he said hopefully. „He has hurt too many people and revoked too many institutions dear to the people of Cuba. His principal support comes from the repressive groups. But his spies are everywhere. The morale of the army is at a new low despite what you hear about salaries and other inducements. „The only way to unseat him is either through the army or through the church. The U.S. government could help by acting as an interested third party - or by just sitting on the sidelines and alowing Cubans to settle their own quarrels."

Whether you hear it from the general who helped Batista to power or from a waitress now working in Miami or from a real estate man, the story of Batista's reign is an unlovely thing. Batista is not the first to plunder Cuba. Virtually every government head since Cuba gained its independence has lined his pockets and then gone off the live in sumptuous exile. Those in power cannot resist the temptation of easy money. Batista's brother-in-law has charge of the slot machine racket. A close friend said that the right contractors get the road and building construction jobs and that the proper kickback comes back to the palace. There are the atrocities and the loot and the prostitution and the censorship. These are the things that Batista stands for, no matter how he attempts to disguise them.

And an hour's flight from the palace in Havana, the man who helped create Cuba's Frankenstein monster cringes beneath the weight of his conscience. The fact that he has a conscience automatically disqualifies him as a Batista man.«

April 14, 1958: »Dictator Fulgencio Batista, who likes to call himself an old newspaperman, maintains iron control over virtually all of the Cuban press through a feudal system of subsidies without which most of the major newspapers would cease to exist. This is a normal procedure even when insurgent forces aren't creating little incidents. Now that civil guarantees have been tossed down the drain and censorship has been imposed, control of the press is complete.

Not a dissident whisper filters into Cuba's newspapers. And newsmen aren't as indignant - at least not openly - as they would be in this country because they, too, are subsidized and without the added money they would scarcely be able to subsist. The result is darkness and ignorance of the true state of affairs for the great majority of the 6,000,000 people of Cuba as well as a fuzzy picture for the outside world. Censorship, enforced by economic necessity, is the great weapon in Batista's arsenal. No atrocity picture is printed. The press doesn't dare to criticize the inhuman Maj. Esteban Ventura Nobo or the other psychopathic characters who enforce Batista's decrees.

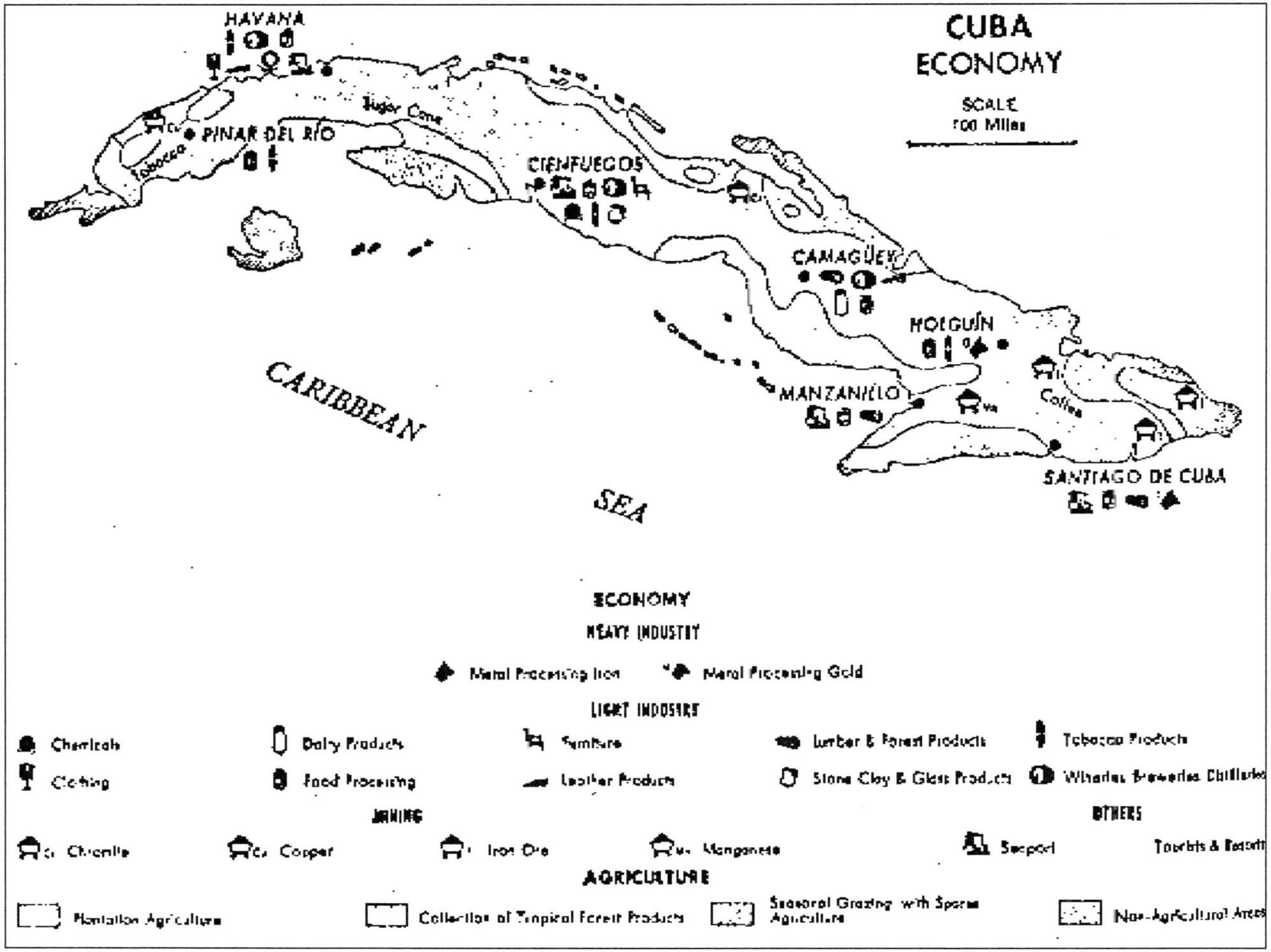
CUBA
ECONOMY
SCALE
100 Miles
HAVANA
PINAR DEL RIO
Tobacco
Sugar Cane
CIENFUEGOS
CAMAGÜEY
HOLGUÍN
MANZANILLO
Coffee
SANTIAGO DE CUBA
CARIBBEAN
SEA
ECONOMY
HEAVY INDUSTRY
Metal Processing Iron
Metal Processing Gold
LIGHT INDUSTRY
Chemicals
Clothing
Dairy Products
Food Processing
Furniture
Leather Products
Lumber & Forest Products
Stone Clay & Glass Products
Tobacco Products
Wineries Breweries Distilleries
MINING
Chromite
Copper
Iron Ore
Manganese
OTHERS
Seaport
Tourists & Resorts
AGRICULTURE
Plantation Agriculture
Collection of Tropical Forest Products
Seasonal Grazing with Sparse Agriculture
Non-Agricultural Areas

Technically, Batista has imposed official censorship some eight times since 1953. Before that, censorship had been imposed only once, by Machado back in 1931 to 1933. Chief of his censors is Evangelina de las Lleras, a member of the underground movement that ousted Machado in 1933. She's a shade over 50 and, purposely or not, unable to see any point of view but her own. Her decisions, however devoid of reason, are final. There are 40 censors in all, one for each of the 16 newspapers in Havana and the others for telephone, magazines, radio stations and the island's four TV stations.

Subsidizing began in 1933, when people within the newspapers were bought. Presidents Grau San Martin and Carlos Prio Socorras followed suit when they came to power. But it was found that a general subsidy was more effective. Batista's tab for purchasing the integrity of newspapers and newsmen runs into millions of dollars each year. The subsidies run from $4,000 per month to as high as $1,OOO per day and many of Havana's newspapers could not possibly make ends meet without this largesse from Batista, the boy who wears a button describing him as Newspaperman No. 1. The button entitles him to hold a job with a guild minimum wage of $22.08 per week, despite or because of which he has managed to accumulate what revolutionaries estimate as $300,000,000.

Any sparks of rebellion among editors are quickly extinguished. Luis Ortega Sierra, a veteran Cuban newsman, was baldly beaten and exiled to Miami and his newspaper, Pueblo, was sold for peanuts. Five papers are controlled or owned directly by the government. One of these is Pueblo, operated by Andres Domingo Morales, a close friend to Batista. On the rolls of Pueblo appears the name of Fulgencio Batista as a reporter. It's an evening paper with a circulation of about 2,000.

Tiempo en Cuba is operated by the strong-armed Sen. Rolando Masferrer. A brilliant lawyer. Masferrer has distinguished himself by his services to the present régime. He commanded a battalion in the Spanish Civil War and is an extreme liberal, though not a Red. He has organized his own police force. He carries a gun and is known as a rough customer. Tiempo en Cuba is the Pravda of the Batista government. Masferrer constantly harasses those around Batista, making them feel insecure and thus keeping them on their toes. The censors don't bother him because they have no need.

Alerta is an evening paper with a circulation of 3,000. It was formerly the property of Minister of Communication Ramon Vasconcelos, a Batista supporter who fell from grace and is now living in Spain. No more patriotic newspaper exists in Cuba than Ataja. It features blue and yellow headlines on white newsprint. The colors of the national police are blue, those of the army yellow, and the Navy, white, and Ataja, which means attack, is circulated in barracks all over the island. Even then, its circulation is only 12,000. It is operated by a pompous little man, Alberto Salas Maro, who stretches out to a height of five feet and has a habit of chinning himself on casino roulette tables for hours at a time.

Republica is owned by Julia Elisa Consuegra, in her fifties and an old friend of Batista. The newspaper has a circulation of 1,000 and was started by former police chief Rafael Salas Canizares - who is a better story than Republica. Canizares clubbed a student to death in 1951 and was indicted in Havana. He was to face the court the same week Batista took power in 1952. Batista had the case taken care of and made Canizares a general in charge of the national police. At the time Canizares was poor. But he took control of gambling until 1956 and upon his death left $14,000,000 to his widow. His death was almost accidental. After the March 13, 1957, attack on Batista's palace, four rebels of the Directorio Revolucionario were executed. Out of retaliation, they shot to death Security Police Chief Blanco Rico in a cabaret, the Montmarte, of which hoodlum Meyer Lansky owned a sizable portion. Canizares heard the killers were at the Haitian embassy and raced off to intercept them. There were a dozen refugees there, but none of them was involved in the Rico killing. Canizares was hunting for them out in the garage when he was met by a young man with a gun. They both opened fire but Canizares fell, mortally wounded. lrindido Martinez, the boy who fired the fatal shot, is still in hiding.

There are the „independent" newspapers that get money and other favors from the government. The 125-year-old Diario de la Marina, once the voice of the church and the Spanish colony, is a morning paper with a circulation of 35,000. Today it gives Batista no cause for worry. Informacion is run by the Claret family, which is close to Batista. EI Mundo was born with the republic 57 years ago and once had a great tradition as an independent liberal newspaper. The owner of record is Amadeo Barletta, an Italian who went to Cuba 20 years ago and - in between visits to other countries and deals with other dictators - has done very well indeed under the Batista régime. Former President Prio is reported to have put up more than half of the purchase price for EI Mundo. Barletta was once Mussolini's consul to the Dominican Republic. When Barletta was thrown into jail there, Mussolini threatened to send his fleet to free him. Barletta has also done business with Peron, as well as with Prio and Grau San Martin. He has had a hectic life. On one occasion, Batista assigned SIM men to guard him and the EI Mundo plant, which didn't do much to help the newspaper's reputation.

Another morning newspaper, Excelsior, has a circulation of 28,000 with the help of a plan whereby they print lottery numbers. The owner is Alfredo Hornedo, almost 80 now, a man with a Texas complex. He has the world's largest theater in the Miramar section of Havana, so big that it's rarely opened because of the expense of operating it. Hornedo also owns El Pais, a lottery paper with a circulation of 40,000. The Havana Post is owned by Clara Park, 55, of New Orleans. It is Havana's only English daily and during the Little Rock, Ark., incident, heavily played up the cause of Gov. Faubus and attacked the stand of President Eisenhower. Mañana is owned by Jose Lopez Viloboy, president of Cubana Airlines, in which Batista is deeply interested.

The great Cuban newspaper, Prensa Libre - Free Press - is not subsidized. It has a circulation of over 85,000 and is headed by Sergio Carbo, a newsman with an excellent reputation. The censorship is evident when you pick up a copy of the usually fearless Prensa Libre. With incidents breaking loose all over the place, with threats of total war by Castro, seizure of arms shipments, the front page heavily played up a chit-chat column which wanted to congratulate one Jose Sierra on his birthday. Reporters are poorly paid. Scale is $22.08 per week, but there is something called the botella. The botella is a government job of doing nothing as a rule. A reporter can have several of these, bringing his salary up to $1,000 per month for the man covering the palace, and somewhat less for those on less important beats.

Stories of U.S. mobsters allied with Batista in the gambling racket were so muffled by the purchased press in Havana that the news of the alliance wasn't exposed until THE NEWS uncovered the story last January. Not only does the subsidized press suppress the news, but reporters working for Batista don't hesitate to attempt to slander legitimate newsmen coming into the country to do an honest job.«

April 17, 1958: »There are more than 2,000 Cuban exiles in Miami, which has been called the Siberia for Latin-America, and the reason most of them are battling the Batista régime is simple - they want to go home. They want to go back, however, with the guarantee they won't be dragged out of their beds during the night by the dreaded SIM (Security Police) and forced to submit to torture and worse.

There's the pianist who says: „Even here, I can feel the hand of Batista. His spies are everywhere in this city - even in New York and other places where Cubans have gone for refuge. I listen to the shortwave broadcasts from Fidel Castro's headquarters in the Sierra Maestra two or three times a week and they give me hope - even though I am not 100% for Castro, either." You hear that often - Cubans who hate Batista are not necessarily in love with Castro. There is a mistaken idea that if you talk or write about the régime's terrorism you have to be for Castro. A large share of the exiles in Miami are for Cuba only. The insurgents, be they Castro's or Faure Chomon's or followers of other rebel leaders, are merely the weapons by which the anti-Red middle class hopes to free its homeland.

There's the exiled newspaperman who says: „Batista is a murderer, but Castro is an ambitious man, and who knows if things will be any better when and if he takes over? Our best hope is a third party - preferably the army - under a non-political man like Gen. Jorge Garcia Tunon, also exiled by Batista." Revolutionaries are common in Miami. They seem to collect in the same places night after night. „I have a family in Havana," said one, „and my sole aim is to go there to live with them again. I saw them eight months ago, but it's too risky for me to make frequent trips. I can only fight against those who keep me from my mother and two brothers."

Portly Dr. Roberto Agramonte, a former sociology professor, his wife, daughter and son - who fought with Castro in the Sierra - are exiles living in a cramped „efficiency apartment." Suitcases are scattered about the place and there is little furniture - the mark of the transient who hopes this is only a temporary stop. Agramonte, Dr. Manuel Bisbe and others in the „26th of July Movement" spoke March 16 at a commemorative meeting at the Flagler Theater in Miami. It was a Sunday morning, but there were about 300 present to pay tribute to the memory of Dr. Pelayo Cuervo, slain as a suspect in the March 13, 1957, attack on the Presidential Palace. Cuervo had no part in the uprising, but he had been a marked man because he couldn't be bought. He was taken from the home of a friend, pushed into a car and shot to death in a Havana suburb.

The people at the Flagler were middle class. Some of them arrived late, making excuses to friends that they had to attend church first. Batista likes to call them Communists, but Reds aren't in the habit of putting church services before revolutionary meetings. Inside, there was emotion-drenched oratory. Batista, say these sober, well-educated people, „has drunk the blood of the Cuban people." The current theme - „Liberty or death." Cuba's martyrs are remembered in Miami - and there are many martyrs, with new ones created by each abortive uprising. „But it's like a chain letter," said a Cuban attorney, „Each person who dies for Cuba inspires a dozen others to take his place in the movement against Batista. Some day - be it this month or this year - we will return to our homes in Cuba." The revolutionaries and exiles don't always find jobs. But they seem to get along - mostly from the bounty of those who have plenty of money and are willing to share it.

Castro has his followers. So does ex-President Carlos Prio Socarras. So do others. Curiously, Batista and Castro profess the same aims for Cuba. They don't want to run the country personally, they say, they merely want a strong, honest group to take over - with free elections, civil rights and all the other benefits the Cubans don't have. Batista turns on his ever-ready charm and tells the world he would like nothing better than to turn over the reins to some deserving characters. In the next breath, he indicates he would like to retain control of the army in case anything goes wrong. Castro has said he doesn't want to be president of Cuba, not even a high officer of the government. He wants to sit on a park bench in the background and make like an elder statesman. „I would act only as the conscience of the administration," he said.

The consensus among the more highly-educated exiles is that Cuba would be better off if neither Castro nor Batista ruled the island. „There are many misconceptions," said an exile. „There is, for instance, a popular belief in the U.S. that if Batista relents in his reign of terror, takes it easy on his enemies, there will be peace. This is not so. There can be no peace while he directs any phase of the government. But on the other hand, I do not believe that Fidel Castro is statesman enough to rule Cuba as it should be governed."

Batista has ruled Cuba for 17 of the last 25 years. The past six years have been the goriest in Cuba's history. How did he get started? Fulgencio Batista y Zaldivar was born of humble parents and was a laborer in a sugar mill, a farm worker, a tailor and eventually a stenographer. He joined the army at the age of 20 and attained the rank of staff sergeant because of his knowledge of shorthand. He came into power through a coup in Sept. 4, 1933, ending the reign of tyrannical President Gerardo Machado. But, though he was now Cuba's strong man, Batista didn't become president until 1940 when a coalition - including the Communist Party he now denounces - elected him. When he was barred by the Cuban constitution from running for a second term in 1944, he put up his own candidate - who was defeated. Batista retired to Daytona Beach to lick his wounds and plan a comeback. When he regained control in 1952 through a coup d'etat, he was hailed as the savior of the people. But the people were soon to find out that this was a different Batista than the one they had known. This one was out to make a fortune and a place in history. He has done both.

PRODUCTION OF MAIN CROPS
(Thousands of metric tons)

	1958	1959	Percent change
Sugar	5,778.6	5,964.2	+ 3
Tobacco	41.6	41.2	− 1
Coffee	29.1	49.2	+68
Rice (unpolished)	222.7	295.5	+32
Cotton	0	1.4	—
Black and red beans	30.0	35.0	+16
Corn	147.0	190.0	+29
Peanuts	7.0	11.0	+42
Potatoes	101.0	113.0	+11
Pineapples	100.0	98.0	− 2
Oranges	73.0	81.0	+11
Cucumbers	18.0	18.0	0
Tomatoes	69.3	73.1	+ 5

CUBA'S CURRENT ACCOUNT
(Millions of dollars)
Aggregates for seven years, 1952-1958

	Receipts	Expenditures	Balance
1. Merchandise	4,818.1	4,636.4	181.7
2. Tourism	247.7	232.9	14.8
3. Transportation	49.7	480.7	−431.0
4. Insurance	5.5	11.8	− 6.3
5. Dividends & interest	51.7	369.1	−317.4
6. Gov't transactions	12.0	9.7	2.3
7. Other services	138.5	33.8	104.7
8. Gifts	17.1	36.5	− 19.4
9. Total (1 through 8)	5,340.3	5,810.9	−470.6

The Cuban Economy in 1958

Castro is now 32. He is a brilliant lawyer, has three university degrees and comes from a wealthy family in the sugarcane business. However, he has a reputation as a young man who likes to run off in the direction of a revolution. In 1946, he was a member of an expedition against President Rafael Trujillo, of the Dominican Republic. The invasion fell through and Castro escaped by leaping into the sea from a ship. He also took part in a revolt in Colombia. Is he Communist? One of his severest critics says: „Castro may have used Reds to gain the ends he seeks, but he's not a Red. He may have associated with them but I'm sure that he was not aware of the political inferences. He has suffered from nothing more serious than adolescent political growing-pains." The Castro „26th of July Movement" originates from his attack on the army barracks in Oriente Province. From that day on, even though Castro's losses were heavy and he had to flee for his life, his name became synonymous with Superman and Robin Hood. There are those who don't believe that Castro will ever really come out of his beloved mountains - that when he does venture out too far he'll be cut to ribbons.

You have to try to divorce the distortions from the realities in any analysis of the Cuban situation. You have to discount the enthusia,sms of Castro's followers as well as the propaganda dished out by the Batista regime. The best way is to talk to the solid, substantial men who have never before entered into a revolutionary movement, who refused to go into politics. These men comprise the great middle class of Cuba. They speak with wisdom and authority. They had made great sacrifices -leaving their beautiful homes in Havana: to live in airless little rooms in Miami, New York and Chicago. Dr. Manuelo Urrutia, who will head the provisional government if Castro wins out, is in New York. He was an honored magistrate for 31 years before he was exiled for daring to indict a police official for murder. Men who have known violence only through hearsay form the nucleus of the underground that goes from New York to Miami and Cuba.

It is work to which they have become accustomed. They don't complain - they merely keep the guns going over to the Sierra Maestra and the Sierra del Escambray. One of them. said: „Castro is almost a prisoner in his mountains. Batista is virtually a prisoner in the barracks at Columbia Military City. But the Cuban people are the real prisoners."«

1959: DEATH PENALTY BY CASTRO TROOPS ON CUBA

Andrew Lopez, *United Press International*

In 1960, according to the jurors in the Pulitzer Prize Photography category, „the outstanding example of news photography is the series of 28 photographs taken by a team of *Associated Press* ... covering the Khrushchev tour of the United States.“ In addition, the jury report classified five other entries of single photographs as follows: Donald Nevin, *Boston Globe*; Andrew Lopez, *United Press International*; Eugene Hackley, *Los Angeles Mirror-News*; Anonymous, *Atlanta Journal*, and Raymond Gora, *Chicago Tribune*. The Board did not accept the *Associated Press* group entry. Instead, the third on the list of finalists was chosen, Andrew Lopez. His Pulitzer Prize-winning photo showed „a priest comforting a condemned Cuban.“

It was the time when the Cuban dictator Batista had to leave the Island and the troops of Fidel Castro got control over the country. Correspondents from all over the world poured into Havana to cover the historical situation. They were given credentials by Castro that allowed them to go anywhere they wished. Andrew Lopez, a veteran news photographer of *United Press International*, covered the war crimes tribunal at Matanzas, fourty miles from Havana. He was an eye-witness when a former Batista army soldier was sentenced to death: Nobody was permitted to take photos but Lopez,with a trick, shot the scene and got the film out.

Andrew Lopez, born on June 10, 1910, in Miraveche, Spain, came to the U.S.A. at the age of five. He visited public schools in New York City and became a naturalized American citizen in 1937. His first journalism job came to him in 1942 as a photographer for Acme News Pictures. The following year Lopez was sent to Europe, covering the landing in Normandy, the battle of Paris and the invasion of Germany. General Dwight D. Eisenhower awarded him the Medal of Freedom for rescuing U.S. soldiers. He then moved to the Asian Pacific war theatre where he covered the atomic bomb tests at Bikini Island and the capitulation of Japan on the U.S. Ship Missouri. More than a decade later, in 1957, Lopez switched to *United Press International*. Beside of his Pulitzer Prize, he won numerous awards for his sports photography. Following is the key photo of his award-winning pictures:

RECEIVING LAST RITES IN FIDEL CASTRO'S CUBA

Andrew Lopez, January 17, 1959, Photo shows Jose Rodriguez shortly before he was to be executed in Mantanzas, Cuba. He was a former Batista army corporal and sentenced to death for war crimes. Immediately after his trial, he was to be shot. After a priest gave him last rites, a rebel major stopped the execution as the order was not yet given officially. Rodriguez was killed next day by a Castro firing squad.

1962: ESTABLISHMENT OF SOVIET MISSILES ON CUBA

Harold V. Hendrix, *Miami News*

When the jurors of the International Reporting category in 1963 started their selection process, among the exhibits was one of the *Miami News* containing six articles only about the escalation of a global crisis between the USA and the Soviet Union, the Cuban Missile confrontation. „Each story," it was said by the newspaper, „was published by the *Miami News* before it appeared in any other paper in the country. With a single exception, each story was first denied or at least denied comment by the appropriate authorities in Washington only to be confirmed later by the same authorities in Washington. The sum of the work, represented by these six stories, is impressive not only because of the accuracy, but also the enterprise of Mr. Hendrix."

„Throughout the year", the background description continued, „reporter Hendrix has been ahead of other United States newsmen in reporting what was going on inside the island of Cuba. Events following his reports testified to an unusual accuracy in a most difficult area of getting the story right, in which the difficullty is made large not only because of the reluctance of usual information sources to speak, but also because of the gossip and rumor." The Pulitzer Prize jurors in their report of March 8, 1963, shared that opinion and declared Hendrix's articles „an outstanding example of international reporting." His reports indicated, the report runs, „that by hard digging he had confirmed the presence of large numbers of MIG-21s in Cuba days before President Kennedy's speech disclosing the extent of the Russian buildup in Cuba." So Hal Hendrix earned the Pulitzer award „for his persistent reporting" on the Cuban missile crisis.

Harold Victor Hendrix was born on February 14,1922, in Kansas City, Missouri. In 1941, he began his studies at the Rockhurst College before he went to the *Kansas City Star* in 1944. He stayed with this newspaper until 1957, treating Latin-American questions as a columnist from 1947 on. When he changed to the *Miami News* afterwards, Hendrix covered this special political field intensively. He took advantage of his membership in the leading journalistic organization for North- and South-America, the Inter-American Press Association, to the board of directors of which he belonged for a while. His various connections rendered it possible for Hal Hendrix to find out from Miami in the second half of 1962 that Cuba was shipping military weapons to other Latin American states; some months later he was the first American journalist to report that Soviet jets, MIG 21s, had arrived in Cuba. Following now are five of his Pulitzer Prize winning articles:

October 7, 1962: »Construction has begun in Communist Cuba on at least a half dozen launching sites for intermediate range tactical missiles, United States intelligence authorities have advised the White House. Although official U.S. spokesmen have declined to disclose the intelligence reports, the *Miami News* has learned that experts have advised President Kennedy that the ground-to-ground missiles can be operational from inland Cuba within six months.

From the type of construction under way it has been determined that the launching pads will have the capability of hurling rockets that could penetrate deeply into the United States in one direction and reach the Panama Canal Zone in the opposite direction. Official observers do not believe that the Soviet Union has yet delivered the intermediate range-type missiles to Cuba. But neither do they now doubt that delivery plans have been made. „The United States has a 'grace period' of about six months insofar as these new missiles are concerned," an official observer commented yesterday. After that, once the installations are complete and the missiles emplaced, any time there is a flare-up in tensions anywhere in the world between this country and the Soviet Union, the Communists in Cuba can rattle the offensive rockets in the Caribbean."

Officials have reported that U.S. plans for a crackdown on free world shipping to Communist Cuba could slow down the launching site construction, but there is no guarantee that the Soviets will not divert their own vessels to this high-priority project. Washington also has been alerted to the fact that Communist Cuba's north coast now is solidly banked with „defensive" short-range surface-to-air missiles, capable of downing an aircraft in a 25-mile range. Officially, the State Department has announced that at least 15 to these SAM bases have been completed - adding that the total may reach 25 or more.

Behind the coastal missile emplacements, now manned jointly by Cuban military and Soviet „technicians," are an undisclosed number of ground-to-ground missile bases already operational. These are reported to have a range of about 35 miles, designed for firing on ships at sea and strategic ground installations. According to reports from Cuba, some of these shortrange „defensive" missiles now are installed within easy reach of the U.S. Naval base at Guantanamo Bay.

Meanwhile, reports from Moscow and Havana point out that shipments of military materials and personnel still are continuing to pour unchecked into Communist Cuba. The State Department has acknowledged that there are now about 4,500 Soviet „military specialists" in Communist Cuba. Outside the department, observers believe the number is closer to 10,000. Since July, according to late State Department announcements, more than 85 Soviet shiploads have arrived in Cuba ports. Red Star, the Soviet military publication, notes that ships „are on the seas daily bound for Cuba with support for our Cuban friends."

The size of Communist Cuba's air force also continues to swell, as intelligence reports disclose stepped-up Russian supply lines. As first reported by The Miami News last month, the Soviets have supplied the Castro régime with at least six supersonic Mig-21 jet fighters. Intelligence sources have reported that there is evidence that at least 25 or 30 more of these most modern Soviet jet fighters will be operational in Cuba soon. Each carries heat-sensing air-to-air missiles and has a maximum speed of 1,685 miles per hour. The Mig-21s are the „frosting on the cake" for Castro's air force.

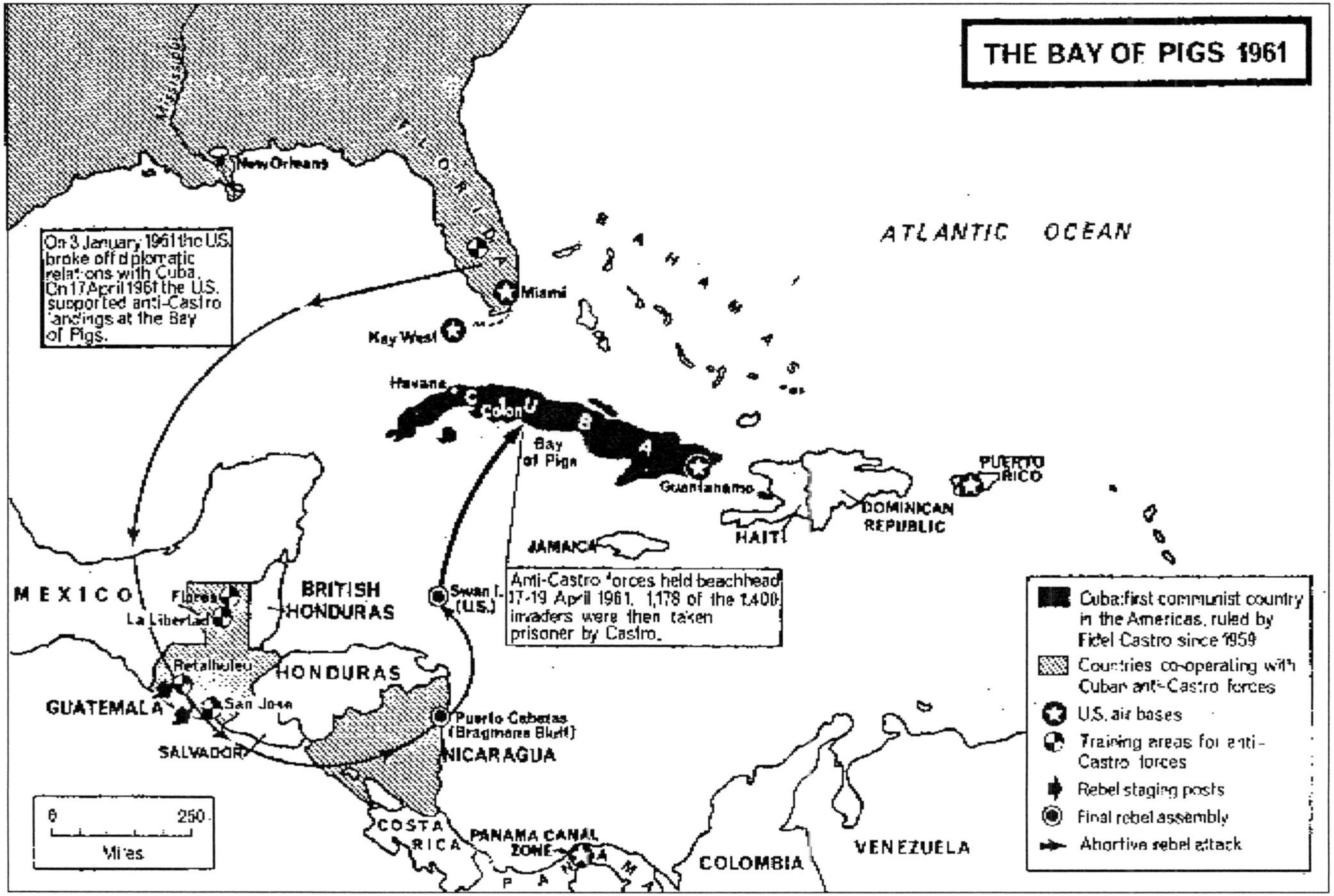
THE BAY OF PIGS 1961
ATLANTIC OCEAN
FLORIDA
New Orleans
Mississippi
Miami
Key West
BAHAMAS
Havana
CUBA
Colon
Bay of Pigs
Guantanamo
JAMAICA
HAITI
DOMINICAN REPUBLIC
PUERTO RICO
MEXICO
Flores
La Libertad
Retalhuleu
BRITISH HONDURAS
HONDURAS
GUATEMALA
San Jose
SALVADOR
Swan I. (U.S.)
Puerto Cabezas (Bragmans Bluff)
NICARAGUA
COSTA RICA
PANAMA CANAL ZONE
PANAMA
COLOMBIA
VENEZUELA
0 250 Miles
On 3 January 1961 the U.S. broke off diplomatic relations with Cuba. On 17 April 1961 the U.S. supported anti-Castro landings at the Bay of Pigs.
Anti-Castro forces held beachhead 17-19 April 1961. 1,178 of the 1,400 invaders were then taken prisoner by Castro.
Cuba: first communist country in the Americas, ruled by Fidel Castro since 1959
Countries co-operating with Cuban anti-Castro forces
U.S. air bases
Training areas for anti-Castro forces
Rebel staging posts
Final rebel assembly
Abortive rebel attack

The backbone of the Cuban air strength, according to published Defense Department figures in the Congressional Record, is about 100 Mig-15, Mig-17 and Mig-19 jet fighters.

On the sea, the Communists have delivered to Castro at least 16 „Komar“ class guided missile patrol boats, each carrying two rockets which fire 11 to 17 miles. It has been reported by Western intelligence that the Soviets have earmarked at least two destroyers and two East German submarines for Cuba. Meanwhile, U.S. Under Secretary of State George Ball last week told a special House committee investigating Cuban arms traffic from the Soviet bloc that United States policy on Cuba „still is based on the assessment that Cuba is not a military threat.“«

October 23, 1962: »The showdown between the United States and Communist Cuba, although long in coming, was inevitable. In retrospect, it began only a few days after Fidel Castro came to power Jan. 1, 1959. Shortly after the bearded revolutionary leader came down from the hills of Cuba's Sierra Maestra mountains when President Fulgencio Batista fled from Havana on New Year's Eve, Castro declared that 200,000 gringos would die if the U.S. Marines ever set foot on Cuban soil.

Since that angry declaration in the lobby of the Havana Hilton Hotel early in January 1959, Castro has been screeching about invasions from the U.S. and working overtime to destroy the U.S. image in Cuba and throughout Latin America. Now the United States has moved to liberate Cuba from Castro and his Communist allies - and mend its shuttered image in Latin America. In launching that decisive last night against Communist Cuba, President Kennedy also has served notice on the world, that the U. S. has drawn a new line on the advance of international communism.

„The line is being drawn on the Cuban problems rather than in Berlin or the Far East, because there is more room to move in the Caribbean,“ commented a U.S. official to the Cuban arena. The most frightening of the apprehensions raised by President Kennedy's address to the nation on the Cuban crisis is that a bearded madman in Havana now has in his hands the dread power to fire missiles or bombs into the U.S. mainland and possibly spark World War III. President Kennedy declared that it shall be the policy of the United States to regard any nuclear attack launched from Cuba against any nation in the Western Hemisphere as an attack by the Soviet Union on the U.S. - requiring full retaliatory response from Russia.

Since the Soviets are cognizant of Castro's history of irrational and unstable behavior, it may be that they would not risk placing any pushbuttons near his itchy trigger finger. Still, it could be difficult even for the Russians in Communist Cuba to keep Castro and his fanatic henchmen away from the pushbuttons. It would still be more difficult to keep them from a capricious attack against the U.S. - if the Castro régime figures it can penetrate U.S. defense. These grim possibilities are certain now to be on the minds of Latin America's heads of state - and they will be a factor in any action taken by the Organization of American States.

OAS action to back up President Kennedy's collision with the Castro-Communist combine is expected to develop quickly, although it may not be unanimous. Brazil is likely to maneuver to throw some kind of roadblock up before the OAS action. Such a move could lead to far-reaching repercussions inasmuch as President Kennedy is still planning to visit Brazil Nov. 12. Mexico, who with Brazil has led the „hands off Cuba" fight in Latin America, has shown signs of changing its posture in light of disclosures of Castro's offensive firepower.

In his speech, President Kennedy astutely pointed out that Mexico City could easily be a target for one of Castro's intermediate range ballistic missiles. Mexico's President Adolpho Lopez Mateos, now touring the Far East, declared today in Manila that Mexico would stand by the OAS in meeting the new situation in communist Cuba. „Mexico signed the Rio de Janeiro pact and in that document it was contemplated the possibility of a country being a victim of an aggressor," President Lopez Mateos said. „In case such an event took place, Mexico would duly fulfill her duties contained in that pact."

In Central America, the U.S. will find solid support of its new tough and determined policy. This means six voices at the OAS Council table - Guatemala, El Salvador, Honduras, Nicaragua, Costa Rica and Panama. On the huge South American continent, Brazil is likely to abstain rather than fully reverse its pro-Cuba and leftist position. Chile and Ecuador, both with a high incidence of Communist activity and facing threats of strikes, may join Brazil. All the other countries - Colombia, Venezuela, Peru, Bolivia, Argentina, Uruguay and Paraguay, are expected to line up behind the U.S. program to rid the hemisphere of the Castro regime.«

October 26, 1962: »Temporarily thwarted by the Umted States' naval blockade around Communist Cuba, the Soviet Union is pressuring desperately for aircraft landing rights in Africa and South America to service an armaments airlift to Havana, The News learned today.

Authoritative sources in Washington disclosed that Soviet representatives are concentrating heavy pressure on Brazil to give them transit rights for medium-range transport planes en route to Communist Cuba. The squeeze is being applied on Brazilian diplomats in Washington and by the Russian envoys assigned to the Soviet embassy in Brazil.

Although Washington sources did not link the Russian pressure on Brazil with President Kennedy's plans to visit there next month, it was reported that the White House has been in touch with the Brazilian government about the projected trip. The expectation now is that the trip, slated to begin Nov. 12 will be canceled. Press Secretary Pierre Salinger said today he probably would have something definite to say on the plans before the day is over. Reports from Brazil say the trip already has been canceled. On the African side of the proposed airlift route, overtures are known to have been made to the government of Algerian Premier Ahmed Ben Bella, who just returned from a visit to Communist Cuba - and the United States. It has been learned that the Russians attempted to obtain transit landing rights at Dakar, but the government of Senegal rejected the proposal.

Soviet affairs specialists interpret the intense airlift pressuring as another indication that the Russians are determined to continue their military buildup in Communist

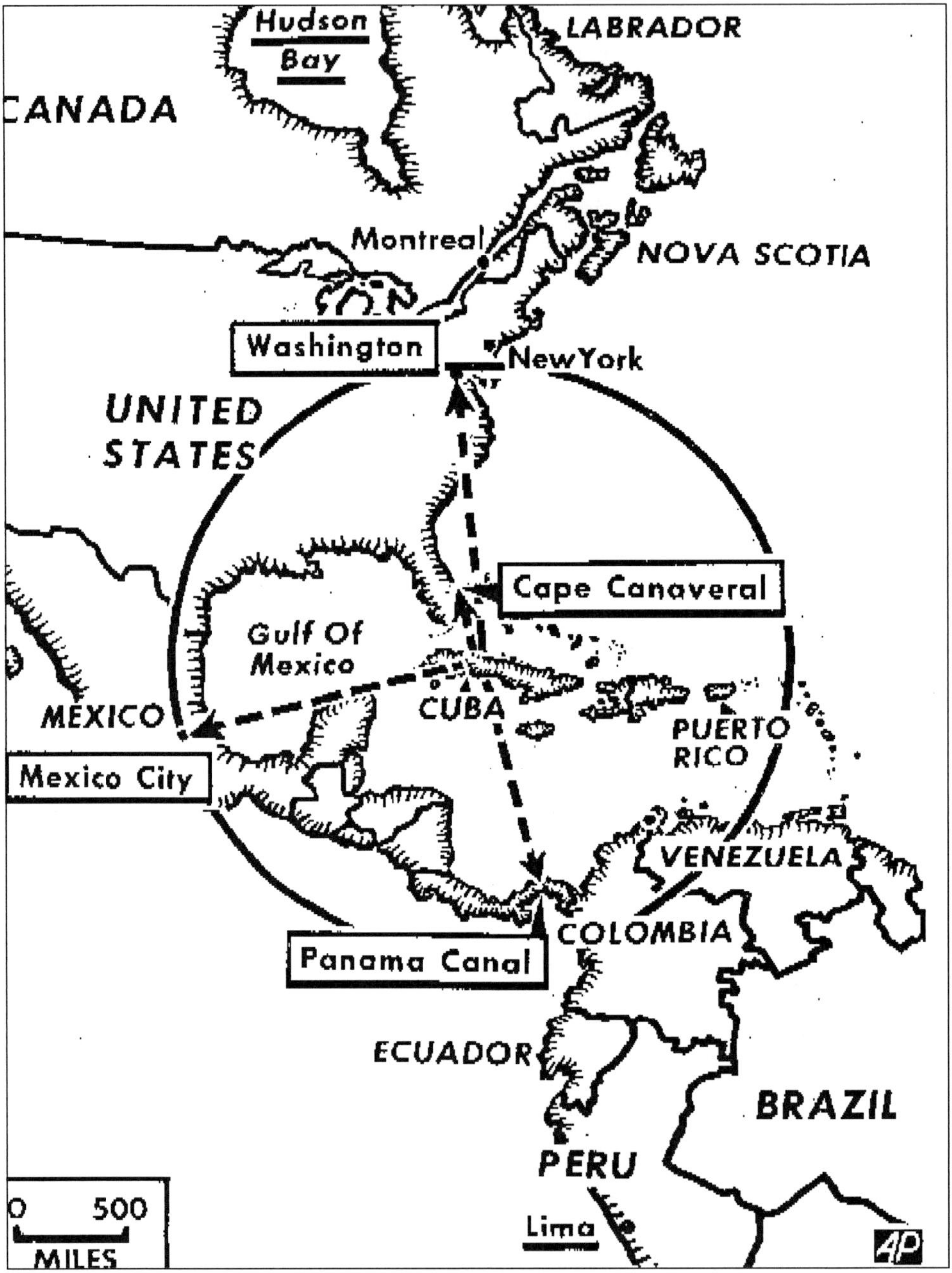

Radius of Cuban Missile Coverage (Arrows Point To Places Within Range)

„A WALL!“

This cartoon, drawn by Pulitzer Prize-winner Frank Miller and published on October 23, 1962, in the *Des Moines Register* of Iowa, illustrates the U.S. blockade of Cuba: President John F. Kennedy had ordered a quarantine of all ships to Cuba containing cargoes of offensive weapons.

Cuba. It is pointed out that medium-range rockets could be landed in Cuba by the Russian Ilyusyin 11-18 turbo-prop airliners modified for such a mission. The African and South American transit stops are needed for such an operation because of the limited flying range of the Ilyusyin. It is not believed that Russia has sufficient longrange air transports to sustain a nonstop airlift service between the Soviet Union or any of its East European satellites and Communist Cuba.

Meanwhile, it was learned that the U. S. intelligence forces have information of additional Soviet supplied firepower in Cuba beyond that which the Defense Department has made public earlier this week. Unofficially, the White House and Defense Department have been alerted to „hard" information that nuclear warheads of the 1-megaton class now are in Cuba under tight control of Soviet military personnel.

It also has been determined that the medium-range missiles already delivered to Communist Cuba include the T-2, T-4 and T-5 models that have been observed at Soviet military displays. All are capable of delivering atomic warheads. The T-2 is propelled by liquid fuel and has an operational range of 1,500 to 1,800 miles, with an inertial or self-contained guidance system. It is about 100 feet long and weighs about 60 tons. The T-2 model has appeared in a number of the serial photographs obtained by the United States in flights over Cuba - some at an altitude as low as 500 feet.

Shipments of the T-4 and T-5 models are known to have been aboard some of the Soviet vessels that have turned back before encountering the U.S. Atlantic fleet. Photographs of the missiles on the deck of at least one Czechoslovakian ship have been obtained.«

October 28, 1962: »In spite of the wordy correspondence racing back and forth between Moscow and Washington over the explosive Cuban situation, direct military action by the United States is inevitable - and likely to be launched soon with lightning swiftness: Without saying so directly, President Kennedy has in effect given the Castro-Khrushchev axis a 48-hour ultimatum to start dismantling the Soviet missile bases in Communist Cuba or face destruction of them by U.S. force. That was couched carefully in his letter last night to Premier Khrushchev dealing with possible negotiations on the Cuban problem. He commmented: „There is no reason why we should not be able to complete these arrangements and announce them to the world within a couple of days."

A possible deterrent of significant proportions to quick U.S. direct action is the proposed visit to Havana by Acting U.N. Secretary, General U Thant. Castro late yesterday extended an invitation to the U.N. leader to discuss with him the question of the negotiation proposals sailing between President Kennedy and Premier Khrushchev. The U.N. chieftain said he would announce his decision today.

Apart from the Castro-Thant matter, President Kennedy and his strategy advisers are known to have concluded that last week's strong support from the Organization of American States is clear authority to use force in dismantling the bases - and ultimately destroying the Communist threat to the Western Hemisphere. The U.S. conclusion was quickly backed up by OAS Secretary General Jose A. Mora, who declared that any measures taken by the United States to dismantle the bases would be „multilateral measures with multilateral support."

The national and hemispheric impetus to take decisive action is not likely to be slowed down by Khrushchev's letter writing, inasmuch as the United States has demonstrated during the week the Kremlin's penchant for false words, statements and pledges with respect to Cuba and other Cold War trouble spots. The buildup of U.S. military force in the United States and throughout the Caribbean which began last Monday continued through last night, and Pentagon strategists were working into the morning. Basic blueprints for an invasion of Cuba, an air strike on the missile launching sites and for numerous other operations in the stack of the Pentagon's „contingency plans" were reported to be under constant review by the Joint Chiefs of Staff and their aides.

Meanwhile, in the Caribbean the close surveillance of Russian and Soviet-chartered ships was continuing without interruption. Observers reported that the string of vessels stretched out across the Atlantic and Caribbean was continuing to inch toward Cuba. So far, according to surveillance reports, at least 17 ships, all presumably loaded with weapons, have turned around before encountering the blockade ring around Cuba.

The Defense Department last night added to the already potent potential strike force of the United States by calling 24 troop carrier squadrons to immediate active duty. The units are used to transport paratroopers and other combat forces. When asked if the callup implied that a Cuban invasion was immiment, Assistant Secretary of Defense Arthur Sylvester declined to reply. Observers in the capital last night carefully pointed out that realistically there was little likelihood of the problem of Cuba being resolved by correspondence or negotiation at this stage.

It also was emphasized that even if Castro or Khrushchev would agree to „defusing" and removal of the nuclear missiles aimed at the United States, more than 250 million dollars worth of Soviet non-nuclear armaments still would be in Cuba and that an invasion threat to the Western Hemisphere by Soviet international communism still would exist. The United States has publicly announced that its policy with respect to Cuba is „to get rid of the Castro régime and remove the Communists from Cuba." Vice President Johnson, for example, has traveled across the United States with that message, and it has been echoed by dozens of other high officials from Washington in recent weeks.«

October 31, 1962: »Now that the tensions over Communist Cuba have eased in Washington, a number of nagging questions are being asked from a number of directions. Two puzzlers are foremost: How could the United States have let the situation reach the point it did in Communist Cuba, and why did the Kennedy Administration deliberately mislead the American public by prolonged withholding and denying of intelligence reports on Soviet activities in Communist Cuba?

Indecision, which has become the hallmark of both the Eisenhower and Kennedy Administrations with respect to Fidel Castro and Communist Cuba, played a tragic role

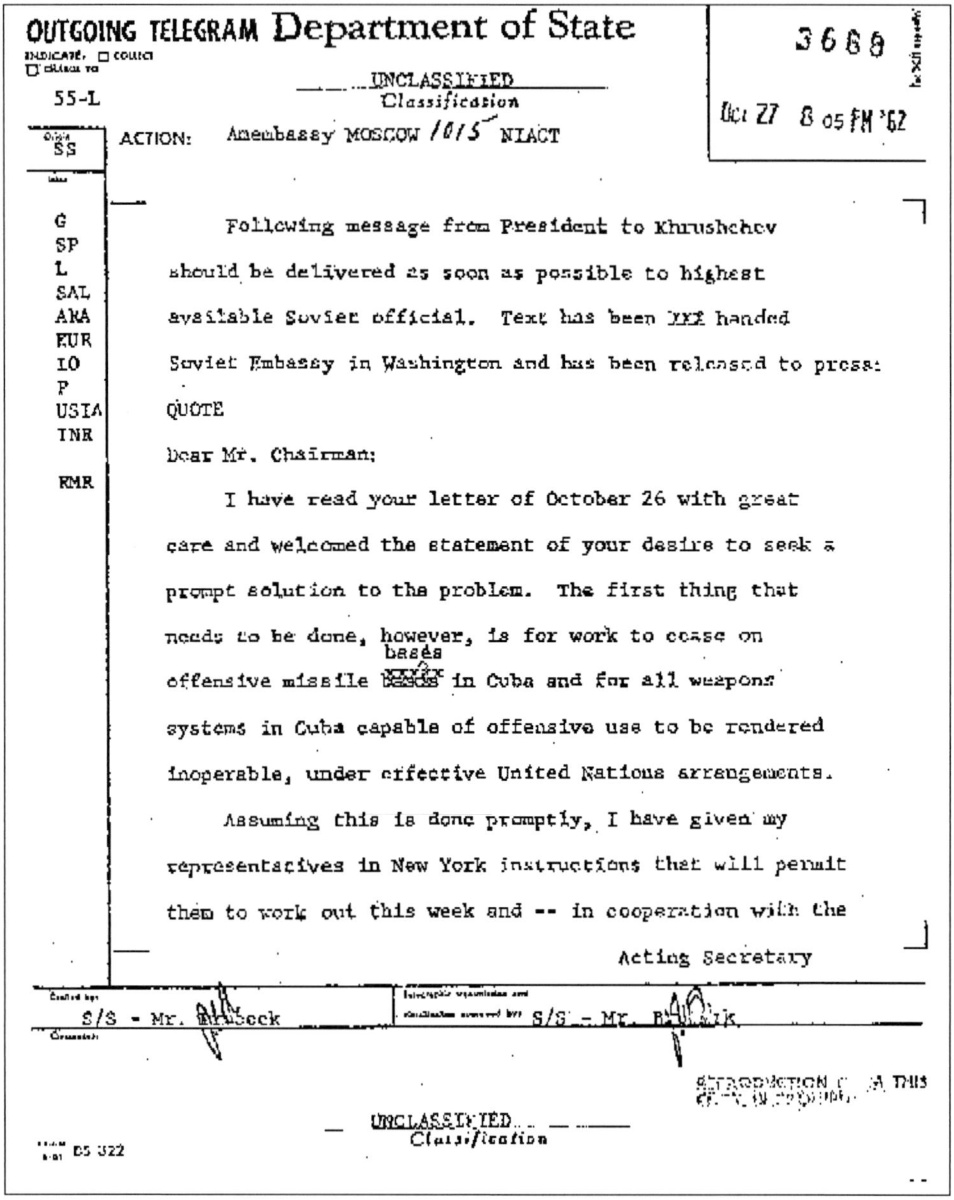

OUTGOING TELEGRAM Department of State

INDICATE: ☐ COLLECT ☐ CHARGE TO

55-L

UNCLASSIFIED
Classification

3668

Oct 27 8 05 PM '62

ACTION: Amembassy MOSCOW 1015 NIACT

SS
G
SP
L
SAL
ARA
EUR
IO
P
USIA
INR

RMR

Following message from President to Khrushchev should be delivered as soon as possible to highest available Soviet official. Text has been XXX handed Soviet Embassy in Washington and has been released to press:

QUOTE

Dear Mr. Chairman:

I have read your letter of October 26 with great care and welcomed the statement of your desire to seek a prompt solution to the problem. The first thing that needs to be done, however, is for work to cease on offensive missile bases in Cuba and for all weapons systems in Cuba capable of offensive use to be rendered inoperable, under effective United Nations arrangements.

Assuming this is done promptly, I have given my representatives in New York instructions that will permit them to work out this week and -- in cooperation with the

Acting Secretary

Drafted by: S/S - Mr. Brubeck

Telegraphic transmission and classification approved by: S/S - Mr. Brubeck

REPRODUCTION ... THIS ...

UNCLASSIFIED
Classification

DS 322

in connection with the first question. There is no pin-point answer to the second, other than the continuing struggle inside the New Frontier between the „hard action“ and „soft action“ advisers on Communist Cuba. This much in the controversy is certain. The State Department and the White House had accurate intelligence several

Page 2 of telegram to Amembassy MOSCOW NIACT

UNCLASSIFIED

Acting Secretary General and your representative -- an arrangement for a permanent solution to the Cuban problem along ~~the~~ the lines suggested in your letter of October 26. As I read your letter, the key elements of your proposals -- which seem generally acceptable as I understand them -- are as follows:

1. You would agree to remove these weapons systems from Cuba under appropriate United Nations observation and supervision; and undertake, with suitable safeguards, to halt the further introduction of such weapons systems into Cuba.

2. We, on our part, would agree -- upon the establishment of adequate arrangements through the United Nations to ensure the carrying out and continuation of these commitments -- (a) to remove promptly the quarantine measures now in effect and (b) to give assurances against an invasion of Cuba and I am confident that other nations of the Western Hemisphere would be prepared to do likewise.

If you will give your representative similar instructions, there is no reason why we should not ~~be~~ be able to complete

these

weeks before President Kennedy finally broke the news in his Oct. 22 television address to the nation.

Page 3 of telegram to Amembassy MOSCOW

UNCLASSIFIED

these arrangements and announce them to the world within a couple of days. The effect of such a settlement on easing world tensions would enable us to work toward a more general arrangement regarding "other armaments", as proposed in your second letter which you made public. I would like to say again that the United States is very much interested in reducing tensions and halting the arms race; and if your letter signifies that you are prepared to discuss a detente affecting NATO and the Warsaw Pact, we are quite prepared to consider with our allies any useful proposals.

But the first ingredient, let me emphasize, is the cessation of work on missile sites in Cuba and measures to render such weapons inoperable, under effective inter-national guarantees. The continuation of this threat, or a prolonging of this discussion concerning Cuba by linking these problems to the broader questions of European and world security, would surely lead to an intensification of the Cuban crisis and a grave risk to the peace of the world. For this reason I hope we can quickly agree along the lines outlined in this letter and in your letter of October 26.

/S/ John F. Kennedy

END

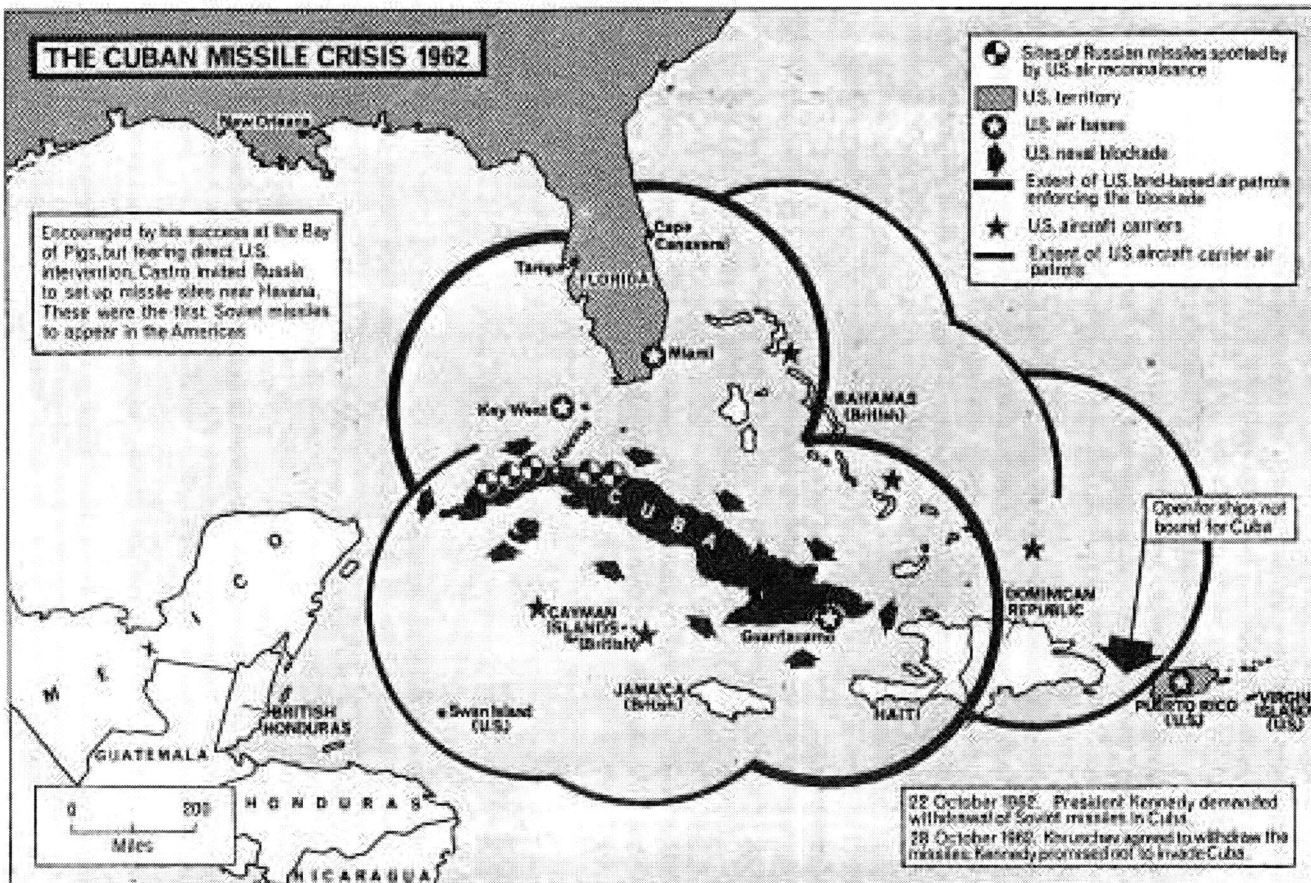
THE CUBAN MISSILE CRISIS 1962
Sites of Russian missiles spotted by by U.S. air reconnaisance
U.S. territory
U.S. air bases
U.S. naval blockade
Extent of U.S. land-based air patrols enforcing the blockade
U.S. aircraft carriers
Extent of U.S. aircraft carrier air patrols
Encouraged by his success at the Bay of Pigs, but fearing direct U.S. intervention, Castro invited Russia to set up missile sites near Havana. These were the first Soviet missiles to appear in the Americas
New Orleans
Tampa
FLORIDA
Cape Canaveral
Miami
Key West
BAHAMAS (British)
CUBA
Guantanamo
CAYMAN ISLANDS (British)
JAMAICA (British)
HAITI
DOMINICAN REPUBLIC
Open for ships not bound for Cuba
PUERTO RICO (U.S.)
VIRGIN ISLANDS (U.S.)
Swan Island (U.S.)
BRITISH HONDURAS
GUATEMALA
HONDURAS
NICARAGUA
0
200
Miles
22 October 1962. President Kennedy demanded withdrawal of Soviet missiles in Cuba
28 October 1962. Khruschev agreed to withdraw the missiles; Kennedy promised not to invade Cuba

The location of the kink, or where the data was bottled up likely never will be admitted. As late as three days before the President's speech, Under Secretary of State George W. Ball declared Communist Cuba posed no military threat to the United States. But, immediately after the President's address, the Cuban crisis and threat to the United States was being described as the most serious and grave crisis faced by the United States and the world since the explosion of World War II.

Three days before the crisis exploded into global size, the Kennedy Administration was insisting that all the Soviet weapons in Communist Cuba were „defensive." Officials scoffed at month-old reports of IRBM missiles in Cuba. It was repeated often in the previous weeks that possibly as many as 15 surface-to-air missile sites (SAMs) with a slant range of 25 miles had been installed in Cuba. Last week it was announced there were as many as 30. The State Department and White House before last week insisted that Castro had only about 60 older model MIG jet fighters in his air force, and „at least one" advanced jet interceptor (MIG-21) that was operational.

But again when the crisis became global, Castro was admitted to have more than 100 operational Soviet supplied jet fighters and at least 39 operational supersonic MIG-21s - plus a number of medium range jet bombers capable of carrying nuclear bombs and striking the United States. Obviously, this jet fighter muscle did not sprout overnight in Communist Cuba. „Hard" intelligence reports placed the planes in Cuba long before last week. Pictures of the Cuban MIG-21s even appeared in this newspaper ... Who was asleep and why?«

1980: FACETS OF THE CIVIL WAR IN EL SALVADOR

Shirley Christian, *Miami Herald*

In 1981, when the jury of the Pulitzer Prize for International Reporting had to select the entries, it finally recommended the three following exhibits in alphabetical order for the Board's consideration: Shirley Christian of the *Miami Herald*, for her dispatches from Central America; Richard Ben Cramer of the *Philadelphia Inquirer*, for his coverage of the Afghanistan revolution; Randall Richard of the Providence *Journal-Bulletin* for his coverage of illegal drug activity in Colombia. „Shirley Christian's work on Central America," the jury report of March 4, 1981, states, „was clearly the most outstanding of any the jury read from that area of the world. She displays a superb eye for detail, and combines great writing skill with her obvious expertise on the complex and bewildering problems that bedevil the region. Her work shows an exceptional ability to combine explanatory and straight reporting, and she does that explaining without ever treading over into advocacy. She is careful to select only relevant information, and has the enterprise to not sit idly by and write, say, about land reform from a bureau office, but goes to the plantation to interview the owner himself, as well as his peasants. Richard Ben Cramers superior writing ability," the jury report continues, „distinguished his reportage from that of any other entry submitted to the jury. A magnificent storyteller, he has an eye for detail and for dialogue that brings the characters to life, makes his situation seem close at hand ... Randall Richard comes from a relatively small newspaper, and the jury was impressed both with the enterprise of the reporter and the newspaper, and with Richard's ability to carry off his assignment." The Advisory Board liked most the Central America stories and bestowed the award to Shirley Christian.

Shirley Christian was born on January 16, 1938, in Kansas City, Kansas. She earned a B.A. from Kansas State College and an M.A. from Ohio State University, where she specialized in Latin American Studies. In 1968 she joined the *Associated Press*, and since 1970 she was an AP correspondent at the United Nations for three years. During her UN assignment she covered China's admission to the world body, Security Council debates on the India-Pakistan war and Yasser Arafat's appearance in 1974. Until 1977, Shirley Christian was an editor on the AP's foreign and world desk. Then she became bureau chief of the *Associated Press* for Chile and Bolivia, with headquarters in Santiago. After twelve years with AP, she joined the Latin America staff of the *Miami Herald* in 1980. She concentrated her writing and reporting especially on Central American topics and received the 1981 Pulitzer International Reporting award for her dispatches from that area written during 1980. Following are several of her award-winning articles:

March 31, 1980: »Explosions and gunfire broke up the funeral Sunday of assassinated Archbishop Oscar Arnulfo Romero, stirring panic and pandemonium that left at least 40 persons dead. Most of those killed were crushed in the fleeing crowd of 75,000 who had gathered at San Salvador's Metropolitan Cathedral for the funeral mass. But witnesses said at least seven of the dead were shot. Medical sources said more than 220 other persons were injured.

The first explosion - possibly a molotov cocktail or a bazooka round - went off in a corner of a nearby plaza about 45 minutes into the mass as Cardinal Ernesto Corripio Ahumada of Mexico was delivering a message on behalf of the Vatican. He had just finished labeling Romero „the voice that cannot be killed" when the violence erupted. Frightened mourners, who minutes before had been singing Christian folk songs and waving palm fronds, surged through Boy Scout lines and scaled a six-foot-high iron fence in a rush to find refuge inside the cathedral. Thousands of persons jammed stomach-to-stomach and head-to-head, inside the church. Dripping wet in the tropical heat, they moaned, cried and prayed as sporadic explosions and gunshots continued outside. Hundreds of shoes, hats, pieces of clothing, including one cardinal's red biretta, littered the steps of the cathedral and the street.

The Mexican cardinal and more than a score of other visiting priests and bishops were conducting the funeral mass beside Romero's silver casket on the steps of the cathedral where the slain archbishop had become an international figure with his weekly homilies condemning violence and repression. An estimated 25,000 militant leftists had just marched into one side of the plaza with left arms outstretched and fists clenched. They joined about 50,000 others - many of them children and elderly - who had been arriving for several hours before the 11 a.m. (noon Miami time) starting hour. Several of the demonstrators made their way through the crowd with an immense wreath of red and yellow artificial flowers, which they threw over the fence onto the casket. Several batches of pamphlets were then thrown into the air around the square.

Then came the first explosion. With it, the crowd moved, as in a great wave, from side to side, then began trying to get through the rope barriers. White-robed priests raised their arms and called for calm without avail from the cathedral steps. The young Boy Scouts blew their whistles. Then two shots rang out. People inside the plaza said they appeared to come from the second story of the National Palace on one side of the plaza. The panic intensified. A much louder explosion came from another corner of the plaza and four cars burst into flames, sending black smoke billowing over the Palm Sunday scene.

Church officials hurriedly picked up the archbishop's casket and carried it inside, where a brick and mortar crypt - finished and white-washed just two hours earlier - was waiting. The Roman Catholic radio station said the body was placed inside the crypt and the crypt closed, apparently without ceremony in the confusion. Romero, 62, was assassinated by an unidentified gunman last Monday at a small hospital chapel. The civilian-military junta now trying to govern the country has vowed to find his killer, and has asked the help of Interpol, the international police organization.

While the church filled with people, there was also an exchange of gunshots on the side street through which the leftists had entered the plaza. Shots were fired at them from inside one of the buildings. The leftist marchers apparently had weapons concealed in purses, satchels or music cases. Those who fired on them from inside the buildings were not visible. Witnesses on another corner, however, saw a man dressed in civilian clothes with a machine gun. No troops were in sight before the mass or after the violence began. Security forces had been ordered to stay in their barracks to avoid confrontation with the left, which has happened so often in this tiny, overcrowded country on the verge of civil insurrection.

Among the people jammed inside the church were a number of visiting bishops and other church dignitaries from around Latin America, the United States and Europe. One tiny woman hung sobbing to the neck of Panama's Archbishop Marcos McGrath, a head taller than most of the crowd. Also visible inside the cathedral was Nicaraguan Foreign Minister Miguel d'Escoto, wearing his white robes as a Maryknoll priest. The Rev. Charles Harper, an American who is president of the World Council of Churches, was also jammed into the frightened crowd. There were no reports of injuries to any of the foreign church dignitaries attending the funeral. Members of the governing junta were not seen at the mass, and church officials said they had not been expected to attend. U.S. Ambassador Robert White was not present either.

Romero had been an outspoken opponent of repression and an advocate of human rights since becoming EI Salvador's highest-ranking churchman in early 1977. As political violence mounted over the past year, he took an increasingly activist role. He said the well-armed right-wing oligarchy and the military bore the greatest blame for the violence, but he also chastised the extreme leftist political and guerilla groups, calling on them to exercise restraint. In a typical Sunday homily, the archbishop would cite the week's political killings - estimated at 700 so far this year - then go into other aspects of national life. He touched on strikes, government policy, kidnappings, the takeovers of farms and factories by the left.

One day before he died, the archbishop admonished security forces to stop killing peasants, who often die by the dozens in supposed shoot-outs where few if any soldiers die. „You have no responsibility to follow the orders of your superiors when they order you to act against the Law of God," he said. „Thou Shall Not Kill." Another of his admonishments to security forces from the final Sunday homily was printed across a banner that hung inside the cathedral when people came to view his body during the past week: „To the soldiers, I implore you, I beg you, I order you, in the name of God, stop the repression."

Archbishop Romero led an active campaign to account for persons missing after arrests and kept a tally of people killed in political violence. Peasants came from allover El Salvador to sit in the foyer of his office with pictures of relatives who had disappeared or been killed. His cathedral and many other Salvadorean churches became targets to be taken and held in the near war involving extremes of the left and right and security forces.

During the past year, as many as 10 churches at a time have been occupied by extreme leftists. The Metropolitan Cathedral was taken countless times. Last May 8, during one such occupation, security forces killed 24 young demonstrators on the cathedral steps. It was a sign of the times that leftists were also occupying the cathedral when the archbishop was killed. But they vacated it to allow his body to be placed in state there beginning last Wednesday.«

April 6, 1980: »Sitting in a wicker rocker on the veranda of the old hacienda, Raul Salaverria carries within him a legend you can read about on the label of a brand of gourmet coffee. „The year was 1863," it says. „Don Onofre Duran, a man in search of a dream, planted his first field of coffee trees on the Apaneca Mountains deep in the heart of El Salvador." Don Raul Salaverria, 73, is a Berkeley-educated country gentleman and the grandson of Onofre Duran. His three sons constitute the fourth generation in one of El Salvador's coffee dynasties - the kind of people referred to as the oligarchy. It is in their historical control of the land, banking, trade and politics that many people find the roots of the convulsions now wracking this tiny nation in Central America. „The patriarch system is what some call it, and I accept that," said Don Raul as he defended a land-tenure system that has kept thousands of peasants tied to him and his family from their birth to the grave. He believes his people love him, and any of them questioned silently agrees. They get wages that average $27 to $30 a week, plus whatever he chooses to bestow in the way of housing, schools, medical care and retirement benefits.

Now, it's all changing. A way of life that made El Salvador's landed gentry a cross between antebellum Mississippi planters and Texas cattle barons is coming to an end. The military-civilian government, trying to hold off a threatened class war, as decided - like so many reformist Latin American régimes before - that the land will go to those who work it. One month ago, Col. Adolfo Majano of the governing junta announced that all farms larger than 1,250 acres - a total of about 560,000 acres, or 10 per cent of all Salvadorean land - were being nationalized. He said there were 376 such farms, belonging to 244 persons, who would be paid in government bonds. As he spoke, teams of technicians from the Agrarian Transformation Institute and army troops were already moving onto some farms.

The agrarian reform decree was part of what Majano described in a recent interview as the decision of the armed forces „to leave the oligarchy to one side and align itself with the people." For nearly 50 years, until Majano and other young officers overthrew the hard-line régime of Gen. Carlos Humberto Romero on Oct. 15, the military's attitude toward the wealthy was what one landowner called „accommodating." One of the results was concentration of land ownership in the hands of very few families. According to Majano's figures, the families being affected by this first phase owned 25 per cent of the arable land and 40 per cent of the best land. Research in U.S. universities shows this concentration had been increasing in the past two decades. At the same time, El Salvador's population was growing at about 3 per cent a year, meaning that an increasing number of peasants had no land, or at best very little.

Raul Salaverria, whose La Labor plantation has more than 3,000 acres, heard the government radio announcement the night of March 6 at his home in San Salvador, the capital. He immediately drove to his farm home near Ahuachapan in western El Salvador.

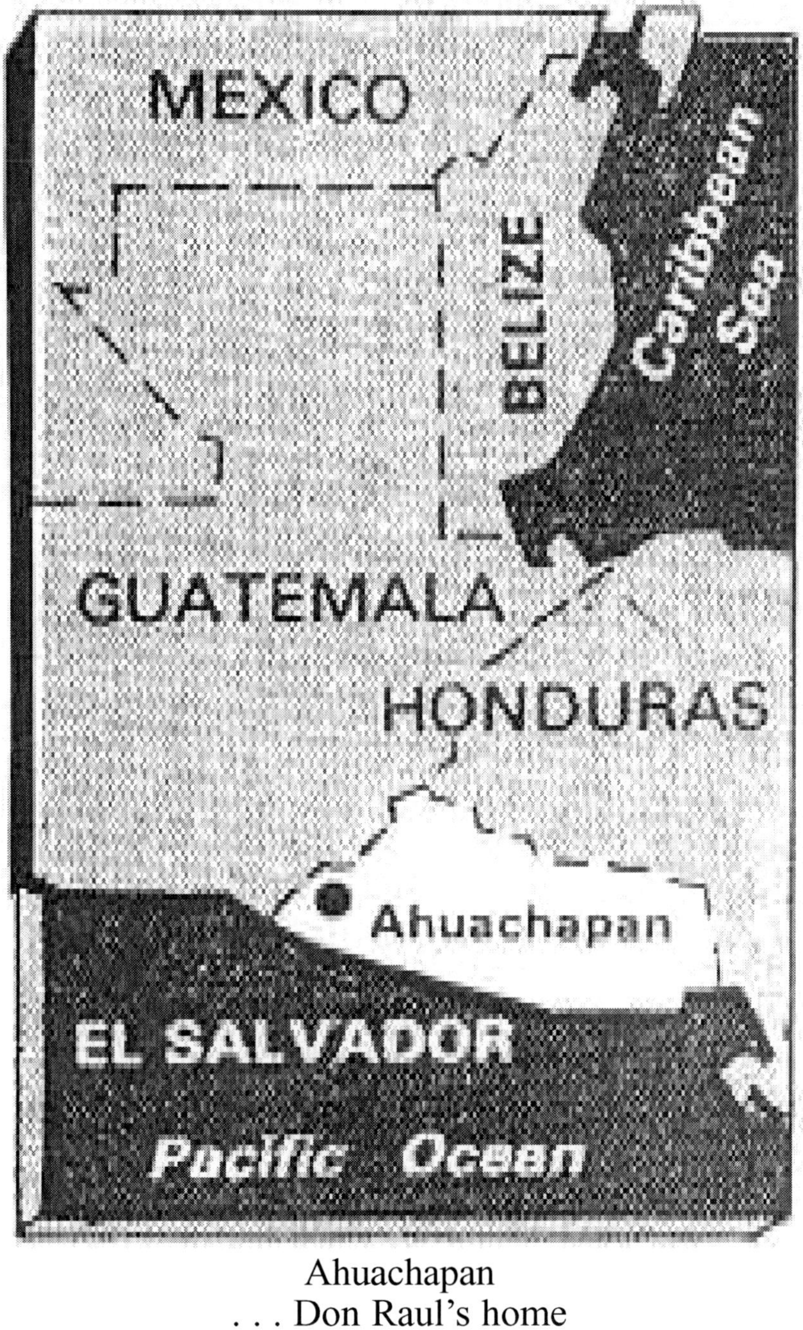

Ahuachapan
. . . Don Raul's home

Here, he was joined by two of his sons and a guard force of about 10 armed men. „The next morning one of my sons called a military friend, who told him, 'We are coming with the law in hand.'" They arrived shortly - an officer, some troops and a helicopter mounted with a machine gun. In the farm office, beneath a portrait of Don Onofre, Raul Salaverria and his sons argued with the officer about the legality of the takeover. As the exchange grew angrier, some shots were exchanged outside between the troops and the guards. Two men were slightly wounded.

The upshot was some kind of standoff. Government agriculture technicians are now more or less camped on the grounds among the peasant houses and outbuildings while Don Raul holds forth in the house. The soldiers are gone and so, apparently, are the Salaverrias' armed guards. „We don't know whose land it is now," said Don Raul. He might - or might not - leave. Maybe he'll give up his stand when the last of this year's coffee harvest is processed. He is entitled to the income from that. He also is entitled to keep the house if he continues to live in it most of the time - the rambling house started by his grandfather, with the garden of coconut palms and flowering shrubs planted when Don Raul and his wife were married in 1930. „I would have gone, but I think the people don't want me to go. I am staying because they asked me to," he said. On the other hand, his honor is intact because he fought, so he wonders if it might not be better to go quietly now.

The peasants working the land - about 1,000 year around, as many as 5,000 during the harvest - are as confused as their patron with the sudden change of status. Told by government officials to elect some leaders and begin to farm the land collectively, they promptly chose Don Raul and his middle son Mauricio to serve on the council. The government overruled them. The army officers and agriculture experts directing the land changeover from a joint command post say this reflects one of the major problems facing the program - that of educating the peasant to his new status and responsibilities. „We want to show him that he is the owner and controls his destiny. We have to encourage initiative," said Luis Napoleon Dominguez Miranda, director of agricultural technology in the Ministry of Agriculture.

Despite the intention to turn over the land to those who work it, ownership will in fact rest with the state. It is the production, the fruit of the labor, in which the peasants will actually share. Dominguez said it is necessary for the land to be worked collectively, at least for now, for several reasons. For one thing, there are so many people on the land in EI Salvador that dividing it into individual tracts would result in what is called minifundia - plots too small to be worked effectively and probably worse than the old system of large holdings, or latifundia. Also, Dominguez said, the peasants cannot handle the debt that would be necessary if they were to buy the land outright now because they are already going into debt collectively to buy seed, fertilizer and other production aids.

One recent Saturday morning, Dominguez and other civilians and army officers stood before an immense map of El Salvador that pin-pointed every farm to be taken under this first phase of the agrarian reform. An anny major displayed a cable stating that farm number 231 had come into state hands at 4 p.m. the day before. With the coordinates given in the cable, he marked it on the map. „The military problem is now over and the technical problems begin," he said.

The takeover is supposed to be followed by the formation of a leadership group and the organization of a cooperative. Then, a survey is to be made to determine what the property consists of and an inventory taken of machinery, debts and other financial information. Next, the new leadership is supposed to form a work plan for this year in an attempt to maintain production. The government is aware that it will be hard-put to maintain production in this first year, but Jose Napoleon Duane, a junta member who is the leader of the Christian Democratic Party, says calculations have been made indicating that enough production can be maintained for internal consumption of such basic commodities as sugar and cotton. One of the goals of the land transformation is to direct the nation's agriculture away from production for export and toward improving the local diet.

The junta is also preparing requests for $240 million in international aid to help finance the land transformation. This will be in addition to about $50 million in general economic and social aid already committed by the United States. Only a few million of the $50 million is intended for the land program. In addition, the junta expects to receive some wheat and soya from the United States. It will be sold for livestock feedgrains, and the money will be used, in turn, for various rural development programs.

Despite the controversy surrounding the takeover of Raul Salaverria's farm, most of the nationalizations have been carried out more peacefully. Such was the takeover of *El Refugio*, a coffee plantation near Santa Ana that belonged to Roberto Daglio. At Daglio's house, on a 4,000-foot mountaintop from which you can see into both Honduras and Guatemala, the furniture is intact, but there is the sense that the house has seldom been used of late. The few books are mostly from the 1950s, like the toys. A radio beside the bar still maintains contact with distant points of the farm. In an ashtray in the master bedroom lie six 38-caliber bullets.

El Refugio is modern and has been well run. Government officials are impressed. Its some 1,300 acres fell into state hands quietly. The armed guards who had been paid by Daglio appear to have joined the peasants in the cooperative venture. „We need for the man who built this to put his ability to work on something else," said a government official, alluding to the fact that the bonds with which Daglio is to be paid can be used to obtain bank credits for industrial development.

But Daglio is far away - in Miami - planning a hunting trip, tinkering with his boat on a Coral Gables Waterway, sipping scotch beside the swimming pool of the Brickell Avenue home of his friend Mauricio Salaverria, the middle son of Don Raul. Daglio enjoys a good life - a big house in San Salvador, another in Guatemala for his mother, a third in South Florida for his American wife and children. Like the three Salaverria brothers, he flies between his homes in his own plane and used to land his helicopter beside the house on the mountain near Santa Ana. He likes gadgets and weapons and is proud of his marksmanship. Outwardly, he is a cheerful and enjoyable companion, but in quiet moments he finds anguish. „It's very difficult to accept that you cannot go back," he said in an interview in Miami. „Sometimes you try to tell yourself that it is best not to return. But the next morning you feel very low."

He still has an insurance firm and a shrimp business in El Salvador, but he expects to lose the shrimp operation any day under another aspect of the junta's nationalization measures. At 45, he is young enough to change businesses. But the idea that the new régime wants him to work for El Salvador brings a bitter reaction. „I understand that we are not really wanted there. There is hatred and resentment toward us."«

December 5, 1980: »The bodies of three American nuns and a Roman Catholic lay worker were dug from a grave on a Salvadorean ranch Thursday, 36 hours after they disappeared while driving into the capital from the airport. U.S. Ambassador Robert White stood by as workers used ropes to lift the bodies out of the four-foot grave. „This time they won't get away with it," White muttered, without indicating whom he meant. The diplomat, whose life is often threatened here, was surrounded by bodyguards.

The victims were Sisters Ita Ford, 40, Maura Clarke, 46, Dorothy Kazel, 40, and lay worker Jean Donovan, 27. Ford,from Brooklyn, and Clarke, from Belle Harbor, N.Y., were of the Maryknoll order. Kazel was an Ursuline nun and Donovan a certified public accountant from Cleveland. The nuns were dressed in casual civilian clothes. All had been shot. One's face was nearly blown off, apparently when a bullet in the back of the head exited through the front. The disarray of clothes caused some at the scene to conclude that two of the victims had been raped. One's blue jeans were on backwards, and the bloody underclothing of another lay beside the grave. Judicial authorities in Canton Santa Teresa, near the plantation, later said all „were raped before they were assassinated." The victims' bodies displayed large-caliber bullet wounds in the backs and the heads, authorities said.

A truckload of security force personnel appeared at the gravesite as the bodies were being brought up, but no officials were on hand to assist in recovering the bodies. The peasants raised the bodies - first Donovan, then Clarke, then Kazel, then Ford - and laid them on the ground. Their faces were first covered with tree branches, then sheets. The Rev. Paul Schindler, an American priest who worked with Kazel and Donovan, supervised the recovery.

The four women disappeared Tuesday evening on the 35-mile trip from the international airport to San Salvador, the capital. Kazel and Donovan had gone there to meet the two Maryknolls who were returning from a meeting in neighboring Nicaragua. Their burned-out Toyota minibus was found the next morning and a search was initiated. Acting Archbishop Arturo Rivera y Damas, White and other officials received word Thursday morning that the women were in a grave on the Hacienda San Francisco near the community of Santa Rita Almendro, about 15 miles from the airport. White had been driving through the area earlier in the morning, apparently searching for some clue to the fate of the women.

Peasants who lived in a house about 100 yards from the gravesite, which was in a pasture surrounded by cornfields, said they had heard a car drive into the area about

U.S. GUNS IN EL SALVADOR

This cartoon, drawn by Pulitzer Prize-winner Ben Sargent and published on February 27, 1981, in *The Austin-American-Statesman* of Texas, opposes the foreign policy of President Ronald Reagan. In contrast to Jimmy Carter's, the Reagan administration thought the developments in Central America were very important. The fear to see the South American countries fall in the hands of socialist leaders, which would have constituted a victory for the Soviet Union, made the U.S. administration support the revolutionists in the respective Central-American countries, like the military insurgents in El Salvador. Reagan's comment in the drawing refers to the fact that the insurgents had formed death squads who also terrorized religious groups: A year prior, Archbichop Oscar A. Romero was assassinated because he criticized the U.S. giving military aid. In December of the previous year, three Amrican nuns had been kidnapped, probably raped and subsequently shot. With regards to the tragic incident, Reagan did not put a stop to deliveries of weapons, instead he merely warned the recipients not to kill any more American citizens - especially U.S. nuns - living in El Salvador.

11 p.m. Tuesday. Then they heard shots. Like most here, they did not venture outside until the next morning when they said they found the four bodies lying alongside the dirt road. The peasants said they contacted the local justice of the peace, who came to the scene with national guardsmen. They inspected the bodies, then told the peasants to bury them. That was Wednesday morning. It is not known who eventually concluded that they were the missing Americans and advised church authorities.

A small group of priests and nuns - Salvadorean and American - embraced each other and fought back tears as Rivera y Damas told a representative of the governing military-civilian junta by telephone of the discovery. Others, at the gravesite, recalled the dead women as hard workers with great senses of humor. „Jean and Dorothy used to talk a lot about their plans for the future," said one nun. „They often said they had plans A, B, C and D, but always ended up activating plan M."

Another friend recalled that the women worried little about their safety in this convulsed Central American nation, often saying that blue-eyed, blonde North Americans were probably the safest people in El Salvador, which is known for treating foreigners with great consideration. In Cleveland, Diocese Bishop-delegate Anthony Pilla released a statement saying, „I am grieved to tell you that our sisters, Ms. Jean Donovan and Ursuline Sister Dorothy Kazel, missioners from our diocese to El Salvador, were among the four bodies found dead .... We were informed that positive identification was made by local officials in El Salvador." State Department spokesman John Trattner said in Washington that the U.S. Embassy in San Salvador had been in touch with El Salvador's government „at the highest levels" since the Americans were reported missing late Tuesday.

„The incident represents another chapter in the continuing struggle in EI Salvador, which demonstrates the futility of violence as a means to resolve problems. We deplore violence against innocent persons once again, and particularly in this case against U.S. citizens," Trattner said. Sister Melinda Roper, president of the Maryknoll Sisters Mission, said: „[Ford and Clarke] chose to remain in El Salvador despite the dangers inherent in the continuing conflict." In his call to the government, Rivera y Damas told a junta representative that people traveling from the airport in recent days had noted an increased level of vigilance by security forces.

Earlier Thursday, before the bodies were discovered, Rivera y Damas was asked whether he thought rightist paramilitary forces or security people had anything to do with the disappearances. „I am inclined to believe they do," he replied. A spokesman for the Maryknoll order said the nuns' friends believe the El Salvador military was responsible for the killings. „Evidence provided by reliable sources indicates the military was instrumental in the death and disappearance of these four women," said Judy Noone, a spokesman for the Maryknoll order in Ossining, N.Y. „Other church people were stopped by the military in the area that same evening" the women disappeared, she said. The two Maryknoll nuns will be buried in El Salvador and a delegation of nuns will fly to San Salvador for their funeral. Ten priests - two Europeans and eight Salvadoreans - have been killed in El Salvador since 1977, including Archbishop Oscar

Romero, shot down by a gunman as he said mass in a hospital chapel last March. Forces of the extreme right are generally blamed in the priests' killings, although in some cases responsibility has been unclear. No one has been charged in the archbishop's murder. The junta has a policy of trying to halt repression by security forces, but the five members virtually concede that they cannot control the situation. An estimated 8,500 have died so far this year in El Salvador's near civil war.

The two Maryknoll nuns, Ford and Clarke, arrived at the airport at 7:30 p.m. Tuesday on a Panamanian airline flight from neighboring Nicaragua, where they had gone to attend a Maryknoll meeting. Kazel and Donovan were at the airport to meet them. The Maryknoll nuns were working in the northern Chalatenango region with refugees who have fled their homes because of military-guerrilla clashes or random violence. Ford had been here several years and Clarke recently arrived from Nicaragua, where she had worked for 20 years. Donovan and Kazel were „10 per centers" - Catholics who heed the call made by the late Pope John XXIll for parishes in developed countries to send 10 per cent of their clerics to developing countries. Both came from Cleveland, as have a number of other Americans working with them near La Libertad, on the Pacific coast near the airport.

A priest familiar with the Chalatenango area said the religious workers there had recently received implied threats on their lives. He said threatening posters had been hung on the doors of their housing complex twice. One poster, he said, claimed the occupants of the house were Communists. The other, he said, told them to go to Cuba to work.

It was the second trip of the day to the airport for Kazel and Donovan. They had gone early in the morning when four nuns were scheduled to arrive, but Ford and Clarke had decided to take the later flight, so Donovan and Kazel had to return to the airport in the evening. An interfaith delegation of Canadian priests, Protestant pastors and lay people had arrived at the airport on a different flight about the same time as the two Maryknolls. The Canadians reported seeing the Maryknolls. The Canadians, from the Inter-Church Committee on Human Rights for Latin America, said the four women were still at the airport when their group left. The Canadians, taking the same road, said they were stopped and checked by a large military patrol, then allowed to continue.

Two of the Canadians, the Rev. Gregory Chisholm of Scarborough and the Rev. Jacques Couture of Quebec, participated in the funeral mass Wednesday for six top leaders of the leftist coalition, the Democratic Revolutionary Front. The six men were kidnaped from a meeting at a high school last week and later found shot to death. When the Canadians left San Salvador Thursday for home, they were escorted to the airport by security agents of the U.S. Embassy. There is no Canadian Embassy here.«

December 7, 1980: »He has tried to be in the middle, and in a country turned against itself that is the most difficult ground to maintain. Now, one side has branded him a Communist, a frightening label for a member of the Salvadorean military. A senior officer has questioned his loyalty. On the other hand, he does not want to be lumped with those responsible for the death of the innocent, for the mangled and tortured bodies found by the dozen every day. Catholic priests, whose opinions he values, constantly remind Salvadorean soldiers that they are not authorized to violate the will of God.

This young officer fixed a drink, then another, and talked, on the patio of his home, about the personal agony that now confronts him and his companeros, the Salvadorean military officers who share his views. Maybe the only choice left for him, he says, is to join the guerrillas of the left. He has been discussing such a thing with people of his confidence. Others are thinking along the same lines, he says. However, that is to get ahead of the story. The story began with a dream, a dream that he fears has come to naught. It was the dream of Oct. 15, 1979, when these young men overthrew the corrupt and repressive régime of Gen. Carlos Humberto Romero and installed a military-civilian junta with a plan to bring social and economic justice and political liberty to a land with little experience in such things. They hoped the coup would head off insurrection from the left. Uncle Sam, traumatized by the Sandinista victory in neighboring Nicaragua just three months earlier, was ecstatic that someone dared seek a middle way here and responded with money and moral support. The young officer was one of the real leaders of that coup, which got most of its impulse from a group of captains, lieutenants and majors.

To represent them on the five-man junta, they elected Col. Adolfo Majano, 42, then the deputy director of the military academy. They chose Majano because he was an honest man, a rare find among the upper ranks of the Salvadorean military. Majano's worst enemies concede his honesty and his intelligence. Majano was to be the vehicle through which they would carry out their program. In an unusual form of military democracy, they formed a sort of parliament of lower-ranking officers to pass judgment on how well the senior officers were doing. Their program called for agrarian reform and other changes to take economic control of the country away from the few, plus an end to repression and to corruption.

Whenever Majano needed them, they would be there to stand behind him. Like elected politicians, they spread the word: A new day had come; the government and military were with the people. They helped deal with the crisis that came along. They also gathered the information that led to the dismissal of 10 per cent of the 15,OOO-member armed forces for abuse of authority. They became known as the Majanistas, a virtual political party within the military.

The first junta and Cabinet set up after the coup ran the gamut of Salvadorean thought from military and conservative businessmen, to centrist politicians, to socialists and Communists. „We are trying to make a revolution with all the existing elements,“ Majano would say. The unwieldy alliance lasted less than three months. When it fell apart, Majano and the other, more traditional military man on the junta, Col. Jaime Abdul Gutierrez forged a pact with the Christian Democratic Party and went back to work.

Washington was even more supportive. It likes Christian Democrats. They are reformminded, but anti-Communist. The new junta said it was fighting for the people against the extremes of right and left. Last March, junta No.2 finally decreed the agrarian reform that junta No.1 had promised. The army itself was used in a lightning takeover of the 300 or so largest *haciendas*, which were turned into peasant cooperatives.

Then the battle got tough. Opposition increased from the political right, dominated by the wealthy families who had owned the big farms. Several coups were attempted through supporters of the right within the military. Majano gradually lost his upper hand in the military and the junta. There was at least one recent attempt to assassinate him. The young officer says much of the reason for the decline in Majano's following was that „the right was buying off officers." Majano's critics within the military say he overstepped the bounds of military authority and tradition in his thorough reform. On the day late last month that six top leaders of the leftist Democratic Revolutionary Front, or FDR, were kidnaped and assassinated with the apparent concurrence of at least some elements of the security forces, Majano left the country in a cloud of mystery. The official story was that he had gone to the United States to visit his children, who are in school there. However, he turned up Friday in Panama, where he made a call for the „Military Youth" to uphold their „progressive" ideals.

The young officer expects Majano back momentarily, but he also thinks the colonel's days in the junta are numbered. Also numbered, he thinks, are the days that he and other hard-core Majanistas will remain in the military. He put this group at fewer than 100 men among about 700 officers. There still are other sympathizers, he says, but it is the small group that „wears the colors." In recent days, he says, many of them have received anonymous notes in the mail or delivered to their homes that say: „You are a Communist son of a bitch." He can't say for certain where the notes originate - maybe with other military men, maybe with rightists outside the régime. In most Western countries the charge would be laughed off. Here, it is taken as the kiss of death; being pegged as an assassin's target. It is the accusation that anyone in this government fears most. This is because EI Salvador, and especially the Salvadorean military, has never ceased to fight John Foster Dulles' battle, has never given up the crusade that Dulles planted throughout the „free" world.

A more or less neutral Salvadorean military officer, now retired, explains the Communist preoccupation this way: „You don't tell military men for 30 years that their primary goal is to kill Communists and then, when they think they finally have some Communists to kill, tell them, 'Don't kill the Communists; talk to them, dialogue with them.'" That, according to the retired officer, is what separates the Majanistas from their more traditional colleagues. Majano has tried repeatedly to open a dialogue with the left; it was reportedly about to bear fruit when the six leftist leaders were assassinated. The young officer is one of those who has dared to question the blind crusade against communism. That, coupled with the implied death threat and frustration about the military hierarchy's inability or unwillingness to control repression, leaves him to believe the only way out for him is toward the left.

While wondering what is best for the future of his small children, he says he may join the guerrillas. He acknowledges that the guerrillas are not doing well in their battle against the security forces but says the military is not doing well, either. The guerrillas, he thinks, are going into „prolonged popular war." The young officer knows that his own political ideas - he says he wants a „very slow movement toward socialism" - may not coincide with those of the Marxist-Leninists who are the majority in the FDR, but he adds: „I don't know how communism would be. They say, for example, that it is anti-Christian. I don't know. But the situation we have now is intolerable."«

December 13,1980: » He gets $50,112 a year, a bullettproof car, a bomb-proof office, plenty of bodygards and a death threat every couple of weeks. Jesse Helms calls him a leftist ideologue; his friends consider him „profoundly moral and patriotic." He is not one of the members of the beleaguered government of El Salvador. He is the equally beleaguered ambassador from the United States of America.

Aftcr a week in which six assassinated Salvadorean leftists were buried, the bodies of four murdered American women were dug out of a common grave and the U.S.-backed ruling fell apart, Robert E. White got the word that he is on what he calls the „hit list" of the incoming Reagan Administration.

While it's not the kind of hit list that is common in El Salvador, White thinks that the news leak of his probable firing or transfer is undermining his efforts to combat a progressive right-wing takeover and unchecked violence here.

He would have preferred a vote of confidence. Instead, local newspaper headlines last Sunday confirmed to all the plotters in El Salvador that the Reagan transition team wants to reduce the influence of „social reformers" in the career Foreign Service, especially White.

The story had appeared two days earlier in *The New York Times*. White, however, fought back with all the verbal talent at his commmand. He dashed off a long. angry telegram to the State Department, then went public. „The leaked report of the Reagan transition team ... has struck a heavy blow at the Chrisitan Democrats and moderate military officers seeking a centrist solution to the problems of El Salvador," he said in interviews here. White also complained about „various mixed and contradicton signals coming out of various people who think they speak for the Reagan Administration. When civil war breaks out in this country, I hope they get their chance to serve."

By Friday, other voices from both incoming and outgoing Washington administrations had joined a shouting match that was starting to crack the calm facade of transition. Lawrence Pezzullo, the U.S. ambassador to Nicaragua and also on the „hit list," spoke up for his colleague. So, too, did Patricia Derian, assistant secretary of state for human rights, who accused Reagan transition team members of making „imprudent statements" that endangered White's life.

The State Department later characterized Derian's statement as private and in no way expressing department views, but Fred Ikle, a Reagan foreign policy adviser, termed her remarks „totally irresponsible."

And Edwin Meese Ill, counselor to the president-elect, said Friday that no authorized member of the Reagan transition team has made any statement that might „undercut the position of any ambassador anyplace." Meese added, „I question in a sense the professionalism of those ambassadors if they're making such reckless accusations."

White said Friday that he, as a career diplomat, has no intention of resigning, because „the whole point ... is that you serve until you are relieved. Now, if a policy were inflicted on me over my objections and I felt strongly about that policy, then I might consider resigning," White told *The Herald*.

„But that's clearly not what we are talking about here .... I don't resign over problem situations. I try to meet them as effectively as I can in order to resolve them. I think the Reagan people have this whole idea turned around and that they are looking at it from the wrong angle," he said. „The fact that certain of us have worked effectively to move the policy of this administration should be a recommendation for us to the next administration."

El Salvador isn't the first place that Robert White has brought his Irish temper, his wit and his compassion to bear on a controversy that has himself as a target. As a 25-year Foreign Service veteran and an ambassador, he certainly is more „hittab1e" now than earlier in his career, but he has been in trouble before.

He was born 54 years ago in Stoneham, Mass., descended from what he calls an Irish „two-boater" family - the poorest of the Irish potato-famine poor who needed two generations and two boat trips to get the whole family to the United States.

White graduated from St. Michael's College in Winooski, Vt., and earned a master's degree at Tufts University's Fletcher School of Law and Diplomacy before going to England as a Fulbright Scholar. He joined the Foreign Service in 1955 and held posts in Hong Kong, Canada and throughout Latin America before going to Paraguay as ambassador in 1977.

In Nicaragua, his distaste for Anastasio Somoza led to his recall. While on a misson for the Organization of American States in Chile, he riled Henry Kissinger and Gen. Augusto Pinochet by denouncing the lack of press freedom there. In Paraguay he gained the animosity of strongman Gen. Alfredo Stroessner by trying to protect dissidents.

When the Carter Administration - on the heels of the Sandinista victory in Nicaragua - adopted a policy of trying to head off leftist insurrection in El Salvador by promoting a moderate reformist government, White voluntered. And although he did not have serious competition for what often seems a thankless job, it did not come to him easily.

Helms, the conservative Republican senator from North Carolina, once labeled White an „extreme leftist," perhaps the nicest thing the senator ever called him. Although he eventually won Senate confirmation by a 71-17 vote, it was only after answering more than 80 questions from Helms in writing.

However, if White has powerful enemies in Washington, he has a fiercely loyal staff here. „Ninety-five per cent of the staff is here because of him," said one embassy official, „and half of them will ask for transfers if he goes."

Visitors to White's San Salvador residence, after running a gamut of sharpshooters and sentries from what may be the biggest contingent of Marine guards in the diplomatic corps, get a surprisingly warm welcome. White seems to glory in the tension, and the attention.

His wife, Mary Anne Cahill White, is here with him, but their five children are not. Since the assassination last March of Archbishop Oscar Romero, San Salvador has heen an „unaccompanied post,“ meaning no spouses or children, except for Mrs. White.

Jerrold M. Dion, White's deputy chief of mission, pointed out that a week and a day after White arrived in El Salvador last March, the ambassador went unannounced to Romero's Sunday mass in the downtown basilica and took communion. The basilica is a couple of blocks from the Metropolitan Cathedral, then in the hands of armed leftists.

„It was a symbolic political act that no other diplomat I know would be willing to do,“ said Dion. „It was a big signal. It turned the extreme right violently against the ambassador, but it led the church to believe that at last someone here would pay attention to it.“

White is also capable of symbolic acts on a spontaneous basis. On the day after the disappearance on the airport road of three American nuns and a religious lay worker, concern arose about a Canadian church delegation preparing to leave for home. White came by the Canadians' hotel early in the morning and escorted them 35 miles to the airport with some of his security people.

Returning from the airport, he received a radio report that the missing women's grave had been located in the area. He found the site and shook with emotion and anger as the corpses were dug up, making clear that he thought security forces were responsible.

Others in the embassy say that if Ronald Reagan, the astute politician, could see Bob White, the astute politician, at work, he might not be so eager to sack him. Besides, with things going the way they are in El Salvador, it's not going to be an easy job to fill.«

December 14, 1980: »Crisis follows crisis in EI Salvador, but in trying to help resolve them the United States has become an elephant struggling in a closet. It has an abundance of power and a shortage of options. The incoming Reagan administration will likely find that it could move only slightly to the right or slightly to the left of the Carter policy of providing moral and financial support - but no military advisers - to the military-civilian régime trying to govern EI Salvador. Any sharp move in either direction, unless it is a pragmatic necessity resulting from a fait accompli such as the Sandinista victory in Nicaragua or the Garcia Meza coup in Bolivia, would violate American traditions and open to public criticism a Reagan administration in its infancy.

Consider first the option of moving further to the left. The Salvadorean Left is made up of a coalition called the Democratic Revolutionary Front, known by its Spanish initials FDR, and a collection of armed guerrilla organizations. Theoretically, the FDR and the guerrillas are separate. In practice, several of the so-called mass organizations in the FDR are controlled by, or closely connected to, the guerilla groups. At the same time, the FDR has some people of unquestioned democratic credentials. One of them was Enrique Alvarez Cordova, the reformed oligarch and former agriculture minister who was president of the FDR until he and several others of the organization's leaders were assassinated two weeks ago. There is also a range of social democrats, Marxist types and Christian Democrats, the latter of whom have deserted fellow Christian Democrats who still share the government with the Salvadorean military.

Moving toward the FDR would mean making some clear signals that Washington and the present Salvadorean government are willing to negotiate. Both say they have been willing all along to at least open a dialogue, but the U.S. position has mainly appeared to be, „we are willing to talk, if they come to us." A so-called „dissent paper" that came out of Washington anonymously a month ago argues for negotiations and insists, contrary to what U.S. diplomats say, that the FDR is putting out signals of a desire to talk. The paper, thought to have been prepared by intellectuals and some former government experts on Central America, suggests that this be brought about through third parties sympathetic to the FDR, particularly the Mexican government or Gen. Omar Torrijos in Panama.

The trouble with this approach is that those who make U.S. policy are convinced that talking to the FDR as an organization, as opposed to talking to its democratic components, is the same thing as negotiating with one of the most unattractive guerrilla movements to be produced in Latin America. The Salvadorean guerrilla left is nervous and trigger-happy. In a country ripe for social and economic revolution, the extreme left defeats itself by killing more soldiers' families than soldiers, burning buses, bombing McDonald's and destroying crops gathered by peasant hands. While the right may kill more, the left hurts itself with the very constituency it pretends to serve. The vast majority of Salvadoreans are still trying to live a peaceful, workaday existence. For them, it may be more disruptive to walk to work or lose their jobs to bombings than to read about nameless bodies tossed by the roadside.

The mass organizations within the FDR are also not without blame in this politically misdirected violence. The Revolutionary Popular Bloc, the largest mass group in the FDR, marched 20,000-strong into the peaceful crowd attending the funeral last March of the assassinated archbishop Msgr. Oscar Romero. Somehow shooting broke out and more than 30 people died, most or all crushed in the resulting panic. Subsequent investigations established fairly conclusively that there were no security forces or snipers in the area and that the Popular Bloc demonstrators accidentally set off an explosion, then panicked and whipped out their own pistols and started shooting wildly. So, while the killers of the extreme right were probably responsible for the assassination of the archbishop, the extreme left carries the burden of the deaths of 30 or more simple, innocent people who went to the plaza that day to mourn him.

But if the extreme left is unattractive to an American government whose traditions demand democracy and oppose the class struggle, then the extreme right becomes repugnant for other reasons. The extreme right in El Salvador is less nervous than the extreme left, but just as trigger-prone. It has more weapons and a better aim. It kills with an unimaginable brutality, chopping off arms, legs, heads and sexual organs with machetes.

The organization of the extreme right is just as shadowy and complex as that of the left. One of its elements is composed of the once big land-owning families who lost their land to agrarian reform earlier this year. This is considered the source of the right's money (the left's comes from $50 million or more gathered from kidnapings), but these people don't pull triggers. There are various paramilitary organizations on the right made up primarily of armed peasants. More important, however, it is conceded by many military men and Christian Democrats in the government that a large segment of security forces - a term that generally exludes the professional army - moonlights for the right, on- or off-duty.

The Reagan election and statements by various Reagan advisers suggesting that his administration would favor more direct assistance to the Salvadorean military for the campaign against leftists has given vigor to the extreme right. So, too, has the general U.S. policy of supporting Washington's friends - i.e., those who oppose communism. Intentional or not, this surge in rightist sentiment came at a time when many Salvadorean business and professional people were moving toward support for the government. If the Reagan administration, however, decides to provide all-out military support in El Salvador and stress a military victory, it must consider the repercussions at home of being even more closely identified than the Carter Administration with a large majority of the deaths. There have been at least 8,500 killings so far this year among El Salvador's 4.7 million people - the equivalent of wiping out a city of 400,000 in the United States.

It has taken a long time for the American people to discover the anguish of El Salvador; but the murder 10 days ago of four American women, three of them nuns, surely did what all those other deaths could not do. Even if yesterday's headlines go away, the vision on network television of the angry and shaken American ambassador watching as the bodies were dug out of a common grave is less easily forgotten. Nor the implication in Ambassador Robert E. White's words when he said he was going to raise „holy hell" with the Salvadorean defense minister. There is strong circumstantial evidence that security forces from the local post engaged in an attempt to cover up the killings. This, in the eyes of diplomats and many people in the government, points to the extreme right.

Ronald Reagan has shown he understands well his constituency. It fears communism. But it is also a constituency that believes in morality, in the sanctity of the person, and that is religious. The issue has already been confronted in the United States at least once. Americans thought they were fighting communism in Vietnam, but when the evening news brought them pictures of American boys setting fire to peasant huts as wrinkled old women stood by helplessly, they realized the issue had another dimension. The choice then was withdrawal, but subsequent events in Southeast Asia and El Salvador's proximity to the United States make that choice unlikely this time around. Facing extremes that represent communism on one side and nun killers on the other, a president who is responsible to American ideals has no choice but to continue the difficult effort to construct a broad middle.«

1982: OBSERVER OF LIFE AND DEATH IN EL SALVADOR

James B. Dickman, *Dallas Times-Herald*

The jury's recommendations, which included two entrants removed from the spot news pictures classification and placed in the Feature award category, were: James B. Dickman of the *Dallas Times-Herald* „for his picture story 'EI Salvador - The Killing Ground', the aftermath of a series of bloody battles." Barron Ludlum, also of the *Dallas Times-Herald*, was praised by the jurors „for his picture story of the courageous battle of an eight-year-old to survive a congenital liver malfunction; this struggle was shared by her mother." The third name on the list was that of John H. White of the *Chicago Sun-Times*, who had won the preceding year, „for his portfolio of pictures which cover the tappestly of life in Chicago, from the grief of a child of Tylenos victim to a tooth operation on an elephant and almost all elements of our society in between."

The jury „was unanimous in its decision selecting Dickman's work as the finest of these three and of what we found to be an extremely strong field of contenders." So the Board accepted this proposal and gave James B. Dickman the Pulitzer Prize „for his telling photographs of life and death in EI Salvaador." The photographer and some of his colleagues from other newspapers had been in the capital San Salvador, when „the military started shooting guerillas right in front of us," he remembered, „we were around the side of a building, staying low, trying to get pictures. I photographed soldiers dragging away bodies. Nobody tried to stop us ... One of the difficult parts is to keep your focus literally and figuratively, on what you are there for. Hopefully you are human enough to be affected emotionally, but you realize that you are documenting it so people back home can see it and it will have an impact."

James B. Dickman, born on March 25, 1949, in St. Louis, Missouri, studied at the University of Texas at Arlington from 1967 to 1969. Afterwards he joined the McKinney Job Corporations of Texas as a photographer. His first newspaper job was at the *Denver Post* before he moved to the *Dallas Times-Herald* in 1970. Since 1987 Dickman freelanced for *Life, Time, National Geographic, Fortune, Sports Illustrated* and other magazines. Once, he spent three months living in a stone-age village in Papua-New Guinea for National Geographic, and he also was a photographer on several book series. Following is the key photograph of his award-winning pictures from El Salvador.

WOMAN TAKEN FROM HER HOME BY DEATH SQUAD

Photo depicts a scene of the civil war in El Salvador, showing a woman who had been forced out of her home by the troops. On election day, the guerillas had tried to keep voters away from the ballots while soldiers had stepped in. In the following battle a dozen guerillas had died. The woman and her husband's tiny cabin had been in the line of fire that had been exchanged between the death squad and the guerillas in San Antonio Abad, a suburb of San Salvador which was also called El Payon. This is where the death squad brought all the persons they thought to be supporters of the guerillas in order to execute them. The soldiers had forced the couple to lie on the ground, originally to question them of their alleged alignment to the leftist guerillas. As one soldier had been about to shoot the man, a sergeant had pulled him back. However, when the couple was allowed to get up, the woman fainted with fear. She was not able to stand up by herself and had to be carried away.

James B. Dickman, July 18, 1982

1984: ILLEGAL U.S. IMMIGRANTS FROM MEXICO

Stan Grossfeld, *Boston Globe*

The jurors listed the three nominations in this category as follows: Stan Grossfeld of the *Boston Globe* who had presented two series, one on Ethiopia, the other one on illegal aliens on the U.S. border with Mexico. In the eyes of the jury, both series showed an „impressive close-up, human element as well as stunning overall shots, a great variety and strong impact." Another finalist was Stormi Greener of the *Minneapolis Star-Tribune* who had shown „pictures of a dying girl that celebrated her life rather than emphasized her dying," the jury report said, „the best photo is of her and friends smiling." Sebastian Salgado Jr. from *Magnum Photos* of Paris was the third contestant on the shortlist for presenting pictures of „strong, beating reality of Ethiopia, with simplicity and high drama in the series and good combination of the general and the specific."

The Board gave the Pulitzer Prize in this category to Stan Grossfeld of the *Boston Globe* „for his series of photographs of the famine in Ethiopia and for his pictures of illegal aliens on the Mexican Border." It was quite a surprise that Grossfeld was not the only winner in the Feature Photography category because the Board also declared Larry C. Price of the *Philadelphia Inquirer* winner in this award group. Both earned the Pulitzer Prize in equal parts, and for both it was already their second honor of this kind.

Stan Grossfeld, born on December 20, 1951, in New York City, graduated from the Rochester Institute of Technology with a Bachelor of Science in Professional Photography degree in 1973. He then started to work as a staff photographer at the *Newark Star-Ledger*. Two years later he switched to the *Boston Globe*. While working as a photographer Grossfeld graduated from Boston University with a Master in Journalism degree in 1980. He published the book *Nantucket: The Other Season* in 1982. The following year he was promoted to be chief photographer of the *Boston Globe*. Stan Grossfeld was made the recipient of the 1984 Pulitzer Prize in the spot news category for his series of unusual pictures which reveal the effects of war on the people of Lebanon. Two years after earning his second Pulitzer Prize, Grossfeld moved up to Associate Editor of the *Boston Globe*. Following is his award-winning photograph from the U.S.-Mexican border:

MEXICANS TRY TO MOVE INTO THE UNITED STATES

Photo shows a group of Mexicans trying to enter the United States illegally by crossing the Rio Grande river, wading neck-high in the murky water. They wanted to work on the fields at El Ranchito, Texas. However, they had to move back towards the Mexican side of the river when a United States Border Patrol Agent came by. The number of illegal immigrants from Mexico to the U.S. was estimated to have skyrocketed in recent years.

Stan Grossfeld, September 9, 1984

1984: PEOPLE FLEEING FROM WAR-TORN EL SALVADOR

Larry C. Price, *Philadelphia Inquirer*

The winner's name could not be found on the jury's list of finalists in the feature photography award category. Instead, his merits were told on the shortlist in the spot news category, from where the Board had switched the entry to the feature group. Without saying anything about the content of Price's exhibit, the jury report only told in general wording that he had shown „initiative in getting where the action was; he came up with exceptional photos out of dangerous situations, showed the desperation of the situations." When Price earned the award, he was praised by the Board „for his series of photographs from Angola and San Salvador depicting their war-torn inhabitants."

The photographer remembered El Salvador as a dangerous story because „you never knew where the enemy was, you never knew what was waiting for you around the comer". Particularly menacing were the right-wing death squads, which murdered more than 50,000 civilians in thirteen years. „These death squads," Price said, „would target neighborhoods in El Salvador, summarily execute people, throw them into the back of a truck, drive them out and throw out their bodies." The dead were often taken to a field of volcanic lava outside of San Salvador. „I drove over late one afternoon", Price remarked, „there had been a whole fresh round of killings. The remains of that persons had been dumped a couple of days before. There were a lot of fairly fresh bones and skulls."

Larry C. Price, born on February 23, 1954, in Corpus Christi, Tx., began his career with taking photos for the Corpus Christi Ray High School newspaper. He attended Sam Houston State University in Huntsville before he transferred to the University of Texas in Austin in 1976 where he worked for the student newspaper *Daily Texan*. The following year he received a Bachelor of Jourrnalism degree. He then joined the *El Paso Times* where he stayed for two years. Afterwards he was engaged as a staff photographer by the *Fort Worth Star-Telegram* in 1979. Larry C. Price was awarded the 1981 Pulitzer Prize in the spot news photography category for pictures from Liberia. In 1983 he switched to the *Philadelphia Inquirer* where he got the post of a photojourrnalist. After winning his second Pulitzer Prize he moved to the *Baltimore Sun*. Following is the key photograph of his award-winning pictures:

FAMILY FLEES FROM EL SALVADOR TO SAFER AREAS

Photo shows a Salvadorian family leaving the region of Jucuaran, in order to evade the fighting which had not ceased since guerillas came to the area six months earlier. The family crossed the Rio Grande de San Miguel climbing the remains of the bridge that used to be there. The Marxist guerillas had destroyed the bridge as they wanted to keep the government soldiers away. However, the troops found another way to enter the region and the fighting commenced. Simultaneously, elections were being held nationwide. The Marxist rebels did not take part in them as a party. By declining to partake in the political progress of El Salvador, the guerilla force made an ending of the war improbable. They were having considerable success, as they controlled almost a quarter of the country. The Salvadorian Army was supported massively by the U.S. forces in their struggle to suppress the rebels. The life of the Salvadorian population was made even more difficult by the raids of the right-wing death squads. The latter had killed more than 40,000 people whom they believed were supporting the guerillas. All the family on the photo had left wear the belongings they could carry and one pig. The promises of democracy and stability, given in the pre-election campaigns, were meaningless to the fleeing peasants.

Larry C. Price, March 24, 1984.

1985: TRAGEDY OF AN VOLCANO ERUPTION IN COLOMBIA

Carol Guzy/Michel du Cille, *Miami Herald*

The five members of the jury whittled down their group of finalists to these three entries: A team of photographers of the *Dallas Morning News* that had submitted a „Portfolio of Pictures from the Mexico City Earthquake". David Walters of the *Miami Herald* also had provided excellent „Mexico City Earthquake Coverage." Carol Guzy and Michel du Cille, also from the *Miami Herald*, had „under deadline and access difficulties brought both the horror and the strongness of the Armero earthquake disaster to their readers." Never before in the history of either photography award had there been three finalists that all depicted similar themes, in this case various forms of natural disasters.

The Board preferred the photographic output of Guzy and du Cille who worked together as a team of two and were praised „for their photographs of the devastation caused by the eruption of the Nevado del Ruiz volcano in Columbia." The two photographers had arrived in devastated Armero in Columbia just thirty-six hours after the volcano exploded." It looked like a tornado came through and wiped everything flat", du Cille remembered, „there were bodies everywhere - it was the smell of death." Guzy had hoped that a thirteen-years-old girl, thin deep in mudwater but alive, could be rescued. But after the photographer returned to the scene, the girl „was gone", said Guzy, „I couldn't believe they had their hands on her and the helicopter was there and they could'nt get her out."

Carol Guzy, born on March 7, 1956. in Bethlehem, Pa., graduated from the Northampton County Area Community College in her hometown with an deegree in nursing in 1978. After having served an internship at the *Miami Herald*'s Broward Bureau she was engaged by that newspaper as a staff photographer. In 2006 Carol Guzy earned her first Pulitzer Prize, shared with Michel du Cille. Two more honors of that kind should follow in future years - Michelangelo E. du Cille, born on January 24, 1956, in Kingston, Jamaica, graduated from Indiana University with a Bachelor's degree in journalism in 1981. He then joined the *Miami Herald* where he won his first Pulitzer Prize, shared with Carol Guzy, another one should follow a couple of years later. In 1988 du Cille became picture editor of the *Washington Post*. Following is one of the award-winning photos from Columbia, taken by Carol Guzy:

A TEENAGER IN DANGER TO LIFE IN COLOMBIA

Photo shows 13-year-old Omayra Sanchez, who had been trapped in volcanic mud that covered her hometown Armero in Colombia. She could not be freed and died after two days of struggling for her life.

Carol Guzy, November 15, 1985.

1992: LIFE OF WEALTHY AND POOR PEOPLE ON HAITI

Liz Balmaseda, *Miami Herald*

„In Miami, with more foreign-born citizens than any other city in the nation", the Managing Editor of the *Miami Herald* stated, „'local' news often happens far away. A dissident uprising in Cuba is big news in Little Havana. A power shift in Port-au-Prince can send hundreds to the streets of Little Haiti - and to the shores of Miami Beach. Liz Balmaseda's intimacy with South Florida's communities makes her work special ... A Cuban American, she distinguished herself as a foreign correspondent in South and Central America... There are also the special gifts Balmaseda brings to her craft - a keen eye for detail, an ear for language, compassion and a sense of outrage. Twice each week, Liz reveals, counsels, sometimes scolds. Regularly, through skilled reporting and writing, she breaks news and tells people things they didn't know." When these words, together with samples of her work, reached the Pulitzer Prize jurors they were impressed and stated in their report of March 3, 1993: Balmaseda „did what the entire U.S. government failed to do. She traveled to Haiti and got the truth... She showed Haiti's elite as well as the poor." The Pulitzer Prize Board shared the praise and gave the award to Liz Balmaseda „for her commentary from Haiti about deteriorating political and social conditions."

Elizabeth R. Balmaseda was born on January 17, 1959, in Puerto Padre, Cuba, admist the Cuban Revolution. Her family emigrated to the United States, and she grew up in Miami, Florida. She received an associate's degree from Miami-Dade Community College, and then a bachelor's degree from Florida International University in communications in 1981. She had been an intern for the *Miami Herald* in 1980, and was hired upon her graduation in 1981 to write for *El Herald*, the *Miami Herald*'s Spanish-language sister paper. She worked in this and several other reporting assignments at the *Herald* until 1985, when she left to become Central America bureau chief, based in El Salvador, for Newsweek. She moved to *NBC News* as a field producer based in Honduras before returning to the *Miami Herald* in November 1987 as a feature writer, earning the Pulitzer Prize in 1993. Following now are several of her award-winning articles:

May 31, 1992: »Port-au-Prince, Haiti - The shame of the new return policy on Haitian refugees is told in a simple number. Only 16 people have been granted political asylum at the U.S. Embassy since February. Sixteen doesn't begin to reflect the reports of violence and repression in the shanly towns, in the mountain villages, in the coastal slums. I've met people in hiding. I know of villagers arrested, of homes ransacked, of schoolchildren surrounded by security forces. The other day I spoke to a Haitian journalist who was beaten by soldiers when he tried to cover an anti-government student rally. So how on earth can they find only 16?

Josef Paunel is not one of the 16. Most likely, he will be part of the huddled masses, stopped at sea with no opportunity to tell their stories on neutral soil, loaded onto a

U.S. Coast Guard cutter and deposited on these docks where cruise ship revelers used to land. On Friday morning, like the masses, Josef is silent as he takes an application from a relief worker before he enters the processing center. The form is in French, a language more likely to be understood by those few who live a world away, in the lush hills ahove the putrid shanty towns that are home to would-be refugees like Josef. No one explains what is printed on the form, that it is for seeking political asylum.

Last Sunday night, Josef crept aboard a Miami-bound refugee boat after dark in the port of Leogane, just southwest of the capital. He didn't know that several hours earlier the president of the United States had ordered all Haitian boat refugees returned without political asylum hearings. If he had known, Josef tells me, he would have gone anyway, „to save my life.“ He had left his home in the Carrefour Feuilles slum because armed men had come looking for him several times. „They came in shadows in the night. Afterwards, there was shooting in the neighborhood,“ he says as he waits in line to receive $15 and a meal card from the Haitian Red Cross.

He didn't know who the gunmen were. Army? Police? Macoutes? Terrorist mobs: known as zenglendo? He wasn't about to stick around to find out. His neighborhood is considered to be one of the most loyal to ousted President Jean Bertrand Aristide, and an area where young men are often harassed by security forces linked to the de facto government.

Josef is 19. I stare at his T-shirt. Three white sailors frolicking in 1940s Hollywood style. „Liberty Blues,“ it says. I ask if he will seek political asylum. He shrugs. He harbors no great hope anyone would believe him anyway. He has no proof. Besides, he doesn't know how much time he has left. „I will be in the street at the will of God,“ he says. I lose him in the crowd, and, for no reason other than to see his face again, I scour the mob of torsos for his benign sailors. I am terrified for him.

George Bush says people like Josef must apply for political asylum at the U.S. Embassy here. But the reason Josef may never join the lucky 16 is because it could be more dangerous to embark on the feared Haitian magouy, the labyrinth of red tape and dead ends. Besides, what address would he give? His mother's? She doesn't even know where he went that night when he fled Haiti. All of the would-be refugees in this teeming depot - 740 in several wooden boats - set sail after Bush issued his executive order May 24. None with whom I spoke said they knew about the order when they left. Few understood how to seek protection from what some described as persecution.

„What is this paper? What does it say?“some of the refugees wondered when asked if they would request asylum. There are all kinds of stories here. There are refugees who admit they left because they wanted to make a little more money. Others say they fled their poverty in desperation. I find 22-year-old Edeline Ketelin in a stained pink dress breast-feeding her 2-month-old baby. With no way to support her baby, she sold her bed and kitchen table and bought a $50 seat on a boat to Miami. But had she known how this voyage would turn out, she says she would have stayed home. Her first time on a boat, she had never imagined the power of the sea. As their wooden boat plied the turbulent Windward Passage, its sail ripped and the crew threatened to start tossing passengers overboard. Edeline could not breathe in the cramped quarters. Her baby was burning up with fever. She believes the U.S. Coast Guard saved them. If she had known about Bush's order, she tells me, she wouldn't have tried to leave Haiti.

I watch the refugees jam into the depot, looking much the way they might have looked on their refugee vessels, rib to rib, shoulder to shoulder melting in the tricks of the gwo lame, the „big ocean." Babies on their mothers breasts. Young men waiting to be fingerprinted. A faded sign overhead proclaims, „Welcome to Haiti." At the fringe of this madness, I approach the vice consul of the United States, a good-natured man named Howie Muir. Pointing to the crush of refugees, I ask him if the consulate is prepared to handle it. Yes, he says, there are three to seven windows open to assist asylum-seekers in filling out their forms. The refugees, he says, could either mail their claims or take them in person. If they are fearful, he says, they can give the name of a trusted contact who would be called by the embassy. He's confident this system will be safe for applicants.

But during the week, sources familiar with cases of persecution told me those in hiding are unlikely to take a number at the consulate. Besides, they have little faith that U.S. officials will grant them asylum, no matter how valid their fears may be. They know refugees are presumed economic until proved political, safe until proved dead. They know few in the U.S. government believe the Haitians because it is so difficult to confirm their stories. Too many times in this complex land, their stories are taken as myths. They simply can't be real because they can't be proven beyond a reasonable doubt. And it doesn't help the refugees that in Haiti hunger and politics bleed into each other, muddling claims of persecution. Still, how could the consulate find only 16?

The dramatic contrast between the swelling tide or refugees and the tricklc of asylum claims raises crucial questions about the U.S. government's procedure for screening those whose lives could be in danger. So far, in Port-au-Prince only 330 have applied for political asylum, according to an embassy source. Of those, 166 were scheduled for interviews with U.S. immigration representatives here. Of 86 applicants already interviewed, only 16 have been approved for asylum. By contrast, in Guatanamo where 35,000 refugees were interviewed following interdiction, 9,700 have been granted permisssion to pursue asylum claims in the United States. That tells me that on neutral soil frightened Haitians feel safe enough to tell there stories, and be heard.«

June 1, 1992: » Port-au-Prince, Haiti - At first, I don't recognize him, his hunched figure taking purposely brisk steps up a garden path. I remember his electric presence in the diaspora, rustic protest signs in his circumference as he rattled fierce, effcient sound bites, the kind that usually earned him a few seconds on the evening news. But now here he is, eyes fixed upon his feet as they shuffle into a dim room, a safe room. Nine months after a coup toppled popularly elected President Jean-Bertrand Aristide, Miami's most vocal Haitian political activist is still in hiding. Gerard Jean-Juste, the Roman Catholic priest who spent more than two decades in exile and returned to his homeland after Aristide won, says he wants to stay right here, in the shadows of an increasingly tense, uncertain, violent Haiti. As I watch him enter the darkened room on this recent morning, a watchful companion in his wake, I know his fear is very real. The night before, the brother of a powerful and vocal Aristide supporter was assassinated as he left his business downtown. The three bullets that killed Georges Izmery, relatives bclieve, were intended for his brother, Antoine, a wealthy merchant who, like Jean-Juste, was vowed to stay and fight the de facto government. The murder confirmed what the Aristide faithful know all too well. „Death is at our doorstep," says Jean-Juste, taking a seat across from me at a friend's table.

For the first time, I find his trademark drama in perfect context. In this safe room he is not an exile barking rhetoric from a fareaway land, as I'm sure many skeptical outsiders saw him years back. He is in Haiti. On the inside. And as we talk, I find he is not afraid to bark just as loud here. It is part of his mandate, even if his president is in exile. When Aristide came to office in early 1991, he named Jean-Juste liaison for the 10th Department, as the exile community is called. After the Sept. 30 coup. Jean-Juste's office was seized, his staff forced to scatter. He was forced into hiding. But he remained quite plugged into the teledio, the rumor mill, the most popular news service in Haiti. And he often broadcasts on Miami's Haitian airwaves what he learns from trusted sources in hiding, in repressed slums, in the city streets.

The other night, for example, he told listeners of Little Haiti's VeyeYo about an army attack against residents of a nearby shanty town several weeks ago. „They raped a 10-year-old girl in front of her mother," he tells me. He tells me about an Aristide militant repatriated from the U.S. Navy base at Guantanamo Bay who was arrested by security forces and disappeared last month. He passes on such reports to human rights groups abroad in hopes of documenting the persecution he hears about every day. His own pursuit of safety has been traumatic. On his trail, security forces have already harassed friends and relatives three times since the coup. One month after Aristide's overthrow, soldiers burst into a safe house and handcuffed his assistant. Weeks later, plainclothes gunmen firing Galil assault rifles in the air surrounded a church rectory where they believed he was hiding. „Where is Jean-Juste?" they demanded. „Bring him down to us!" Claiming to be soldiers, the gunmen beat a seminarian and threw rocks on the roof of the church.

I find it remarkable that he is here. Beyond the risk he lakes, he is away from the politically ignored exile community at a time when it may need him the most. In his exile years, he organized activc communities in several American cities and Canada. As executive director for the Haitian Refugee Center in Miami, he needled U.S. authorities for more humane treatment of Haitians, staging rallies and protests. His activism won him a cold shoulder from church authorities in Miami. It is ironic that after 26 years in exile, after so many struggles against Haitian dictatorships, so many press conferences, so many marches, after waiting so long, he savored Haitian democracy for just eight months.

Eight delicious months. That's one month less than the military-backed government has been in power. And now Jean-Juste hides. He rarely sleeps in the same place two nights in a row. HIs friends and contacts use different names when they call. „A lot of people think I'm in the States," he said, seeming impressed that he could keep a low profile for so long. Frankly, I, too, am impressed. As we say goodbye, he tells me his thoughts arc with his „constituens" in the 10th department, the Haitians who listen to Creole radio in the kitchens of Miami restaurants, in the factories, in middle-class offices, in the tiny shops along North Miami Avenue. For them, Jean-Juste, voice of Haitian exiles, has this perfect sound bite: „Don't give up in the struggle for democracy. It's worth giving one's life for Haiti and its peoplc."«

June 4, 1992: »Port-au-Prince, Haiti - Those are the neighbor's children dancing in the rain, thrusting their faces skyward, trying to catch the raindrops in their mouths, singing a song that gets lost in the deluge. Those are not the children of Morales Leger. His children are inside, dry, pleased nevertheless to witness the downpour on such a suffocating day. From his house across the alley, he and I watch the neighbor's girls in their euphoric convulsions, drenched, entranced. Morales, a man of 64, has put out large tin pots to catch the clean rainwaater, a blessing on this humid Feast of the Ascension. He pulls his young son close to him, kissing his cheek, explaining that „he easily gets the flu."

The sudden storm caught me as we talked in his home. Entirely by chance. I found myself dropped in the middle of daily life in a squalid shanty strip where a desperate existence churns on endlessly, even on feast days. The rain hammered on the tin roof, veiling doorways and windows in misty curtains. A shower of relief.

To arrive at his house, I crossed the ancient slaughterhouse, walked along the muck-filled canal where pigs slept. The stench of human and animal and vegetable waste clung to my face like a mask. I took quick, shallow breaths through my mouth. A young woman bathed in the pig water, scrubbing her arms with a pink bar of soap, as if the rosy suds could extinguish the film of God-knows-what -is-dumped-in-there. I had passed more than a dozen wooden doorways framing swollen, naked children. Inside, their mothers and sisters and maybe cousins lounged in a darker dimension. Because this was a holiday, no one was working. Normally, this place is alive from 4:30 a.m. with wailing animals and haggling merchants who later sell the fresh, warm meat at the market.

Then I slipped into the home of Morales Leger. Within dim, green walls there are two beds over which gauze mosquito nets dangle. There is a pink, child-size potty chair where his youngest girl, Philocles, 2, fidgets, naked. We talk about his life. He has not worked steadily in years. He was a sergeant in the military for 26 years, though he says he is not a political man. He left the service 17 years ago and has worked odd jobs since. He married a woman much younger, Margareth Coustan, 28. He delivered their four children in his home, on their matrimonial bed. He writes their names in my notebook in a spidery hand: Gina, 8, Philomene, 5, Philippe, 3. Philocles, 2.

He lifts the youngest from her chamber pot, slides a piece of cardboard over it's seat, and kisses the girl gently. "My consolation," he whispers, kissing her again. Then it begins to rain. I ask him about Haiti, about politics and refugee boats, and the régime du jour. But he shakes his head. „It is a divine presence that guides us. That is all,“ he says, offering me a seat in his home. The rain is powerful and relentless. In a while, his wife arrives, soaked and shivering. From what I can understand, she brings back what the market ladies don't sell.

A 25-year-old neighbor named Jonny explains that friends sometimes help her buy food. „She has many mouths to feed,“ he says. „She has plenty babies. And another is on the way. Margareth is five months pregnant.“ Why so many babies? I ask. Morales answers for her. „They are my security,“ he says, clutching his chest. „They are my future.“ The gray canal outside his window has become a swift river rushing away. After the rain, everything along the alley glistens, and in the distance a rainbow has appeared.

A couple of days later, I watch a storm approach from my hotel balcony high above the capital. The city seems to dissolve gradually into silver sheets of water that sweep inland from the bay, across the slums and markets. I think of the slaughterhouse and the resilient souls who dwell on its fringe. Probably, they're happily getting wet. I know I learned something that afternoon at the house of Morales Leger. I learned that neither poverty nor politics can break the Haitian spirit. I learned that sometimes it can rain on the most putrid of days.«

June 5, 1992: »Port-au-Prince, Haiti - These are two stories of young men who hide, two stories of cries for help. The first is Michelete Pierre Joseph, a 22-year-old mechanic forced to leave home last fall, when soldiers stormed his house. The second is Paunel Joseph, a 19-year-old student from the same poor neighborhood. He, too, was forced to run away after gunmen burst through his door, shooting in the dark. Both are fervent supporters of ousted president Jean-Bertrand Aristide. Both believe they are hunted by military thugs. Both were returned to Haiti in a U.S. Coast Guard cutter.

Both had families, means of support. Neither had economic reasons for leaving, or any great desire to live outside Haiti - until fear made them run. Their stories illustrate the risks run by young men these days in poor slums like Carrefour Feuilles, the Aristide stronghold where both lived. Even supporters of the de facto government acknowledge that security forces are targeting Aristide loyalists there, searching their homes, arresting them, beating them. Fearing a dechouke, a popular uprising, the military appears to have launched a preemptive strike against members of Lavalas, Aristide's „tidal wave“ party.

On Oct. 1, the morning after the military coup that ousted the populist president-priest, soldiers invaded Michelete's home, shooting in the air, demanding to see him. While his sister told the gunmen he wasn't there, Michelete scrambled over a wall and made a run for a nearby town. He knew these were men from the police station near his house. They knew him quit well. On election day, in December 1990, Michelete operated a voter registration booth from his house. He also had campaigned for Aristide, sticking posters all over his neighborhood.

The police beat his mother and his young nieces, whom the guards scorned as „lavalas children.“ Escorted by religious workers, his entire family, including his wife and 2-year-old daughter, went into hiding. They left behind a humble but comfortable home filled with food and clothes and appliances - proof that they did not flee for economic reasons. Michelete hid for two months with friends, turning his back on a job that paid him up to $500 a month. On the night of Dec. 13, he boarded a small refugee boat. As he and 20 other refugees sailed toward Cuba, they were stopped by a Coast Guard cutter. Michelete wound up at the U.S. Navy base at Guantanamo Bay, Cuba, for two months. In interviews, he told U.S. immigration officials why he left home.

But on Feb. 1, an official told him he would have to go back to Haiti. He wept openly as he stepped onto the docks in Port-au-Prince. An American television crew spotted him in the crowd and asked where he lived. The crew journalists from Christian Science Monitor television, accompanied him to his home. That same day, military men in civilian clothes came and asked where he had been. Sensing danger, he called the journalists, who helped him into safety. Late that night, soldiers showed up at his house to take him away. The journalists wrote a letter to the U.S. Embassy on Michelete's behalf. „We believe he is in political danger and deserves your attention." Michelete went to the embassy twice. He was interviewed without a lawyer present.

Last month, he received a form letter in French from the U.S. government: „Dear Mr. Pierre: We regret that we cannot approve your request to be admitted into the United States as a refugee." From a list of standard reasons, officials had checked three boxes: First, they said, his claim did not constitute persecution, according to U.S. immigration law. Second, they said, his statements did not support a wellfounded, reasonable fear of persecution. Third, they said his claim of persecution „is not consistent with what is known and accepted as real conditions or practices in your country of origin."

Read: Things like this don't happen in Haiti. „I give up. They beat my mother. They want to kill me. My family is in hiding. 1 can't see my wife and my baby, and still, no one believes me," Michelete told me this week, tears of rage rising in his eyes. The odyssey of Paunel Joseph began two weeks ago, when he says gunmen burst into his house at 3 a.m., firing into the air and demanding that everyone come out. Paunel's father, a mason, had campaigned for Aristide in the neighborhood during the elections. But that morning, Paunel wasn`t sure if the gunmen were from the nearby police station or if they were zenglendo, a gang or common criminals. In fear, he hitched a ride to the port of Leogane and, with thc help of a man he met along the way, got on a refugee boat.

It wasn't until last week, after a Coast Guard cutter brought him back from the high seas, that he was told his parents had disappeared that morning and that the men who took them away were police. He has been afraid to go back home, to the house friends say has been vacant since Paunel fled. Friends have warned him to stay away. I met him at the docks on the morning he was repatriated, Several days later, he showed up at my hotel to tell me his parents were missing. From his shirt pocket, he pulled out the application he got at the docks to begin his political asylum process. He would fill it out, he told me.

On Thursday, he returned with an appointment card. He has been given interview No. 417 at 8 a.m. June 11. „But if they ask about proof, I have nothing to offer them,“ he told me. „What about the fact your parents are missing?“ I asked. „Is that enough?“ he wondered. I didn't want to tell him about Michelete, about how his odyssey turned out. I didn't want to tell him what I really thought, that most likely it would make no difference that he is afraid, that he hides, that his parents have vanished. Not in the eyes of those unwilling to accept that in Haiti such things happen every day. No, it probably would make no difference at all.«

June 15, 1992: »Petionville, Haiti - „This,“ says the wealthy factory owner with a sweep of his hand across the restaurant filled with elegant patrons, across the kirs and the five-star rum cocktails, across the trays of delicate canapes, across the smoke rising from Campari lips, across the faces that belong to families with important names, „this is Haiti.“ He is a man nearing middle age, a handsome man with an acquired distrust of foreign journalists. He, as many here tonight, doesn't like reporters because always, when the conversation turns to Haiti's domestic situation, they talk in comparisons between the very rich and the very poor, comparisons that inevitably leave the elite in a rotten light.

I'm afraid we've fallen into this kind of dreaded conversation tonight. It is Friday night Happy Hour at La Belle Epoch, an upscale nook in the mountain suburb of Petionville. For years, this weekly happy hour has been a ritual of the bourgeoisie on „the hill,“ one of the few things you can count on - other than blackouts - in this unpredictable land. I ask the wealthy man how he feels about living this way while his compatriots in nearby shanty towns have - sewage dumps for front yards. Must be frustrating.1 suggest.

„No, it is not frustrating,“ he says, putting down his tumbler of scotch to make a point. „You see, I can drink this whiskey with a clean conscience. I know that while I am here, there is a man starving in Cité Soleil. But my consience is clear. I work 18-hour days. I have helped build schools in the slums. I have given jobs to those people. I cannot do anything to stop them from starving.“ He tells me how he will lay off most of his workers tomorrow morning. The embargo imposed after the coup that ousted President Jean-Bertrand Aristide, he says, is strangling his business.

All through the night, as I mingle with regulars under slow ceiling fans on the terraced cafe. I know this is a Haiti far different than the one I've seen so far. I sit with women who look like they've stepped off the pages of French fashion magazines, shimmery hose, silky scarves, their faces watercolors of perfect shadows and light. This is the world of the MREs, those who are often labeled by outsiders as Haiti's „Morally Repugnant Elites.“ Haitians who care more about whether their Limoges dishes match their antique tables than the alarming infant mortality rate. Of course this is a stereotype. But it is a fairly accurate label of those who really believe the educated few, the wealthy few, should decide for the impoverished masses because they are too poor and stupid to know any better.

Tonight, I hear such convictions. I sense an intensifying anger toward foreigners. Over and over again. I hear how the wealthy Haitians feel misunderstood, beleaguered, besieged by internationa1 pressure to foster democracy, to help create a middle class, to respect the results of the December 1990 election that brought Aristide to power. „Why don't they just leave us alone," they say. „Haiti is our business. Don't force democracy down our throats." In the powerful and healthy sectors of the capital, the fact that Aristide won by a landslide - the fact there was a democratic election to begin with - is almost anecdotal. He is out of the picture.

Even though their votes are few, their influence is massive. „You will see Aristide has very little to do with anything in Haiti," one member of the elite told me on my first night in Haiti. „He is nothing." What about what the masses want? I had asked. „Doesn't matter," she responded with a grin. Tonight's happy hour is not a very happy one. It is still uncertain who the next prime minister will be. The word in the clusters of guests is that Marc Bazin, who lost to Aristide 17 months ago by a landslide, is a shoo-in.

Days later, he was indeed nominated, and Friday he won approval of the Senate. He is likely to be approved within days by the Chamber of Deputies. If any politician exemplifies the Haitian elite, it is Bazin, a man who demanded that his campaign workers wear coats and ties to strategy meetings. Perhaps he is most reflective of the elite in the very fact that although he lost the election, he could still win. Because he has the money. Because he has the education. Because he has the support of the right people. The troubling thing about the Haitian aristocracy is that in too many cases education has not brought awareness. It has brought arrogance.

Despite their exposure to democratic ideals abroad, many haven't a clue what democracy is. „Aristide blew his chance. Now we have to step in and get things done right," one wealthy patron tells me. An elegant woman leans across the table and says: „Democracy cannot happen overnight. You cannot wipe away an entire class, just for the good of democracy." As I get up to leave, the wealthy factory owner reminds me not to write about the fictional Haiti that most jourrnalists write about, the one where people say they are politically persecuted and yearning to be rid of the oppressive forces in their society. „Remember," he says, „this is Haiti." I said goodbye and stepped out of the party into the enormous world that is the other Haiti.«

1994: CELEBRATION OF MILITARY RULE'S END IN HAITI

Carol Guzy, *Washington Post*

There was absolutely no complications when the five jurors picked their recommendations as follows: Denis Farrell of the *Associated Press* had documented the first free elections in South Africa after the end of Apartheid. The photographs by Carol Guzy of the *Washington Post* from Haiti, in the words of the jury, had „not only captured the horror of a broken society in chaos, but also a remarkable spirit of survival and hope in a people oppressed for generations." David Leeson of the *Dallas Morning News* was praised for helping lead a Texas family to safety, as he himself had contributed to the rescue of this family from a flooded river.

The Board favored the work by Carol Guzy who was announced as winner of the Pulitzer Prize „for her series of photographs illustrating the crisis in Haiti and its aftermath." Guzy had covered Haiti since the early 1980s, returning on her own when she could not convince an editor to send her. It was in September 1994, when U.S. troops landed in Port-au-Prince to help return president Jean-Bertrand Aristide to power. Guzy photographed, she remembered, a „very joyous democracy march" when someone threw a grenade into the crowd, „so people were killed and wounded. I hit the ground with everybody else ..."

Carol Guzy, born on March 7, 1956, in Bethlehem, Pa., graduated from the Northampton County Area Community College in her home town with an associate's degree in nursing in 1978. Two years later she received an associate's degree in applied science from the Art Institute of Fort Lauderdale. After having served an internship at the *Miami Herald*'s Broward Bureau she was engaged by the newspaper as a staff photographer. In 1986 Carol Guzy gained the spot news photography Pulitzer Prize shared with Michelangelo E. du Cille for their pictures of the devastation caused by the 1985 eruption of Columbia's volcano Nevado del Ruiz. After having worked for the *Miami Herald* for eight years Guzy switched as a staff photographer to the *Washington Post*. She earned her second Pulitzer Prize in Photography about a decade after the first one, - a third award of that kind should follow a couple of years later. Following is the key picture of her 1995 award-winning photographs:

JOY AND CELEBRATIONS IN HAITI

Glee - a rejoicing crowd celebrates the resignation of General Cedras and the return of their president. An Aristide supporter exclaimed, „For the first time since the coup, we own the streets. We can breathe, we can shout ...“

Carol Guzy, October 11, 1994.

1997: THE EFFECTS OF DRUG CORRUPTION IN MEXICO

Sam Dillon et al., *New York Times*

In 1998, when the jury of the Pulitzer Prize for International Reporting had to select the entries of this award category, it finally recommended the following exhibits to the Board's consideration: Nicholas D. Kristof of the *New York Times* was chosen „for his ability to offer insight on a wide variety of complicated international topics ... Kristofs work ranges widely from malaria's deadly comeback, to the wounds of war in Japan, to the three overlapping wars in the Congo." Next, the jury report mentions John Pomfret of the *Washington Post* for a series „on Laurent Kabila's rise to power in Zaire and his army's complicity with Rwandan Tutsis in exterminating Hutu refugees ... Pomfret brought to his task a rare ability to master a new part of the world, with impressive investigative acumen and a dogged determination to get a story that the new Congolese government had every reason to keep obscure."

The *New York Times* staff was third on the jury's list. The newspaper's series „on corruption in Mexico and the drug trade provides a powerful application of investigative reporting - including impressive sourcing and corraborating documentation. Together, the stories make an unassailable case; they are equally revealing of the flaws of U.S. intelligence-gathering on the subject. Uncovering critical facts in the 'drug war' is difficult enough. But to get to the corrupt core in such a secretive and dangerous environment represents a major journalistic achievement." The Pulitzer Board was impressed by the eulogy on the last exhibit and bestowed the 1998 award for International Reporting on the *New York Times* staff „for its revealing series that profiled the corrosive effects of drug corruption in Mexico."

The newspaper was honored for articles written by Sam Dillon and Julia Preston of the *New York Times*'s Mexico City bureau, Tim Golden, a national correspondent, and Craig Pyes, a freelance journalist. Stephen Engelberg served as editor of the award-winning series. These five journalists undertook something almost unheard-of in foreign correspondence: a major investigation of a foreign country, one vital to United States security. Drawing on classified intelligence documents and interviews with key officials in both Mexico and the United States, the series of articles explored how Mexico's drug barons had acquired the money and power to subvert an entire nation, bribing officials for protection and having Mexican journalists who dared to report on them either prosecuted for criminal libel or killed. The series had a significant effect not only in the United States but also in Mexico, where the press faced legal constraints and the threat of violence in pursuing this kind of investigation. It was mainly the work of Sam Dillon and Julia Preston that earned the *New York Times* team the 1998 Pulitzer Prize for International Reporting. Following are several of their award-winning articles:

February 23, 1997: »The Governor of the Mexican state that borders Arizona is collaborating with one of the world's most powerful drug traffickers, creating a haven for smugglers who transport vast quantities of narcotics into the United States, according to American officials and intelligence. Officials said this conclusion was based on a wealth of evidence, including „highly reliable“ informers' reports that the Governor, Manlio Fabio Beltrones Rivera, took part in meetings in which leading Mexican drug traffickers paid high-level politicians who were protecting their operations.

According to the accounts, Raul Salinas de Gortari, the brother of the former President, received suitcases full of cash and was responsible for distributing the money to those attending. Present and former officials said the evidence of Mr. Beltrones' role was so detailed and compelling that the United States had included his name on a confidential document provided to the transition team of President Ernesto Zedillo listing more than a dozen officials suspected of corruption. Another Mexican Governor, Jorge Carrillo Olea, was included on the American blacklist because of reported entanglements with major drug dealers.

While Mr. Zedillo did not name either man to a federal post, both continue to wield considerable power in their states and nationally through their prominence in Mexico's governing party. Both seem to enjoy a tacit immunity from concerted criminal investigation in Mexico and the United States. Although Mexican governors are popularly elected, presidents have the power in practice to force their removal. Mr. Beltrones, in an interview, denied any links to drug traffickers and disputed American law-enforcement officials' assertions that Amado Carrillo Fuentes, one of Mexico's most wanted drug kingpins, was operating with impunity in his state, Sonora. In addition, Mr. Carrillo Olea, who presides over Morelos, the state just south of Mexico City, disputed charges that he had cooperated with traffickers.

In a four-month investigation that draws on intelligence documents and interviews in the United States and Mexico, The New York Times examined how both governments handled the allegations against the two Governors. The result is a picture of official frustration on both sides of the border and, several officials asserted, a case study of why drug traffickers' political patrons often go unpunished.

Despite the recent disclosures about official corruption, U.S. officials say the Clinton Administration is planning to certify later this month that Mexico is cooperating with anti-drug efforts. Senior administration officials say that decision reflects a belief that Mexico's leadership is doing all it can against staggering odds. But many law-enforcement officials say it also shows that the Clinton Administration considers the narcotics fight less important than fostering commerce with this country's third-largest trading partner. Thus, these officials assert, intelligence reports suggesting corruption among Mexican politicians like Mr. Beltrones receive little attention in Washington. Similarly, agents working in Mexico feel they will get little support if they scrutinize the activities of powerful Mexican officials.

President Clinton praised Mexico last week for arresting the head of its anti-narcotics program on drug charges, citing the act as evidence that corruption, even „at the highest levels,“ was not being tolerated. Privately, however, American officials acknowledge that Mexican traffickers' political patrons are seldom the targets of law-enforcement officials in either country, even though they play an important role in the drug trade. In a previously undisclosed draft analysis, intelligence officials assert that Mexican traffickers take in as much as $10 billion annually, then spend as much as 60 percent of that money on bribes for officials at all levels. Officials say much of the derogatory information about Mr. Beltrones and Mr. Carrillo Olea, a former director of Mexico's anti-narcotics program, has been gathered through intelligence reports from informers, ranging from inside accounts to raw gossip. Their volume, specificity and persistence over time have persuaded many U.S. officials that the allegations against the Governors are well founded.

But officials said such material was of little use to prosecutors, who build their cases around witnesses willing to testify in American courts. In addition, American law-enforcement officials acknowledge a reluctance to invest time and money in pursuing corrupt foreign officials. „In Mexico," said one American prosecutor in a border state, „political protection is difficult to prove. If we could prove it, we'd have them all under indictment. There's a big difference between knowing something and proving it in a court of law. You have extremely reliable intelligence sources, but unless you can prove it, why burn your sources? You'd have their body parts spread all over Sonora."

Mr. Beltrones, for his part, says the reports collected by American intelligence and drug agents were fabricated by political rivals. „This sounds like a novel, filled with horror and error," he said. „At what time of the day do I govern, if I'm spending my time on all these crimes?" Wilburn Sears, a veteran agent with bulging forearms and a walrus mustache, took charge of the Drug Enforcement Administration's five-person office in Hermosillo, the capital of Sonora, in 1991. He soon came to the realization that

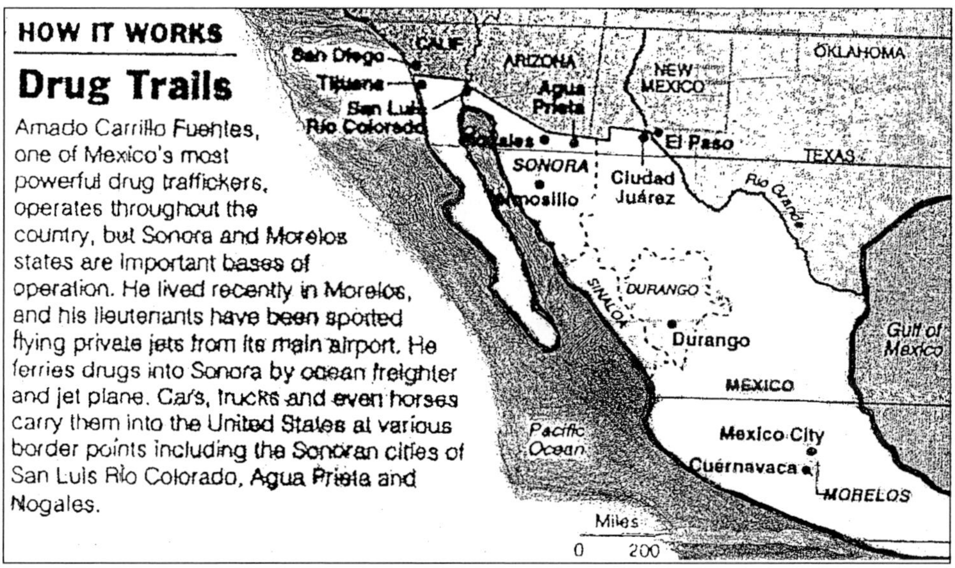

the state was overrun by traffickers. Mexico's second-largest state in size, Sonora was ideal terrain for smugglers, a sprawling region of cattle ranches and desert landing strips etched with rail lines and lonely roads leading north to more than 300 miles of remote border. Vast quantities of marijuana were pouring up the highways. Passenger cars were ferrying methamphetamines over the line into Arizona. And the traffickers were traveling in and out of Hermosillo and other Sonoran cities in long convoys or in private jets, under the noses of state and federal police officers.

„The feds were protecting the airports," Sears said in a recent interview. „They were doing everything out there except kick-starting the narcos' airplanes." It was in those years that Mr. Carrillo Fuentes began the ascent that would make him one of Mexico's shrewdest and most influential drug smugglers. The nephew of one of the country's narcotics pioneers, he had been building his organization in the late 1980s, wooing marijuana farmers to the south in Sinaloa, the heroin clans of Durango and especially the cocaine barons of Cali, Colombia. Most of all, he had cultivated the skills of Mexican narcotics diplomacy and knew what it took to buy protection from powerful politicians.

In a lengthy 1994 study, the Drug Enforcement Administration's analysts in EI Paso, Texas, painted a detailed picture of how Carrillo Fuentes cultivated Mexican police officials and political leaders, including Mr. Beltrones and Mr. Carrillo Olea. According to the classified analysis, based on field reports from more than a dozen American agencies, the trafficker has „purchased influence at various key levels in the Mexican government," giving him „powerful connections" that ensure safe passage of his drug loads through Mexico to the United States.

In the early 1990s, Mr. Carrillo Fuentes was moving to make Hermosillo a strategic staging area, American officials said. He was living in a pink stucco mansion down the street from the American consul's residence in a palm-fringed neighborhood. He had begun construction of a much more extravagant, onion-domed house - locals called it a Thousand and One Nights - a few blocks north. And among other properties he or his associates had acquired was a communications center across town.

In August 1991 Mr. Beltrones was elected governor, and in October he moved into the colonial-style governor's palace in Hermosillo. He was a rising star in the governing Instituutional Revolutionary Party, one of a handful of ambitious 40-something leaders sometimes called the „babysaurs," to distinguish them from the older „dinosaurs" who have long ruled the party. During his early career, Mr. Beltrones had been the understudy to Fernando Gutierrez Barrios, Mr. Salinas' interior minister and one of the pioneers of Mexico's secret police. Some have seen Mr. Beltrones as a possible presidential candidate.

But about the time that he took the oath of office, American officials began picking up reports from confidential informers documenting his ties to Mr. Carrillo Fuentes. In an interview, Mr. Beltrones raised his voice when reporters described D.E.A. reports alleging that he had accepted payments from Mr. Carrillo Fuentes. „These reports are incredible in every sense, filled with fantasy and lies," Mr. Beltrones said. The D.E.A, he added, „is completely out of focus.“ As evidence of his hostility to drug trafficking, Mr. Beltrones asserted that he had virtually driven Mr. Carrillo Fuentes from Hermosillo. A high-ranking Mexican official said that Mr. Beltrones learned of Mr. Carrillo Fuentes' residences in Hermosillo shortly after he took office. Months later, the official said, Beltrones ordered aides to videotape Mr. Carrillo Fuentes' arrival at the local airport in a Lear jet, and his travels about the state capital in a convoy guarded by police vehicles. The governor delivered the videotape to President Carlos Salinas de Gortari, the official added, and federal authorities later confiscated four of Mr. Carrillo Fuentes' properties, including the onion-domed mansion. „How would the D.E.A explain that I'm the one who took away this man's houses?“ Mr. Beltrones asked.

American officials and reports acknowledge that four of Mr. Carrillo Fuentes' Hermosillo houses were seized. But they said his organization continued to use at least eight other properties, including the communications center. The officials maintain that Sonora remains one of Mr. Carrillo Fuentes' most important operating bases. In the early 1990s, Mr. Carrillo Fuentes set out to increase his air smuggling operations, and for that he needed help at the highest levels of the federal bureaucracy. Under Mexican law the federal government enforces the drug statutes. At the time, Mexican authorities were working with their American counterparts to perfect a radar network that tracked aircraft flying north from Colombia. The system allowed controllers to follow unidentified planes on a walllsized screen in Mexico City and to scramble interceptor aircraft if the planes entered Mexico.

Mr. Carrillo Olea, a former army general whom President Salinas appointed to oversee the drug intelligence center created with American help, was in charge of the radar system. American officials spoke highly of him, and many reacted with disbelief to the first intelligence reports that he was helping the traffickers. But by 1992, additional reports persuaded analysts at El Paso's intelligence center that Mr. Carrillo Olea was helping Mr. Carrillo Fuentes. (The two are not related.)

As one intelligence document reads: „Reporting from 1992 indicates that the former Mexican coordinator against narcotics trafficking, Jorge Carrillo Olea, was at that time Amado Carrillo Fuentes' most influential associate in the Mexican government. Carrillo Olea was in charge of controlling the radar detection in Mexico, and by utilizing the information provided to him, he was able to ensure safe passage of Carrillo Fuentes' aircraft.“ In an interview last week, Mr. Carrillo Olea, now Governor of Morelos, called these accounts „a complete barbarity.“ „What can I say about a thing like this,“ he asked „except that it is a rotund and absolute lie? It has no foundation whatever.“

American officials say that reports about Mr. Beltrones' drug activities have come from nearly two dozen sources inside the Mexican government and its law-enforcement agencies. The 1994 D.E.A study of Mr. Carrillo Fuentes described how his smuggling organization, identified by his initials, A.C.F., expanded „full force“ into Sonora. „Manlio Fabio Beltrones Rivera is well documented as being associated with the A.C.F. organization,“ the report reads. It quotes a commander of the Federal Judicial Police as stating that Mr. Beltrones is „involved in protecting drug traffickers passing through

Sonora.“ In 1994, Sears searched the D.E.A.’s computerized intelligence files and found numerous references to Mr. Beltrones and members of his family, according to a memo Mr. Sears wrote. „The Governor,“ the document noted, is mentioned in cases „from San Diego to Tucson.“

Among the most persuasive intelligence reports, officials said, are accounts of regular meetings at a ranch in which Mexico’s most notorious traffickers gave cash to Raul Salinas, who in turn distributed it to the senior politicians present. Mr. Salinas, whose brother was President of Mexico at the time, is now awaiting trial in Mexico City on charges of murder and financial wrongdoing, and investigators have found more than $100 million in his overseas bank accounts. He maintains that his fortune has legitimate sources. Mr. Beltrones was said to have attended three meetings at the ranch from 1990 to 1993, and the officials said Mr. Carrillo Fuentes was present for at least one.

In August 1994, the State Department sent William Francisco, a former Army infantry officer, to serve as the senior diplomat at the American Consulate in Hermosillo. Almost immediately he trained his sights on the Governor, raising questions about the reports of corruption and misconduct, which were being ignored by other American officials. Mr. Sears and his D.E.A. staff in Hermosillo were busy trying to keep track of the five major mafias operating all across northwest Mexico. They spent much of their time traveling between Hermosillo and the distant border gateways of Tijuana or Cludad Juárez.

„They gave me a new car,“ Mr. Sears said, „and I put 35,000 miles on it in seven months. We were just keeping our heads above water. There were so many reports of corruption about everybody that most of the time we didn’t even write it up. We just had to accept the fact that corruption exists.“ Mr. Francisco felt otherwise. Shortly after his arrival, he received a briefing from Mr. Sears about the major Mexican traffickers and studied the intelligence report naming Mr. Beltrones as an associate of Mr. Carrillo Fuentes.

Then, Mr. Sears recalled, Mr. Francisco traveled south to the state of Sinaloa and came back with new reports about the pervasive influence of traffickers. At his request, Mr. Sears checked D.E.A.’s computerized intelligence files and found extensive references to Mr. Beltrones. In an unusual step for a State Department official assigned to an obscure consulate, Mr. Francisco began recruiting his own sources about the drug trade and Mr. Beltrones’ role in it. When Mr. Francisco heard a report that Mr. Beltrones was being considered for a post in President Zedillo’s cabinet as head of Mexico’s powerful Interior Ministry, he grew downright alarmed.

On Nov. 15, 1994, after just 12 weeks as consul, he stalked into his office and fired off an urgent cable to the embassy in Mexico City. „Request for assistance to verify and further develop info of allegations of extensive criminal activities by Sen. Gov. Manlio Fabio Beltrones Rivera, who may be under consideration to become the next Secretary of Gobernación,“ Mr. Francisco headlined his dispatch, using the Spanish term for Mexico’s Interior Ministry.

Mr. Francisco complained that the D.E.A. and customs agents in Hermosillo were too preoccupied with minor traffickers and should instead pursue political figures like Mr. Beltrones, whom he termed „a truly major kingpin player." His cable - which mixed drug, intelligence with lurid tales about the personal lives of Sonoran officials - stunned Mr. Sears and officials at the embassy in Mexico City. Although Mr. Francisco had no direct or specific evidence to document his allegations, he called for a criminal investigation that could lead to Mr. Beltrones' indictment in the United States.

The cable reached the desk of the American Ambassador, James Jones, and American officials said he viewed it skeptically. Jones was instinctively cautious about the reliability of law-enforcement intelligence reports. In addition, several officials said, the criminal investigation of a foreign official poses daunting political and practical difficulties. Collecting intelligence on an official like Mr. Beltrones is one thing. But several officials said that building a criminal case against him - linking him to specific drug shipments or conspiracies that violate American law - would be quite another.

Informers willing to whisper an allegation under cloak of confidentiality would have to be persuaded to travel to the United States to testify before a grand jury, and perhaps later at a public trial. That would endanger not only their careers but their lives. Even if all these difficulties were overcome, the accused official would have to be extradited to the United States for trial. Mexico has never before extradited a Mexican citizen accused of narcotics trafficking. (Juan Garda Abrego, a Mexican trafficker, was expelled to the United States a year ago, not extradited, and he holds American citizenship.) „Indicting a public official of a foreign government is cumbersome to say the least," the official said. „And then getting them out of Mexico - it never happens."

Mr. Francisco's recommendation was never seriously considered by the embassy's top officials. Virtually everyone there reportedly regarded it as quixotic, even „goofy," as one put it. In fact, officials said, the idea of launching an U.S. criminal inquiry into Mr. Beltrones' dealings was not raised with senior officials in Washington.

As it happened, Mr. Zedillo and his advisers, preparing to take office on Dec. 1, 1994, had already given American officials a less public means of dealing with allegations involving officials like Mr. Beltrones. „The Zedillo administration wanted names of people believed to be corrupt, or possibly in the pay of traffickers, whom the United States would not like to see in the new Government," a former American official said.

Mr. Jones gave Mr. Zedillo's transition team a list of about 15 current and former Mexican officials. It included Mr. Beltrones and Mr. Carrillo Olea, three officials said. A senior Mexican official said in an interview that neither Mr. Beltrones nor any other of Mexico's 31 active governors was ever considered for a post in Mr. Zedillo's Cabinet. The Zedillo Government apparently has never followed up on the American warning by investigating either Governor. But embassy officials felt that delivery of the list had shifted all responsibility onto Mexican authorities, where it belonged.

Early in 1995 the embassy's No.2 official, David Beall, telephoned Francisco and lectured him about the cables he had written, American officials said. Mr. Francisco interpreted the call in subsequent conversations with associates as an order to stop reporting on the Governor. A senior American official denied that. „He may have been told, 'For your own safety and for the integrity of what law enforcement is trying to do, don't be a cowboy,'" the official said. „But he was not muzzled."

Still, if he stopped filing cables, Mr. Francisco continued to voice suspicions about Mr. Beltrones' activities. He even shared his opinions of the Governor with Nicolas Escalante Barrett, Mexico's consul general in Phoenix, who reported the incident to Mexico's Foreign Ministry. American officials and Mr. Beltrones said they believed that the Foreign Ministry complained to the American Government about Mr. Francisco's conduct. In September 1995, Mr. Francisco was transferred to Frankfurt. He declined to be interviewed for this article. One senior American official insisted that Mr. Francisco's transfer was a „routine rotation." Others disagreed. „He was a loose cannon," an official said. „He was probably going to get himself killed if we didn't get him out of there." Mr. Carrillo Fuentes has continued to consolidate power. His success at sending cocaine-laden aircraft undetected into Mexican airspace and his largess have led Mexicans to nickname him Lord of the Heavens.

In January, Mexican troops stormed a ranch in Sinaloa during a wedding reception for Mr. Carrillo Fuentes' sister, hoping to capture him. But word leaked, and he slipped away. In the days that followed, authorities acknowledged that three private jets, operating without flight plans, had ferried wedding guests to Sinaloa from the airport in Cuernavaca, the capital of Morelos state, where Mr. Carrillo Olea is governor. American narcotics officials say that Mr. Carrillo Fuentes has been living in Morelos, where he owns many properties, and that his fleet of narcotics jets frequently lands and takes off unchallenged from the Cuernavaca airport. Mr. Carrillo Olea said in an interview that his aides had traced ownership of all residences identified as belonging to the trafficker, without finding his name. Any further investigation, he said, is the responsibility of federal authorities.

Mr. Beltrones is wrapping up his six-year term as one of Mexico's more popular governors. He is working closely with Gov. Fife Symington of Arizona on a plan to improve cross-border commerce and investment. Recent developments have left Mexico's antinarcotics program in chaos. The commander of January's failed wedding raid was Gen. Jesus Gutierrez Rebollo, then the national anti-narcotics coordinator. He was arrested last week and accused of having accepted payments from Carrillo Fuentes for seven years, ever since he was put in a command post in the anti-drug program.

Mr. Carrillo Fuentes' capture was intended as a dramatic symbol of progress in the drug war weeks before March 1. By that deadline annually, President Clinton certifies that drug transiting or producing nations are pursuing serious anti-drug efforts. Instead, the trafficker is still at large and still spending his billions. „Money corrupts," said Doug Wankel, who just retired as D.E.A. operations chief, „and in Mexico it's getting to the point where the traffickers can corrupt absolutely."«

March 9, 1997: »The owner of a department store in the provincial capital of Culiacán was driving to work one morning last September when three unmarked sedans without license plates surrounded his gray Oldsmobile. As passers-by watched in terror, four men brandishing assault rifles hauled the man, Rómulo Rico Urrea, from his car, forced him into one of theirs and sped away. Mr. Rico has not been seen since Sept. 25, 1996. But a notebook dropped in his car by one of the kidnappers, as well as evidence gathered by military investigators, links the abduction to Gen. Jesus Gutierrez Rebollo, the former head of Mexico's anti-drug agency who was arrested last month on charges of collaborating with one of the country's most powerful cocaine barons.

Mr. Rico is one of at least 51 Mexicans who have disappeared in the last three years after kidnappings in which there were signs of Government security force involvement, according to lists compiled by relatives, human rights organizations and the press. Now, evidence is emerging to tie many of the abductions to the war against powerful drug traffickers, which has increasingly been under the command of Mexico's military. „We are everyday citizens under attack, caught in the crossfire between narcos, authorities and narcoauthorities," said Lucfa Jurado, whose husband, a semiprecious-stone trader from the border city of Ciudad Juarez, was seized on the front step of his home on Oct. 6, 1996. „It has gotten to the point where it can happen to anyone."

A majority of the victims have no proven ties to drug traffickers or other criminal activities, relatives and human rights leaders contend, although a number have had brushes with the authorities. „They tend to be businessmen, students and other citizens who were going about their lives," said Oscar Loza of the Commission for the Defense of Human Rights in the state of Sinaloa, where at least nine people have disappeared.

Mexico's military has traditionally played a supporting role in the fight against drug trafficking, mainly eradicating narcotics crops. Shortly after he took office in 1994, President Ernesto Zedillo, facing widespread corruption in the state and federal police, began to place military officers and troops in key positions in the battle against the drug cartels. Gen. Gutierrez was appointed Mexico's chief anti-drug official in December 1996, and army officers were given command of state and municipal police forces in Sinaloa, through which large quantities of drugs flow. Just last week, the army took over narcotics operations in the border state of Baja California.

Since the arrest of General Gutierrez, who was highly decorated, a number of families of missing Mexicans have come forward after enduring their anguish in silence for months and even years. The number of known victims is growing. There is evidence that in addition to Mr. Rico, five men who disappeared since last September in northern Mexico where abducted in operations commanded by General Gutierrez and carried out by his deputies during his two-month tenure as head of the national drug agency or before that, when he was the senior commander of the Fifth Military Region in central Mexico. The abductions in which General Gutierrez appears to have had a role are only a fraction of those reported. The general's lawyers did not respond to requests for comment.

The disclosures about the kidnappings raise new questions about General Gutierrez's ascent to the highest position in Mexico's war on drugs, and about Mr. Zedillo's moves to expand the role of the armed forces in the anti-narcotics campaign. Several months before Defense Minister Enrique Cervantes Aguirre recommended

General Gutierrez to the President for the top anti-drug job, the Mexican military had substantial evidence implicating the general's two closest aides in the kidnapping of Mr. Rico. Both aides were arrested with their commander on drug charges on Feb. 18. The kidnapping allegations apparently never reached the highest levels.

Mr. Cervantes acknowledged that neither he nor President Zedillo had had any doubts about General Gutierrez until about two weeks before his arrest. Mr. Rico's relatives say they believe that he came under suspicion of drug trafficking because Miguel Angel Rico Urrea, his brother, was falsely accused on drug charges in 1992 and served prison time before he was cleared. A judge ordered his release, but the day he was to leave prison he was murdered.

On Sept. 16, 1996, soldiers in Culiacán swarmed into the home of Enrique Rico, another brother. The raid, conducted without a warrant, was led by a brash officer who identified himmself with a name that later proved false. R6mulo Rico was seized nine days later. At first, federal police agents told his relatives he was in custody at their headquarters. But 24 hours later the same agents denied they had ever seen him, relatives said. At about the same time, Mr. Rico's wife of 33 years, Teresa, received an anonymous telephone call from a man who said her husband had been detained by someone named Horacio Montenegro Ortiz. The caller said he had seen Mr. Montenegro escorting his prisoner onto a military plane at the local airport.

The family did not recognize the name at the time, but it turned out to be significant. Mr. Montenegro, a former army captain, had long worked closely with General Gutierrez. Later that day Mr. Rico's family discovered a notebook that one of his abductors had accidentally dropped between the front seats of his car. The scribbled, sometimes encoded phrases showed that the writer was a military officer who was in Sinaloa pursuing an inquiry into the murder in Mexico City on Sept. 14 of a leading anti-narcotics police commander, Ernesto Ibarra Santes. The huge operation to find and capture Mr. Ibarra's killers was commanded by General Gutierrez, senior army commanders recently confirmed.

Unlike many families of the disappeared, the Ricos did not remain silent. They took the notebook to military and police authorities and human rights groups in the state and the capital, raising questions about the mysterious Mr. Montenegro. In October, shortly before General Gutiérrez was appointed commissioner of the National Institute to Combat Drugs, more than a hundred federal legislators signed a petition calling for a deeper investigation into Mr. Rico's kidnapping. And the military told the family that it was opening its own inquiry.

One man who took up the case was a newly appointed Attorney General, Jorge Madrazo Cuellar, a former human rights lawyer. But the Federal Judicial Police under his command steadfastly denied knowing anything about Mr. Rico, Mr. Madrazo said in an interview. So he sent the Rico family to General Gutierrez, recently appointed to the drug agency at the time, thinking he was „the right man to conduct the investigation." „We were surprised at how pleasant and friendly the general was," Mrs. Rico said bitterly in an interview. „I thought I had finally found the person who was going to give me back my husband."

In 10 meetings with her, Mrs. Rico said, General Gutierrez never acknowledged that he had directed the operations in Sinaloa at the time of her husband's kidnapping or that Mr. Montenegro had become his deputy in the drug institute, where the conversations took place. Defense Minister Cervantes confirmed in a speech on Feb. 18 that Mr. Montenegro, „a man with a disastrous reputation," was under military investigation for the Rico kidnapping. He added that last year General Gutierrez had disobeyed „explicit orders" from the high command to dissociate himself from Mr. Montenegro.

Another piece of evidence linking General Gutierrez to the kidnapping became clear after his arrest. Mexican television broadcast film of Capt. Javier Garcia Hernández,

A department store owner was kidnapped in the city of Culiacán.

an army intelligence officer and aide to General Gutierrez who was arrested on drug charges the same day as his commander. Relatives who had witnessed the raid at Enrique Rico's home said they recognized Captain Hernández as the brash officer who had commanded the search. In late February, military officials told the Rico family confidentially that the notebook in Rómulo Rico's car belonged to Captain Garcia Hernández.

In recent days, a half-dozen northern Mexican families, with nine disappeared relatives among them, have come together to somber meetings in the cramped Mexico City apartment where Teresa Rico and her children have taken refuge. They found one another through human rights organizations they had approached after General Gutiérrez's arrest. As they sadly share photographs of missing loved ones, they worry about their own safety. Human rights activists who helped them have received death threats, apparently to stop their publicizing disappearance cases. In interviews the activists confirmed the threats and asked not to be identified.

Gilberto Chaldez, the 22-year-old nephew of two hoteliers who were abducted from the border city of Tijuana, said he had broken down as he watched the televised announcement of General Gutiérrez's arrest. Mr. Chaldez, a burly man with a buzz cut, had to stop to control his sorrow once again last week when he recalled his reactions. „We were sure those men participated in kidnapping my uncles," Mr. Chaldez said. „We thought it meant they would finally be released."

Rogello Verber Mondaca, 59, is the father of two men who were kidnapped by uniformed army troops from a highway south of Tijuana on Jan. 6. Mr. Verber Mondaca, who until a few years ago was the Deputy Police Chief of Tijuana, called on his friends in local law enforcement to help him mount a statewide search for his sons Rogello and Raul, to no avail. His son Rogello, 28, suffers from advanced Hodgkin's disease and has a catheter in his heart for treatment, Mr. Verber Mondaca said. He produced news photographs and clippings showing that General Gutierrez was conducting anti-drug operations in the area at the time his sons disappeared.

Mrs. Jurado and her family have become outraged about the official response to their quest for her husband, Ruben Guillermo Jurado, 39. A senior official of the state of Chihuahua, where the Jurados live, confirmed in an interview this week that Mr. Jurado had been seized by armed men wearing federal drug police uniforms. Nevertheless the official, who insisted on anonymity, said state investigators believed that Mr. Jurado might have been kidnapped by drug traffickers, because of „narcotics-related wrapping materials" found in his home.

The Jurado family indignantly accused the authorities of inventing charges against Mr. Jurado. They point out that the police never searched his residence or workshop, before or since he disappeared. Some relatives have nearly despaired of going through Mexican institutions. Maria de los Ángeles de Beltrán, whose husband, Manuel, disappeared in 1994, wrote to the United States Secretary of State, Madeleine K. Albright, pleading for help. „Our Government doesn't fight drug trafficking," Mrs. Beltran wrote angrily. „It just administers it."

July 11, 1997: » Early last year, a handful of senior American officials in Washington received an alarming secret intelligence report on Mexico. It was on its face, officials said, the sort of document that can force policy makers to change the way they think about a country or a region. In a matter of just weeks, the National Security Agency reported, Mexican drug traffickers had laundered some $6 billion in illicit profits through their country's financial system. The spy agency based its conclusion on an elaborate surveillance of the contacts between drug gangs and their business associates.

Almost immediately, State Department officials delivered an angry protest to the Mexican Ambassador over the apparently vast breach in his country's defenses against drug trafficking. Then, however, American officials' outrage gave way to chagrin. The agency, they realized, was asserting that Mexico had taken in a flood of dollars nearly equal to its entire foreign investment that year without any discernible impact on its economy. „It just couldn't have happened," one official said. And he added, „You have to ask: 'Which reports am I supposed to believe?'"

An examination by The *New York Times*, based on scores of interviews and a review of classified documents, indicates that the agency's discredited assessment was by no means an isolated lapse in the annals of United States intelligence on drugs and corruption in Mexico. Rather, as the United States weighed momentous decisions about Mexico in the 1990s - from the North American Free Trade Agreement to the $12.5-billion bailout of the Mexican economy after a currency crisis - American policy makers were blindsided by some important developments, misinformed about others and inattentive to many more.

After insisting for years that Mexican corruption was an old affliction being cured by a new generation of political leaders, senior American officials have begun to acknowledge that the growing power and influence of Mexico's drug traffickers have led to a law-enforcement crisis so deep that it threatens the stability of a country that shares almost 2,000 miles of border with the United States. Yet a good deal of the information upon which that conclusion is based had languished in the files of American law-enforcement agents and intelligence -officers for years, officials said. Only rarely did such intelligence command the time of senior policy makers. Even less frequently did it prompt them to take any action.

„A lot of this information has been out there, in the bowels of the system," said Donald F. Ferrarone, who, before his recent retirement as head of the Drug Enforcement Administraation's field office in Houston, oversaw investigations that dealt closely with the political protection of Mexican drug traffickers. „But it has been ignored, because people don't want to believe it, the extent and degree of corruption." Allegations over almost two years of drugrelated corruption in the inner circle of former President Carlos Salinas de Gortari have forced American officials to rethink the issue.

The governing party's loss of control of the lower house of Congress in mid-term elections last week now raises the possibility that Mexican legislators will examine more closely than ever the misdeeds of the ruling elite. In recent weeks, senior Clinton Administration officials have begun to plot a wholesale reorganization of the Federal

Government's drug-intelligence apparatus. Officials said the overhaul will seek to pool some information that is now tightly held by different agencies, disseminate important material more quickly, and thin out a vast intelligence bureaucracy in which different offices perform similar work.

But many officials argued that the failures of American intelligence on Mexico are even deeper and more serious than policy makers have acknowledged. And the problems, by all accounts, have been as much ones of demand as of supply. Law-enforcement agents who worked in and on Mexico while Mr. Salinas was a prized ally of the United States said they were often discouraged by political pressure to keep the drug issue from jeopardizing improvements in the economic relationship between the two countries. At crucial moments, they asserted, intelligence struggled with policy and policy won.

For their part, many officials in Washington said they could not help but grow skeptical of the intelligence after being deluged with vague, uncorroborated informants' reports and analysis that was either so thin on evidence or so carefully hedged as to be of little use. At the height of such problems, during the American debate over the free-trade accord that was approved in November, 1993, Mexico's strategic importance to the United States came into focus as never before. The personal reputations and political strength of Mexican leaders became central questions of American foreign policy.

Yet in the case of Mr. Salinas' influential elder brother, Raul, American investigators did little more than file away allegations that he was not only taking kickbacks on government contracts but cutting deals with cocaine traffickers, officials familiar with the reports said. Drug-enforcement agents said they dropped an inquiry into telephone calls by drug traffickers to the Mexican President's offices after they had trouble figuring out whom the traffickers had called. American officials so thoroughly failed to share information on Carlos Salinas' Deputy Attorney General, Mario Ruiz Massieu, that three different agencies raised questions about his conduct without ever hearing of Customs Service reports that suitcase after suitcase of cash had been deposited in Mr. Ruiz Massieu's account in a Texas bank.

Nearly a year after Mr. Salinas left the presidency, a secret Central Intelligence Agency assessment of his own reported misconduct argued that at the least, his hands-on governing style made it „unlikely that he had no knowledge of his brother's affairs or the shady dealings of other close associates." But while a fuller understanding of the drug traffickers' penetration of Mexican politics may await the outcome of criminal investigations that now extend from San Diego to Switzerland, the revelations of wrongdoing have already contributed to a reordering of United States policy.

In a recent interview, the newly departed American Ambassador to Mexico, James R. Jones, recalled his arrival here four years ago. His priorities were to manage trade, promote investment and push for more democratic politics. Then, the list began to change. „The majority of my time," he said in May, as he prepared to leave the country, „is now spent on administration-of-justice issues, corruption and narcotics trafficking." As Carlos Salinas took office at the end of 1988, the perspective of United States officials could hardly have been more different.

The Drug Enforcement Agency and the C.I.A. had traced a growing traffic in drugs through Mexico since the mid-1980s, when the United States began to increase pressure on Colombian smuggling routes through the Caribbean. But through the early 1990s, officials said, American experts remained convinced that Mexican traffickers had nothing close to the financial clout or political influence of their Colombian partners. American officials also drew a sharp distinction between the young, American-trained technocrats whom Mr. Salinas brought to power and the more experienced, conservative - and corrupt - politicians whom he appointed in areas like law enforcement, national security and the ruling Institutional Revolutionary Party.

At the start of his six-year term, Mr. Salinas seemed to attack drug trafficking with a new zeal. Having been told by the Bush Administration that the problem could obstruct closer economic ties, Mr. Salinas ordered the seizure of more drug shipments, the eradication of more drug crops, and the capture of a powerful drug trafficker, Miguel Ángel Felix Gallardo. John D. Negroponte, the United States Ambassador to Mexico from 1989 to 1993, gave voice to the prevailing optimism. In a confidential memo-randum to law-enforcement officials at the embassy, Mr. Negroponte hailed Mr. Salinas' early steps as „clear proof that Mexico is interested in meaningful cooperation with the United States to reduce this flow of drugs." In a recent interview, he recalled: „I don't think we ever doubted Salinas' personal integrity. He was a very disciplined guy. He always wore that Casio sports watch. He worked like hell."

MOUNTAINS OF DRUGS ARE SEIZED
A Mexican soldier carried cocaine to a pile for incineration in Matamoros in April. The cocaine was part of a shipment of about 10 tons that was found inside a tanker truck.

Several law-enforcement officials who served at the embassy were more skeptical. But they said they also had trouble making their case at a time when the drug problem, like other sources of friction between the two countries, was supposed to be „managed“ so as not to threaten growing investment and trade. As United States law-enforcement officials had untangled a Mexican cover-up of the 1985 assassination of an American drug-enforcement agent, Enrique S. Camarena, many became convinced that drug corruption reached the highest levels of the Mexican Government. They believed that unless that system was dismantled, drug interdiction efforts were condemned to futility.

Now, American agents were being told to simply do the best they could. „There was a sense that Mexico was a place that we were just going to have to deal with in the shape that it was in,“ said Matthew J. Maher, a veteran of the Camarena investigation who served as the Drug Enforcement Administration's international-operations chief until 1994. „The only questions you asked were whom you could deal with and how far you could go. It was a matter of finding a path through the minefield.“

Moves toward the trade agreement increased contacts between the two Governments geometrically. But that only reinforced Washington's belief that a new political day had dawned in Mexico. „Every American official who came through there met with the Mexicans involved with Nafta,“ Mr. Negroponte said. „That was the prism through which the American Government was looking at the Mexican Government. We certainly felt that the reformers were in the ascendancy.“

Those bright, English-speaking officials seemed to sustain an American faith: that the more Mexico opened up to competition, the more its Government would have to scale back its economic role - and the less chance Mexican officials would have to demand bribes in return for waiving rules or awarding contracts. Drugs figured little in the equation. But just as Mr. Salinas embraced a trade deal with the United States, the scope of Mexican trafficking began to change as well.

Colombian cocaine producers had already made Mexico their main route to the thriving American market. Then Mexican traffickers, who had been working for fees of $1,000 or $2,000 for every kilogram of cocaine they smuggled, began to demand their cut in kind. The economics were simple: by taking their payment in cocaine and greatly expanding their distribution network, especially in the western United States, the Mexicans began to increase their profits between 5 and 10 times, officials said. And as the value of their smuggling routes rose, so did their payments for protection to politicians, judges, prosecutors and the police.

New trade regulations began opening the already porous border even more. But drug-intelligence officials said it would still take several years before the implications of this change - and the threat it posed to Mexican security - were fully grasped by American policy makers. While Carlos Salinas was being celebrated in Washington and on Wall Street as the man who might lead Mexico into the developed world, American officials began hearing a very different picture of his inner circle from a source they knew well.

In 1991, a Mexican Federal Police commander who had carried out sensitive operations for both Salinas brothers came forward with some startling, specific allegations. The commander, Guillermo Gonzalez Calderoni, spoke to officials from the Drug Enforcement Administration, the Federal Bureau of Investigation and a United States Attorney's office in Texas. And he told of drug payoffs and dirty political tricks at the highest levels of Government.

By 1993 at the latest, American officials said, Mr. González Calderoni had told them that Luis Medrano, a close associate of one of Mexico's biggest drug traffickers, had told him of paying Raul Salinas two years earlier to help their trafficking group acquire two seaports that the Government was planning to sell to private investors. American officials who dealt with the case said Mr. González Calderoni's claims were strongly debated within federal lawenforcement agencies because he was widely thought to have had his own corrupt ties to Mr. Medrano's boss, Juan Garcia Abrego, and because Mexico had unsuccessfully sought his extradition.

None of what Mr. González Calderoni had to say fit readily into any active drug investigations, the officials said. None of it, without further confirmation, was enough to open a new inquiry into drug-related corruption. So in the end, they said, his reports were simply filed away. „I don't think he was ever looked at as being a serious witness in corruption cases," one former official familiar with the debriefings said. „Back in 1993, it was very unpopular to say anything against Mexico, basically because of Nafta. Who was going to go and do a direct investigation against the President's brother? You just put it away, and it goes into the batter."

Eventually, Mr. González Calderoni's allegations circulated throughout the Government. The C.I.A., in particular, viewed him as a less than compelling source. He came to personify, one official says, „the difficulty of getting hard, reasonably credible information on these kinds of allegations." Several other knowledgeable officials put the C.I.A.'s struggle with Mexican corruption in a different light. Throughout the first half of the decade, they said, the agency that is supposed to be the primary source of information for American policy makers about internal workings of foreign governments spent relatively little time trying to verify the sort of charges that people like Mr. González Calderoni made.

The C.LA. station in Mexico City has generally been the agency's most important in Latin America. But former American intelligence officials said that during the latter half of the cold war - when the city was a hub of Soviet espionage, a crucial base for Cuban agents and the common sanctuary for leftist Central American guerrilla groups - turning a blind eye to the drug-related corruption in the Mexican internal-security apparatus was often a condition for securing its assistance.

The quid pro quo became evident as early as 1982, after federal prosecutors in San Diego indicted the chief of Mexico's internal-security force on charges of helping to run a huge cartheft ring. The prosecutors promptly received a cable from the United States Embassy in Mexico City telling them to desist; the Mexican official, Miguel Nazar Haro, was an „essential contact" of the C.LA. station there. Mr. Nazar Haro remains a fugitive from prosecution in the United States and his whereabouts are unknown.

Mexico is one of two dozen foreign nations where the agency is authorized by a 1986 Presidential decision directive to conduct covert anti-drug operations, intelligence officials said. One official said it is also among the handful of nations where the C.I.A. has even broader authority under a top-secret appendix to the Presidential order. Yet until recently, several officials said, C.I.A. officers in Mexico have been far less active against the drug and corruption problems than their counterparts in Colombia, who trained elite anti-drug forces and guided operations against the leaders of the Medellin and Cali cocaine cartels.

„In Colombia, you had the agency pushing and clamoring and trying to get in on it," said a retired American official who worked in both countries. „In Mexico, you had to go down there and try to get them jump-started. They were not focused on drugs. And a lot of the D.E.A. guys there didn't want them involved anyway." Mexico has also been something of a stepchild to the secret coordinating group that has orchestrated the increasingly cooperative efforts of United States law-enforcement, intelligence and military agencies in the Andes, officials said.

The existence of the panel, called the Linear Committee, has not been previously disclosed. But officials describe it as an unusually successful collaboration directed by the C.LA.'s Counternarcotics Center and the Drug Enforcement Administration to find weak points in the linear chain of cocaine production and distribution. Until late 1995, several officials who have sat in on its deliberations said, the Linear Committee's priorities were very much in the Andes. Only after most of the main Cali cartel leaders had surrendered or been arrested did it turn more intently to the major Mexican traffickers.

Some officials said that shift has already shown some results. Last year, the committee helped coordinate the pursuit of Jose Luis Pereira, the principal contact between the jailed Cali cocaine baron Miguel Rodriguez Orejuela and a powerful Mexican drug trafficker, Amado Carrillo Fuentes, whom Mexican officials confirmed today had died after plastic surgery last week to change his appearance. Mr. Pereira, a Bolivian known by the code name Jota, was captured by the Mexican Army after a lengthy surveillance of his safe houses by the C.LA., officials said. He was then deported home on a plane that stopped in Miami, where federal agents were waiting for him. He pleaded not guilty and is now standing trial on federal drug charges.

United States officials explain some of the lapses of intelligence efforts in Mexico by noting that probably nowhere else abroad do American officials deal with a more complicated mesh of economic interests, national-security concerns, law-enforcement problems and domestic political considerations. But many officials also attributed some of the shortcomings to a chronic inattention by American policy makers.

In the months surrounding the agreement's approval in November 1993, officials said, few policy makers even noted reports by the Defense Intelligence Agency indicating that a shadowy armed group appeared to be active in the southern Mexican state of Chiapas. Similarly, though some finance and intelligence officials were concerned in late 1994 about the overvaluation of Mexico's peso, C.I.A. analysts decided not to issue a warning about the problem just a few days before the currency collapsed, according to intelligence officials. At the State Department, copies of an intelligence report titled „A Peso Problem“ sat mostly unread on the shelves.

„We have had, historically, a great deal of information from down there, but nobody wanted to look at it, because they didn't know what to do,“ said former Senator Dennis DeConcini, the Arizona Democrat who was chairman of the Senate Select Committee on Intelligence until the end of 1994. „They were afraid of how bad it might be, and how they would be able to justify the economic policies,“ said DeConcini, who, at his own request, received regular briefings on Mexico from the C.I.A.

Senior officials who dealt with Mexico under the Bush and Clinton Administrations said it was far easier to get the National Security Adviser or Secretary of State to focus on a shortterm problem like Haiti's elections than to devote 20 minutes to a question of Mexico's longterm stability. In early 1995, for instance, a powerful group of Deputy Secretaries ordered a far-reaching assessment of Mexico's turmoil and its implications for American policy. It was typical, officials said, that this effort was eventually forgotten, and the study never completed.

Nor have United States officials had much success in acting to stop Mexican corruption, even in the rare instances when they have had information they considered solid enough to act on. One such case, in 1992, began when American drug-enforcement agents in El Paso raided the home of a mid-level cocaine trafficker and happened upon a fascinating video cassette. Several officials who saw it said the tape showed the trafficker, his wife or girlfriend and several associates cheerfully shooting off automatic weapons with a friend in military fatigues. The friend turned out to be a Mexican Army general, Javier Escobedo.

When the video cassette reached the United States Embassy in Mexico City, Mr. Negroponte, the Ambassador, saw it as an unusual opportunity and he immediately delivered a copy to Mexico's Defense Minister. After being confronted with the evidence by his superiors, however, General Escobedo chose neither to turn informant nor face a court martial. Instead, the officials said, he drove to the grave of his father, who had also been an army general, and shot himself to death. The circumstances of his suicide were never disclosed.

In the fall of 1994, as Washington's Mexico specialists tried to make sense of a guerrilla uprising, a tumultuous presidential election campaign and the assassination of two major ruling-party political figures, many of them began to take the corruption problem more seriously. So did many Mexicans. Ernesto Zedillo, who was elected President that August, pledged to clean up the country's judicial system, and Mr. Jones, the Ambassador, offered information that he said might help the new Government keep out corrupt officials.

Diplomats at the embassy saw the exchange of information as a unique opportunity to deal with the problem. But by the way it was handled, the episode seemed to demonstrate American ambivalence about the issue once again. Mr. Jones asked several of the embassy's senior law-enforcement and intelligence officials to draw up a list of current and former Mexican officials who they thought should have no place in the upper ranks of an honest new régime.

The list they produced - a copy of which was obtained by a reporter and confirmed in its contents by three knowledgeable American officials - catalogues a much wider presumption of corruption at the senior levels of the Salinas Administration than United States officials have ever acknowledged publicly. Among its 18 names are those of a former Interior Minister, a former Defense Secretary, and a former Attorney General; three officials who had been in charge of anti-drug efforts, Mr. Salinas' former national security chief, and his former drug intelligence chief. It also includes several veterans of the Federal Security Directorate, the state-security force that collaborated closely with the C.I.A. until it was disbanded in 1985.

Those officials who could be contacted by a reporter uniformly denied having ever done anything wrong and said they had no idea that they had been included on the American blacklist. In any case, United States officials did not press the point. Mr. Jones sent the list without first clearing the action with the State Department or White House. He later described it as a mere „exchange of information." A second list of about 30 lower-ranking Mexicans, against whom the embassy officials felt they had weaker evidence, was never sent at all.

A senior American official said at the time that the list had been a great success because none of those it named were allowed into Mr. Zedillo's government. But that does not appear to be true. Among those on the list is Wilfredo Robledo, the senior operations official at Mexico's national-security agency, the Center for Investigations and National Security. Mexican officials who work with Mr. Robledo said he remains on the job and in good standing. Officials at the center and Interior Ministry, which controls the center, did not respond to telephone calls asking for comment.

American law-enforcement and intelligence officials said one of their basic problems in understanding the growing political influence of Mexican drug traffickers stemmed from the failure of government agencies to share information. While law-enforcement agents are building their cases, their practice is to guard what they know as closely as possible. After it comes out in court, they say, they generally have little time to try to evaluate the strategic significance of the information they have gathered. C.I.A. analysts who want to borrow such files often have to go to another agency's offices to read them. Often as not, policy makers are the last to find out what law-enforcement officials already know. „There is an impenetrable firewall," one State Department official said, „between what U.S. attorneys are doing and what the policy side of the house knows."

Rarely, however, has the system appeared so uncommunicative as in the case of Mr. Ruiz Massieu, a Deputy Attorney General who was both a close aide to Carlos Salinas and a brother of a leading politician said to have been killed on the orders of Raul Salinas. American officials began to suspect Mr. Ruiz Massieu of corruption after Mr. Garda Abrego, the trafficker, escaped just ahead of a 1993 raid to which he was apparently tipped off. That December, Mr. Ruiz Massieu opened a bank account in Houston. A few months later, his closest aide began arriving there with suitcases and boxes stuffed with hundreds of thousands of dollars in cash.

Customs agents in Texas recorded shipments that would eventually leave more than $9 million in the bank. But even after a suspicious bank officer called them to inquire about the money, Customs officials said, the agents did not investigate further. „Their sense was that there was something wrong there," the head of the Customs Service's financial investigations division, Alan Doody, said of the agents in Houston. „But the realization came pretty quickly that this guy was part of the ruling elite. There was a whiff that something wasn't right. But in order to do something about it, you need more than a whiff."

In Mexico City and Washington, other American law-enforcement officials were getting more. Some informants told of large gifts to Mr. Ruiz Massieu and his wife. Others described a huge smuggling case in which Mr. Ruiz Massieu and his deputy exonerated corrupt Mexican police agents. The success of Mexican anti-drug operations plummetted. Even then, officials said, Customs, F.B.I. and drug-enforcement officials shared little information about the case. Senior officials in Washington and Mexico learned of Mr. Ruiz Massieu's Texas deposits only after he was arrested at Newark International Airport as he tried to flee to Europe in March 1995.

When word of Mr. Ruiz Massieu's fortune reached the American Embassy in Mexico City, Jones assembled law-enforcement and intelligence officers in „the bubble," a secure room adjoining his office. He asked what evidence they might contribute to the case on Mr. Ruiz Massieu's apparent corruption. „All of our great minds said they didn't have any evidence against him," one official at the meeting recalled.

In explaining their belated apprehension of the traffickers' connections to the Salinas Administration, law-enforcement and intelligence officials make an insistent point: Mexican political tradition dictates absolute loyalty until a president steps down. The airing of corruption allegations almost always comes later. Mr. Zedillo appeared to underscore that point as he began his term. Within little more than three months after he took office, Raul Salinas was arrested on murder charges, Mario Ruiz Massieu was accused of taking bribes from drug traffickers, and Carlos Salinas was forced into exile, his reputation in shreds.

As Mexico was being rocked by those tremors, American officials took inventory of the corruption allegations they had against leading members of the Mexican elite. Perhaps the most comprehensive such search was ordered by senior law-enforcement officials in March 1995, as Republicans in Congress fought Mr. Clinton's plan to rescue the Mexican economy. The review turned up all kinds of accusations, officials said, none of them entirely convincing.

„There was just no smoking gun," said Robert Nieves, who joined the search as the Drug Enforcement Administration's chief of international operations. „That doesn't mean that it wasn't meaningful. But you couldn't go to court with that information." How deeply American agencies dug into such matters is unclear. Several officials who read much of the C.I.A.'s reporting on Mexican corruption between 1992 and 1995 said the reports rarely indicated that intelligence officers had done any significant investigation of the claims of their informants.

United States law-enforcement officials who were stationed in Mexico City said they had little choice but to look skeptically at the allegations they heard. Within the Mexican police and security apparatus, they said, leaking negative information about one's political enemies to American officials was a basic weapon of bureaucratic struggle. „Now, all of that information is almost 100 percent," said a former law-enforcement official who processed some of the most explosive accusations against Mexican officials, politicians and businessmen. „But at the time, we had to ask ourselves, 'Is it possible that it goes this high up?' We were afraid to write it up sometimes because we thought people would say we were crazy."

More recently, even as events in Mexico have forced the Clinton Administration to reassess drug trafficking and corruption here, American intelligence efforts have continued to run into problems. The fall last February of Mexico's drug-enforcement chief was a case in point. The official, Gen. Jesús Gutiérrez Rebollo, was arrested on charges of working for Mr. Carrillo Fuentes, the powerful cocaine trafficker who apparently died last week at a Mexico City clinic. Eight days earlier, the bald, rock-jawed Mexican officer had stood at attention in Washington as the White House drug-policy chief, Gen. Barry R. McCaffrey, described him as „an honest man and a no-nonsense field commander."

As commander of a five-state military region that has its headquarters in the western city of Guadalajara, General Gutiérrez Rebollo had been credited with the capture of one major cocaine trafficker in 1995, the arrest of another last August and the seizure of a plane loaded with millions of dollars in drug profits in between. The prevailing view, said a White House official who reviewed background information about the general from the Central Intelligence Agency and the Defense Intelligence Agency, was that he was „a soldier's soldier."

That no other army commander had taken remotely so much initiative in the fight against drug trafficking did not stir much doubt among experts who assessed his appointment for the two intelligence agencies and the Drug Enforcement Administration. Rather, according to several officials familiar with their reports and briefings, the intelligence analysts appeared to take their main cues from American drug-enforcement agents stationed in Guadalajara. The agents, who had dealt with the general on several cases, thought he was all business.

Some of the analysts did note that General Gutiérrez Rebollo had managed to avoid the regular rotations to which other commanders were subjected. But officials said that their reports and briefings raised no particular alarm that he had remained for more than six years in Guadalajara, the Beirut of Mexico's drug underworld. It is an established pattern of Mexican corruption that successful police commanders sell protection to one trafficking group while attacking others. But it went unnoticed among drug-intelligence analysts, officials said, that General Gutiérrez Rebollo had been vigorously attacking the Tijuana-based drug gang run by the Arellano Felix brothers while virtually ignoring their rival, Mr. Carrillo Fuentes.

Had United States officials queried senior Mexican law-enforcement officials, they might have confirmed that the general had balked at turning over suspected associates of the Arellano Felix gang whom his officers had captured, tortured and held incommunicado. Had they asked officials in Guadalajara, they would have heard about serious allegations of misconduct against a close aide whom General Gutierrez Rebollo had placed as head of the state police. After the state government dismissed the aide, the general hired him back as chief of investigations at Mexico's drug-enforcement agency. „He was showing results," said one American official who dealt with General Gutiérrez Rebollo. „His methods were overlooked."

By the time of his arrest in February, American drug-enforcement officials had heard from several informants who questioned the general's honesty. The reports were not vigorously pursued, officials said. Since the Gutiérrez Rebollo episode, officials said, the C.I.A. has instituted a new system to warn of such problems. Every biography the agency's analysts produce on a Mexican official now includes a caveat: just because no negative information has turned up does not mean that the official can necessarily be trusted.

By late 1995, the new director of Central Intelligence, John M. Deutch, was sufficiently dissatisfied with the agency's reporting on Mexico that he ordered intelligence officers and analysts to redouble their efforts. Mr. Deutch, who lived briefly in the Mexican city of Cuernavaca as a boy, took over the post with the Clinton Administration still feeling the sting of Congressional and public anger over the peso crisis. Officials said he included Mexico for the first time on the list of strategic priorities for the C.I.A. He asked his officers to focus on the stability of Mr. Zedillo's government and the threats it faced from both drug corruption and guerrillas.

Nearly two years later, the White House's drug-policy chief, General McCaffrey, suggested that the problems of intelligence on Mexico are still far from solved. Fresh from his own embarrasment with the fall of General Gutiérrez Rebollo, General McCaffrey said in an interview that he has begun an effort to create „a newly defined architecture" for the myriad agencies that collect information to support anti-drug efforts. General McCaffrey said the goal of the redesign will be to establish new „roles and missions and a hierarchy" for such agencies as the Drug Enforcement Administration's El Paso Intelligence Center, the C.I.A.'s Counternarcotics Center in Langley, Va., the Treasury Department's Financial Crimes Enforcement Network outside Washington, and the National Drug Intelligence Center in Johnstown, Pa.

„We need to make sure that this extraordinary amount of information that we've got supports real-world people involved in drug interdiction better than it does now," he said. General McCaffrey said he had briefed the Secretaries of State, Defense, Justice and Treasury on the idea, described it to the Congressional intelligence committees, and gotten the acting Director of Central Intelligence, George J. Tenet, to join him in leading a study group that is design a new structure by this fall.

But other officials said there is already strong opposition to the idea, particularly in the Justice and Treasury Departments. Some officials in those agencies said they were concerned about protecting sensitive or confidential information, such as the details of continuing investigations or income-tax returns. Other officials said that to pool any of their information would be to cede power. „Call me when it happens," one senior official said. „Something like that might work in the military, but those guys don't fight like they do in Washington."«

August 18, 1997: »As the man in the videotape begins to spill the inner secrets of Mexico's most violent drug gang, he appears nervous, chewing off pieces of his left thumbnail and gulping water. Alejandro Enrique Hodoyán had been a minor though well-placed member of the drug organization, running guns and errands. On the tape, he sits center stage, recounting in a soft voice how his brother and a circle of their childhood friends joined a criminal enterprise that killed dozens of police commanders, prosecutors, drug rivals and innocent bystanders.

„Killing is a party for them, it's a kick," Mr. Hodoyán tells Mexican investigators. „No remorse at all. They laugh after a murder, and go off and have a lobster dinner." His testimony, which produced eight hours of videotape and more than 200 pages of transcripts, is viewed on both sides of the border as a law-enforcement triumph, a breakthrough in Mexico's flagging fight against drug traffickers. Mexican officials say his disclosures have already prompted the dismissal of „several dozen" detectives and police commanders accused of ties to the Tijuana-based organization, which is led by the Arellano Félix brothers.

But behind the image on the videotape is a tale of a middle-class family torn apart, with brother turned against brother in a violent drug culture. It is also a story of kidnapping and coercion that highlights some of the perils for the United States in working with the secretive Mexican military, which has been given a central role in the drug war despite its lengthening record of corruption and brutality.

Mr. Hodoyán, an American citizen who was born in San Diego and lived most of his life just across the border in Tijuana, was abducted and detained illegally for 80 days by Mexican military officers. Soldiers tortured him with cigarette lighters and electric shocks to the eyelids, according to an account he later gave his family. The Mexican military eventually turned Mr. Hodoyan over to American officials who are preparing a major, new indictment against the Arellano Félix organization. Some American officials involved in the case now acknowledge they were too willing to turn a blind eye to the methods used by the Mexican military to secure Mr. Hodoyán's cooperation.

American diplomats in Mexico learned of Mr. Hodoyán's captivity shortly after he was imprisoned, but did nothing to help him. After his family reported him missing to United States officials, a law-enforcement agent assigned to the American Embassy interviewed him at an unused barracks, where he was blindfolded and handcuffed to a steel bed. The embassy official assigned to follow up on the agent's report of a captive American citizen took no action. United States officials later described that as an egregious failure to deliver the basic protections guaranteed citizens in trouble in foreign lands.

Donald R. Hamilton, the embassy's spokesman, otherwise defended its handling of the case, saying Mr. Hodoyan did not complain to any American official in Mexico of torture or suggest that he was under duress. The account of Mr. Hodoyán's experiences was pieced together from interviews with his family, American officials in Mexico, and Mexican justice officials who knew him as an informant. It is also based on confidential Mexican court documents as well as audio tape-recordings, obtained by the *New York Times*, of telephone calls he made to his family in Tijuana last year when he was a military prisoner.

In December 1996, the military officer who supervised his interrogation and handover to the Americans was appointed Mexico's top anti-drug official, in part because of successes he scored in the drug war using information supplied by Mr. Hodoyán. Two months later, that officer, Gen. Jesus Gutiérrez Rebollo, was jailed on charges of collaborating with another drug lord, a bitter rival of the Arellano Félix brothers. Mexican officials now suspect that much of the information the general extracted from Mr. Hodoyán went directly to the rival drug organization. Since then, the military has dismissed and is investigating 33 other officers, including four generals, on corruption and narcotics charges, defense officials said.

In the end, Mr. Hodoyán was not much help to American prosecutors. After 10 days in San Diego, he suffered what family members described as a psychological breakdown. Under pressure to give evidence against his brother, he disappeared across the border to Mexico where he had numerous enemies, including the Arellano Félix gang, which, he was told, had put out a contract on his life. Alejandro Hodoyán known to his family and friends as Alex, seemed an unlikely candidate for a career in crime. His mother Cristina, who is 55, is a prim, devoutly Catholic woman from an upstanding Mexican family. His father, Alejandro Hodoyán Ramirez, 63, is a respected Mexican civil engineer. The Hodoyans hoped to raise their children with the best of the American and Mexican cultures. Their three boys and a girl were all born in San Diego, but the family lived just across the border in Tijuana, a city where the multibillion-dollar drug trade has in recent years become a lure even for privileged and educated young people.

The Hodoyán children came of age in Tijuana discos where teen-agers experimented with cocaine in the free-wheeling way of wealthy American youth, They also mingled with Mexican gang members who were rising stars in the cocaine business. One of the flashiest was Ramón Arellano, a leader of the gang who met members of the Hodoyán family at a society wedding in Tijuana. It was a sweltering summer day, but Mr. Arellano sported a mink jacketand leather pants. He was wearing a big thick chain with a big gold cross encrusted with emeralds," said a Hodoyán relative, who asked not to be identified, „Everything about him made you turn around and say, who is he?" Mexican court documents describe Mr. Arellano as a compulsive murderer who has killed several times for sport and is implicated in more than 60 homicides. He and his brothers began their careers as provincial drug dealers, but shot and bullied their way to seize control of drug-smuggling along a western swath of the United States-Mexico border. One by one, friends the Hodoyans had known since childhood were drawn into the Arellanos' circle of riches and violence.

Fabián Martínez González, a grade-school classmate of Alex Hodoyán's younger sister who teased the girls by lifting up their skirts, grew up to become el Tiburón, or the Shark. He is accused of being one of Mr. Arellano's most feared gunmen and is wanted for murder in Mexico. Emilio Valdez Mainero was a boyhood buddy Mr. Hodoyán chose years later to be the godfather at his first daughter's baptism. Mr. Valdéz Mainero became a top operative in the organization, arranging drug shipments and assassinations, the Mexican and American police have charged in court. „In Tijuana the Arellanos bought their way into the cream of society," said a Mexican anti-drug prosecutor who asked not to be identified. „In a normal situation, a family like the Hodoyáns would never find themselves involved with traffickers."

Mr. Hodoyán, the oldest of the Hodoyán children, is a 35-year old law-school dropout and cocaine addict who never held a steady job. An even-tempered man with an amiable face, he started doing small favors for the Arellanos and eventually helped them import rifles and grenades to arm their hit squads. In return they gave him loads of cocaine and marijuana to move across the border, allowing him to keep the proceeds, he told Mexican prosecutors. Alfredo Hodoyán, 25, the rakish and strong-willed brother who is Alex's youngest sibling, took on a more violent role in the gang, according to his brother and other associates. He joined one of the cartel's hit squads and is wanted on murder charges in Mexico.

On September 10, 1996, the Arellano gang sent Alex Hodoyán to Guadalajara, the central Mexican city that has emerged as a battleground for competing drug gangs. His mission, he later said, was to find a new „safe house," a local base for the group's operations. He was walking straight into a military trap. Seven weeks earlier, gunmen for the Arellano organizaation had bungled a plot to assassinate Amado Carrillo Fuentes, the leader of a rival cartel. Instead they killed two army soldiers who were at the scene. The killings infuriated the soldiers' commander, Gen. Gutiérrez Rebollo, a bulldog of an officer with a shaven head who was in charge from his headquarters in Guadalajara of a vast military region encompassing much of central Mexico.

On the afternoon of Sept. 11, Alex Hodoyán went to an existing Arellano safe house in a working-class neighborhood. A squad of General Gutiérrez Rebollo's intelligence troops, wearing black uniforms, was watching the house and seized him. By law, the Mexican armed forces can hold criminal suspects for no more than 48 hours before turning them over to the civilian authorities. But General Gutiérrez Rebollo kept Mr. Hodoyán incommunicado for the next two months, mainly in a vacant army base on the outskirts of Guadalajara. The troops had no arrest warrant and filed no report to the police.

Mr. Hodoyán's kidnapping and secret detention have been described in separate, mutually corroborating accounts by army officers who are now testifying against General Gutiérrez Rebollo in two trials. Their statements are contained in confidential court records. According to the officers, the windowless bunker where Mr. Hodoyán was shackled hand and foot to a bed was General Gutiérrez Rebollo's private interrogation center, where illegally detained suspects were questioned for days and weeks.

After Mr. Hodoyán was released, he said the soldiers had tortured and threatened to kill him. „They told me I had arrived in hell," he said in a statement he dictated to his parents months later. According to Mr. Hodoyán, the soldiers forced soda water spiked with searing hot chile peppers up his nose until he was nearly asphyxiated. He said they had burned the soles of his feet with lighters and had applied electric shocks to his eyelids and toes. Within days, several witnesses said, there was a change in Mr. Hodoyán's demeanor. He began to cooperate, almost too enthusiastically, with his captors. Drawing on his prodigious memory, he poured out what he knew about the Arellanos in manic bursts.

Mr. Hodoyán's claims of torture have not been confirmed by independent witnesses, and the statement he gave his family, which he never signed, remains the only record of his first days in captivity. Two Mexicans who saw Mr. Hodoyan in later weeks of his detention say they noticed a fresh scar in the middle of his forehead. He told them that he had been tortured, but said he could not discuss the details. The scar, he said, was where skin peeled away when his duct tape blindfolds were changed.

General Gutiérrez Rebollo played his prisoner with a maestro's touch, according to the officers who testified in the trials against him. He waited 13 days before visiting Mr. Hodoyán. Then he came on as the consummate good cop, pretending to scold his subordinates for treating the prisoner harshly and ordering them to loosen his manacles and upgrade his food. Mr. Hodoyán soon became devoted to his jailer. When allowed, he trailed behind General Gutiérrez Rebollo. A Mexican drug prosecutor who saw the two men together toward the end of Mr. Hodoyán's captivity said they were „like father and son."

General Gutiérrez Rebollo had good reason to court Mr. Hodoyán. On Sept. 14, three days afrer Mr. Hodoyán was abducted by his soldiers, a hit squad linked to the Arellanos assassinated a top Mexican anti-drug prosecutor in Mexico City. Soon after, Mexican officials sent their American counterparts information developed by General Gutiérrez Rebollo indicating that Alfredo Hodoyán, Alex's brother, was a triggerman in the killing. The Mexicans said Alfredo was hiding out near San Diego with Emilio Valdez, the godfather of Alex Hodoyán's daughter, who was wanted in Mexico on another murder charge.

American federal agents arrested Mr. Valdéz and Alfredo Hodoyán on Sept. 30 in San Diego, and at Mexico's request United States prosecutors opened an extradition case to return them to Mexico for trial. General Gutiérrez Rebollo set out to convince Alex Hodoyán to testify against his friend and his brother. In Mexico, where ties of blood and ritual kinship are nearly sacred and the law absolves suspects from incriminating immediate relatives, it was a formidable undertaking.

As soon as the Hodoyán family realized Alex was missing, they turned to the American authorities for help. On Sept. 20, Adriana Hodoyán, Alex's sister, called the U.S. consulate in Guadalajara to say she believed that her brother, an American citizen, had vanished there. Five days later, Adriana Hodoyán, who is 30, traveled to Guadalajara and gave the consulate a photo of Alex and a detailed account of the travel route he had planned.

On Oct. 7, when Alex Hodoyán had been missing for nearly a month, his sister called the consulate again. She was frantic. According to American officials, she said there were reports that Alex had been detained on Sept. 11 by the military authorities in Guadalajara. American diplomats in Guadalajara made what they later described as routine phone calls to local police stations and jails to see if he was there. „It was just a usual-suspects thing," a United States official in Guadalajara said, just another of the 71 cases the consulate handled in 1996 of Americans who went missing in that region.

No one at the consulate ever spoke with the Mexican military. „We would have no reason to call the military," an American official said, explaining that the armed forces do not usually detain people under Mexico's legal system. But on Oct. 7, the day of Adriana Hodoyan's most urgent appeal for help, one arm of the United States Government learned that the Mexican military knew exactly where to find Mr. Hodoyán. Officers at the Defense Ministry in Mexico City invited an agent from the United States Bureau of Alcohol, Tobacco and Firearms to question an exceptional informant they had about arms smuggling to Mexican drug traffickers. Not long after General Gutiérrez Rebollo had captured Mr. Hodoyán, he had informed his superiors about him.

The A.T.F. bureau declined to make the agent who questioned Mr. Hodoyán available for an interview. His account was relayed by officials in Washington and Mexico who said they had reviewed reports the agent filed at the time. American officials said the Mexican armed forces had provided an airplane to fly the A.T.F. agent to Guadalajara. Two Mexican officers, in plain clothes, drove the agent to the base where Mr. Hodoyán was held and accompanied him into the meeting.

In the bare room, the agent introduced himself to Mr. Hodoyán, blindfolded and cuffed to a bed. The agent later told colleagues that it bothered him that he could not see the prisoner's eyes. Nevertheless, for nearly two hours the American agent probed to find out what the prisoner knew about the traffic of weapons. „The amazing thing is, the guy just doesn't shut up," said a United States official who questioned the A.T.F. agent about Mr. Hodoyán. „He is talking, talking, talking. He immediately implicated his brother and himself in a number of crimes."

Mexican officers told the A.T.F. agent that Mr. Hodoyán had been blindfolded to prevent him from seeing the American's face, since the prisoner, they said, was a „dangerous and violent criminal." The echo-filled room and strangely empty military barracks struck the A.T.F. agent as an „unusual but not inappropriate" place for the meeting. After two hours, the official said, the agent believed that he „had a live one." He began to make mental plans to take Mr. Hodoyán to the United States as a witness in gun-running cases.

That was when Mr. Hodoyán, who had spoken throughout the interview in Spanish, announced that he would not need a visa. „I was born in San Diego," he said. „I am an American citizen." Mr. Hodoyán volunteered nothing about mistreatment by the soldiers, American officials said, and the statement he later gave his family suggests a reason. General Gutiérrez Rebollo's officers, he said, warned him before the interview that if he told the AT.F. agent about his torture, „he would be the last person I would ever cross a word with."

The day after the interview, Mexican military officials told the A.T.F. agent that the general had changed his mind and was not ready to release Mr. Hodoyán. The agent remained uneasy about what he had seen. He consulted with the No.2 official in the embassy, Charles H. Brayshaw, who sent him to the consul general for Mexico City, a senior diplomat who handles problems involving United States citizens. For half an hour, the agent described the American imprisoned in Guadalajara. According to American officials, the consul general, Thomas L. Randall, told the A.T.F. agent he believed that Mr. Hodoyán was probably one more Mexican trying to get out of a jam by claiming to be an American.

Then, several officials said, Mr. Randall did nothing further about Mr. Hodoyán. „He didn't tell anybody above, below or alongside," a diplomat said later, calling Mr. Randall's performance „a clear case of nonfeasance." „Had this person done even the minimum which duty, regulation, law and custom indicate, the consular service would not have been ignorant of Mr. Hodoyán's detention," said Mr. Hamilton, the spokesman for the embassy in Mexico City. Mr. Hamilton refused to identify the consul involved in the case by name. A Washington spokesman for the A.T.P. bureau, Patrick D. Hynes, said classified memos showed that the agent had met with the embassy's consul general, which was the position Mr. Randall held at the time. Other officials confirmed that it was Mr. Randall, who was recalled from Mexico to Washington late last year and retired from the Foreign Service in January 1997. Reached by telephone at his southern California residence, Randall said he had no recollection of Mr. Hodoyán's case.

„I'm sure I would have done whatever needed to be done," he said, calling it „convenient" that embassy officials had heaped all of the blame on the one person involved who was no longer in government service. Mr. Brayshaw did not inquire again what had become of Mr. Hodoyán because he assumed that the Consul General had done his job, Hamilton said. In late October, General Gutiérrez Rebollo was sufficiently confident of his-new informant's cooperation that he allowed him to call his family and tell them he was still alive. They were elated but deeply worried. After the first contact, Mr. Hodoyán was allowed to call his parents regularly, and as he talked in guarded language, they realized that he was informing on the Arellano gang and was under pressure to turn on his own brother.

For his parents the conversations were agonizing. Their eldest son was in the custody of powerful Mexican military officers who, Alex hinted, would think nothing of killing him. The officers were trying to pit Alex against their youngest son, who was in jail in San Diego fighting extradition to Mexico on a murder charge that could put him in prison for decades. Mr. Hodoyan's mother and father urged him to remain loyal to the family and his circle of childhood friends. But Mr. Hodoyán was bitter that the Arellano gang had sent him into an ambush. And General Gutiérrez Rebollo was leaning heavily on Mr. Hodoyán to talk by offering to place him in a Government witness program where his past criminal record would be erased.

Tape-recordings of some of Mr. Hodoyán's phone calls to his family were made available to The *New York Times* by participants in the events who requested anonymity. They depict a man overwhelmed by irreconcilable pressures and dominated by a captor who both terrifies him and inspires his devotion. Cooperating with General Gutiérrez Rebollo, he argued, was the only way he could survive to see his two young daughters again. „I love my brother, Mama," Mr. Hodoyán told his mother at one point. „But my daughters come first."

In one conversation his father asked him what he wanted to tell his brother Alfredo and his brother's lawyers. „Tell them I made a deal with the general, and the general is keeping his word to me," Mr. Hodoyán said. „He even bought new clothes for me." „He spared my life and I want to keep my word to him, too," he said later in the conversation. At one point, the elder Mr. Hodoyán told his son that a Mexican lawyer who had defended the Arellanos was offering to help get Alex out of military custody. Alex exploded, saying: „I don't matter to them! I never did. They just want to help me now because they have problems with the military and the police. They see the end coming." „My stomach is starting to hurt," he said as he raged at the Arellanos. Finally he broke down in sobs. „I don't want them using me," he said, cursing the Arellanos.

Mr. Hodoyán made it clear that General Gutiérrez Rebollo had promised him that his statements against Alfredo could not be used in any Mexican or American court because they were brothers. „My son, it's a trap - you're in a trap, try to understand," Cristina Hodoyan entreated in a phone call on Dec. 10. „You are helping the man who is accusing your brother!" „He can't," Mr. Hodoyán insisted. „ Alfredo is my brother. He can't." His parents hoped that if Alex was freed, he would testify in the effort to block Alfredo's extradition in San Diego. But they warned Alex that he would have to reveal that he had been tortured by the troops. Alex Hodoyán panicked, afraid that General Gutiérrez Rebollo would retaliate if he denounced him. „No! No! They never did anything to me, Mama, please try to understand," he said. „I thought I explained that to you. I can't say anything about that until I finish what I am doing here."

Alex's father suggested to his son that he was suffering from Stockholm syndrome, which occurs when kidnap victims become attached to their kidnappers. Alex rejected the idea with a fervor that suggested he knew it could be true. „Look, Papa, everything they promised me they have done," Alex Hodoyán said of the military. „I don't want trouble. I don't want them to kill me. I don't want that." Mrs. Hodoyán said she felt torn apart by the clashing interests of her two sons. „Alex, above all, we have to be united," Mrs. Hodoyán said, her voice taut with pain. Alex replied: „I am not sure if I can help Alfredo, but at least I am sure I will be free and clear for the rest of my life. But if they hurt me here, who will take care of my little girls? They will be left without a father."

General Gutiérrez Rebollo won the fight for Alex Hodoyán's allegiance. In the last days of November 1996, he summoned Mexican civilian prosecutors to Guadalajara. In three days of declarations, including the sections on videotape, Mr. Hodoyán once again told all he knew about the Arellanos - this time for the legal record. Speaking to the police video camera in measured words and abundant detail, he accused his brother Alfredo of taking part in not one but several killings.

„Prior to the murder the witness's brother arrived at the hotel," the record of Mr. Hodoyán's testimony reads, referring to the April 1996 killing of a Mexican boxer said to have encroached on the Arellanos' turf. Alfredo Hodoyán and one other gunman „were responsible for finding the victim, whom they murdered in the hallway that connects the restaurant and the bathrooms of the hotel."

In December, after General Gutiérrez Rebollo was promoted to head Mexico's anti-drug agency, he offered agents from the United States Drug Enforcement Administration a chance to debrief his informant. The D.E.A. had been told of Mr. Hodoyan's military detention more than a month earlier by the A.T.P. agent who questioned him. Still, the drug-enforcement agents eagerly accepted the offer as a rare chance to cooperate with the Mexican military and improve their relations with the general. „He was showing results," the law-enforcement official said. „He was a very confident guy who projected the sense that 'we're the military - we're going to get the job done.' His methods, frankly, were overlooked."

By February, Mr. Hodoyán had completed his transformation from hostage to informant. He had been given immunity from prosecution in Mexico in exchange for his testimony. He moved about freely at the federal drug agency in the capital, where General Gutiérrez Rebollo had been transferred. On Feb. 10, D.E.A. agents flew Mr. Hodoyán to the United States. They interviewed him, and hoped that he would eventually be a cooperating witness against the Arellanos. The D.E.A. did not allow its Mexico agents to comment about their role. But James J. McGivney, the agency's spokesman, said Mr. Hodoyán had given no indication he had ever been mistreated. „Every time the D.E.A. saw this guy, he was walking around having a good time," Mr. McGivney said. „When we see him, he's not bruised, not beaten, no chili peppers up his nose, no signs of duress."

Soon after he arrived in the United States, Mr. Hodoyán, his 32-year-old wife, Bertha Gastelum de Hodoyán, and his mother met with the American prosecutor who was handling the extradition of his brother. The mother said she had prodded Alex to tell the Assistant United States Attorney, Gonzalo P. Curiel, about his torture in Mexico. But according to both women, Mr. Curiel was reluctant to listen. They said he replied, „This is more than I want to hear." Mr. Curiel declined to be interviewed, noting that he is barred from discussing pending cases.

On Feb. 18, the fragile world Mr. Hodoyán built as an informant imploded. Mexican military officials announced the arrest of General Gutiérrez Rebollo. They released photographs showing that as drug czar he had lived in a luxury apartment owned by Amado Carrillo Fuentes, the leading trafficker. Mr. Hodoyán reeled. His savior was just another drug don. The information he had given to redeem himself had probably just gone to benefit another cartel. Meanwhile, one of the Arellanos top gunmen, Fabian Martínez, „the Shark," placed several calls from hiding to the Hodoyans, saying he knew Alex was an informant.

Then the American prosecutor, Mr. Curiel, said he intended to put Mr. Hodoyán before a grand jury investigating Arellano operatives, including his brother and his friend Mr. Valdez, Mr. Hodoyán's family said. He would have to go briefly to jail, but then he, his wife and daughters could join a witness protection program. „I'll never forget what he said," recalled his wife. '"You know what?' he said, 'I'd rather have them kill me.'"

Before dawn on the morning of Feb. 20, Mr. Hodoyán committed what a United States official described as a „totally irrational and suicidal act." He bolted from San Diego and appeared, wild-eyed and disheveled, at his parents' home in Tijuana. „He was crazy, loco, desperate," Bertha Hodoyán said. „He was crying, telling us he was sorry. Completely neurotic. He was just like a little child, crying and crying." Thirteen days later, when Mr. Hodoyán was driving in downtown Tijuana with his mother, armed men blocked the path of their vehicle, dragged him out, shoved him into another car and sped away. He has not been heard from since. .

His brother Alfredo and his friend Mr. Valdéz remain in prison in San Diego fighting extradition to Mexico. Their lawyers have asserted that the statements of Alex Hodoyán and other witnesses provided by Mexico were obtained through torture and are thus invalid. Mr. Curiel acknowledged recently at a court hearing in San Diego that the allegations of torture were plausible and serious, but said they should be investigated by the Mexican authorities.«

December 29, 1997: »Hoping to build a new bulwark against the flow of illegal drugs from Latin America, the United States is providing the Mexican military with extensive covert intelligence support and training hundreds of its officers to help shape a network of anti-drug troops around the country, United States and Mexican officials say. The officials say the assistance has included training, equipment and advice from the Central Intelligence Agency to establish an elite army intelligence unit that has quietly moved to the forefront of Mexico's anti-drug effort, sometimes ahead of a new civilian police force that the United States is also pledged to support.

The effort has proceeded despite growing American concern that it may lead to more serious problems of corruption and human rights in one of Mexico's most respected institutions, United States officials say. A new United States intelligence analysis of the military's drug ties, for instance, will cite evidence of extensive penetration of the officer corps, two people who have seen draft versions of the assessment said. Clinton Administration officials have described the American aid as a stopgap. Echoing Mexico's President Ernesto Zedillo, they insist that the military's law-enforcement actions will be limited and temporary, helping to disrupt the country's thriving drug trade only until its badly corrupted federal police forces can be overhauled.

But according to many officials, the Pentagon and the C.I.A. have pressed their help partly out of their need to find new tasks after the cold war. They hope to use the aid to expand their roles in the anti-drug campaign in Mexico and to improve their relationships with a secretive, nationalistic neighboring army that has often looked at them with suspicion, the officials said. „They didn't have anybody to play with on the Mexican end of the drug issue, so they went for the military," a former senior official who was involved in American policy in Mexico said, referring to the Defense

Department and the C.I.A. „They knew the risks, but they thought they could control the situation.“

Some of those risks have resounded in recent news reports: the jailing of army generals on charges of protecting major drug traffickers; allegations that military officers have been linked to the torture and disappearance of criminal suspects; failures of due process and proper legal procedure by soldiers stepping in for the police. Other pitfalls have been less apparent. Some officials, for instance, worry that American intelligence officers may face conflicts in trying to build good relationships with Mexican Army officers to sustain the cooperation, and trying to remain watchful of military corruption at the same time. A few other current and former United States officials date their unease to what they described as a disastrous C.I.A. program in the late 1980s to deploy a Mexican Army strike force against the traffickers. The force was disbanded after several failed operations, one of which resulted in the killing of four Mexican civilians.

Mexico has loug stood out in Latin America for the sureness of its civilian control over the military. But American officials said they had been troubled by indications that some officers, detailed to the federal police have operated with considerable independence from the judicial authorities. With the Mexican Army searching for new missions, many American officials doubt that it will limit its participation in law enforcement to the two-year deadline that Mr. Zedillo and his aides set last summer.

„The whole thing has snowballed,“ said a senior American official who, like others, would discuss the matter only on the condition that he not be identified. „We are now seeing two separate anti-drug efforts in Mexico - one by the military and one under the Attorney General. If I were in the Attorney General's office, I would be asking whether it has gone too far.“ To some degree, the policy debate is fueled by old rivalries between American lawenforcement agencies and their intelligence and military counterparts. But the two sides also have some philosophical differences, which center on the question of whether United States support for the military complements or competes with efforts to transform Mexico's crippled criminal-justice system.

„They have basically to rebuild their entire police force,“ a senior drug-enforcement official said of the Mexican Government. „You can't do that in a year or two. And the longer the emphasis is put on the military, the longer it is going to take to get the police up and running.“ The Pentagon spokesman, Kenneth H. Bacon, disputed the idea that the two directions of American anti-drug aid in Mexico were at cross purposes. „There is no conflict,“ he saId. James R. Jones, who left Mexico City this summer after serving for four years as the United States Ambassador there, echoed that view, and denied that American officials had encouraged the Mexican military's new role.

„The temporary detailing of military officers to civilian law enforcement was the Mexicans' and Zedillo's decision - we had nothing to do with that,“ Mr. Jones said. „Our efforts to improve the quality and exchange of intelligence information and our training programs for certain military units had nothing to do with their decision.“ The C.I.A. 's chief spokesman, Bill Harlow, declined to comment on the agency's activities in Mexico. Despite a widespread belief in the corruption of Mexico's federal and state police, Mexicans and their political leaders have been wary about seeking the help of the military to enforce civilian laws. In the late 1970s Mexican officials turned to the army to help drive marijuana and heroin-poppy growers from their sanctuaries in the rugged folds of the western Sierra Madre. Their sweep succeeded in temporarily dislodging the traffickers, and it institutionalized a program in which about 20,000 of the army's 150,000 soldiers are detailed to drug-crop eradication campaigns.

For an army that has relatively little to do in securing the country's borders, the drug eradication program has been a source of pride. Yet even while it avoided police-type activities, the military was shaken during the 1980s and early 1990s by public allegations that some senior officers - including a former Defense Minister, a Secretary of the Navy and several senior army commanders - colluded in the drug trade. After Carlos Salinas de Gortari became President in late 1988, American officials said, they gave relatively little thought to the Mexican Army becauseiof their hopes that at least one of the Government's many police-reform campaigns would succeed. Some also harbored cause for concern in the experience of the Mexican Army strike force created years earlier.

With anti-drug efforts stalled in 1987, American agents developed information that big traffickers were building nearly impenetrable compounds in the countryside. Working with the military, current and former officials said, C.I.A. officers helped form what they envisioned as an elite team of about 50 soldiers that would strike more effectively and operate more securely than the police. Mexican law-enforcement officials were told nothing of the plan, they said.

The team's first operation, against a stronghold of a cocaine smuggler in Sinaloa state, ended with one soldier's capture by a police agent working for the traffickers, two former officials said. The next foray went considerably worse. On the morning of April 11, 1988, helicopters swung out of the dawn sky near the northern town of Caborca, a sanctuary of a reputed marijuana smuggler. „The idea was that you could take a well-trained military unit and go in there and boom - take everybody out," a former official said.

The soldiers did take everyone out, but they did so at what turned out to be a workshop in a residential neighborhood, killing four apprentice welders. Former officials said the Mexican Attorney General at the time, Sergio Garda Ramirez, was so mystified that he asked whether American agents had carried out the raid themselves. Eventually, the military issued a terse statement taking responsibility for the attack but not disclosing the C.I.A.'s involvement. After a third, unsuccessful raid on another suspected drug base, the program was shut down for good, the officials said.

Mexico was near the same point in its political cycle - the end of a six-year presidential term, a period when corruption has historically flourished among outgoing officials - when United States officials looked to the military again in 1994. The idea of greater army support for the police was raised first by American diplomats and again during a visit by the United States Army Chief of Staff, Gen. Gordon Sullivan, current and former American officials said. But at the time, they said, it was rejected by Mexican justice officials.

Mr. Zedillo, who took office on Dec. 1, 1994, has called drug trafficking one of Mexico's most serious problems of national security. United States officials strongly endorsed that view, briefing his aides on such developments as the use of passenger jets to fly cocaine into Mexico from Colombia."The military was the only trained, disciplined force that you could use to deal with this situation in the short term," one of Mr. Zedillo's closest aides said. „There was no one else."

Mr. Zedillo first brought army commanders into the redesign of the Government's drug-control strategy. He then authorized them to work with United States officials in an ultimately abortive effort to deploy its aging F-5 fighters to chase drug jets. Finally, he began allowing military officers to replace federal police agents in several border cities plagued by smugglers. In October 1995, when William J. Perry made the first official visit to Mexico in memory by an American Secretary of Defense, anti-drug aid was at the center of several cooperative ventures he proposed to Mexican military officials, Mexican and United States military officials said.

„You were looking for general ways to engage, military to military," a Pentagon official said. Within months, a first group of young Mexican Army officers were training in anti-drug operations at Fort Bragg, N.C. Of some 3,000 Mexican soldiers who are expected to have passed through Defense Department training courses by next fall, 328 young officers will have completed special 12-and 13-week programs intended to create a corps of anti-drug specialists. Those trainees are being sent in turn to train air-mobile special forces units that are now stationed at the headquarters of the 12 regions and 40 zones that make up Mexico's military geography.

Defense Department officials said the anti-drug curriculum of the units, called Air-Mobile Special Forces Groups, ranged from air-assault operations and military policing to human rights. The Pentagon has also given Mexico 73 aging UH-1H helicopters to transport those troops. The helicopters may be used only for anti-drug operations. But Mexican and United States military officials said there was nothing to stop the transfer of American-trained army officers to similar special forces units that might be deployed against leftist insurgents in southern states like Guerrero and Chiapas.

American officials said that what is perhaps the most significant United States support for the Mexican military's anti-drug efforts is probably the least visible. It comes, they said, in the training, equipping and operational support of C.I.A. officers for a special force of the army intelligence section called the Center for Anti-Narcotics Investigations. The unit, comprising some 90 carefully chosen young officers, began to come together about three years ago, officials said. Like the civilian intelligence groups the C.I.A. works with in Mexico, the military anti-drug force is not supposed to be an „action" unit like the group trained by the agency in the 1980s. But it does appear to sometimes take the lead in raids as well as surveillance actions.

Several American officials compared the program to the C.I.A.'s work in Colombia, where the agency has been credited with critical help in the capture of major drug traffickers. A key difference, they noted, has been Mexico's extreme sensitivity to anything involving the C.I.A. Officials familiar with the operations of the intelligence team said that after a clumsy start - at one point its agents lost track of an important Bolivian drug broker they had under surveillance because they insisted on asking a superior for instructions rather than simply follow him - it has emerged as probably the most active of all Mexican anti-drug units.

Officials said the unit played a central part in the pursuit of Amado Carrillo Fuentes, then Mexico's most important trafficker, before he died during plastic surgery last summer. It also worked closely on the investigation of Mr. Carrillo Fuentes' organization after his death, and on a series of raids against the Tijuana-based drug mafia run by the Arellano Felix brothers. Yet reviews of the unit, which is known by its initials in Spanish as the Clan, have been mixed.

Officials said some Mexican prosecutors have complained privately that the unit's officials have demonstrated spotty notions of the law, at times handing captured suspects over to the civilian authorities without ever gathering evidence to hold them. Some Mexican police investigators have also questioned why - if the United States is willing to provide the sort of sophisticated surveillance and intelligence-gathering equipment that it is said to have given to the Clan - it will not offer the same support to new anti-drug units created in the Attorney General's office. American officials said questions had been raised about the unit's integrity after two of its agents were dismissed this year for what one official described as „unprofessional conduct." Some have also wondered about its independence - from both Mexican civilians and American intelligence officers. „It could be a time bomb," a former intelligence official said, „because they have a lot less control over that unit than they think they do."

The Mexican Army's Chief of Staff, Gen. Juan Heriberto Salinas Altes, praised the unit, saying it has gathered important information for both army special-forces troops and the federal police. He denied, however, that the unit has any formal or continuing relationship with the C.I.A. „There could have been some contact, but it was not any official contact," General Salinas Altes said in an interview, his first since becoming Chief of Staff three years ago.

For their part, Clinton Administration officials said the closer military relationship of that anti-drug cooperation had already paid dividends for the United States. In recent months, they noted, Mexican officials agreed to streamline procedures by which United States drugsurveillance planes are allowed to fly over Mexican airspace, and those by which Coast Guard ships can dock at Mexican ports. The impact of American support on the Mexican military's anti-drug efforts remains somewhat to be seen. Thus far, Defense Department officials said they knew of no instance in which special forces officers trained in the United States had been sent off on an American-donated helicopter in the pursuit of a drug flight.

But many United States officials said it had already become evident that although the Mexican officer corps may be more resistant to the traffickers' bribes than the police, it faces a more serious threat than most American officials foresaw. Clinton

Administration officials were shocked this year when the army commander installed as the Zedillo government's drugenforcement chief, Gen. Jesus Gutierrez Rebollo, was arrested for taking bribes from Mr. Carrillo Fuentes, the trafficker. Since then, though, it has become clear that the episode was not an isolated one.

Other high-ranking officers have been implicated in connection with Mr. Carrillo Fuentes' organization, including one retired general who was arrested after the wedding of the trafficker's sister. Several more senior officers have been arrested for their supposed ties to the rival trafficking organization run out of Tijuana by the Arellano Felix brothers; one has been charged with offering $1 million monthly bribes to another army general who serves as the Attorney General's representative there.

Still, United States officials are divided between those who see new proof of the military's vulnerability and those who see evidence of an institution fighting aggressively against temptation. Mexican officials, not surprisingly, side strongly with the latter camp. „If there is action, there are going to be people hurt," General Salinas Altés said. „We have people killed. We have people wounded. We have people in jail."

General Salinas Altés has himself been a focus of the American scrutiny. According to officials familiar with American intelligence reports in which the Chief of Staff is mentioned, he first came to the United States' attention after he moved from Baja California in 1988 to head the Ninth Military Region headquarters in the city of Acapulco. There, he spent six years in charge of drug-eradication efforts in Guerrero, the state that is Mexico's leading producer of heroin poppies. After he became Chief of Staff in December 1994, two American officials said, General Salinas Altés was again briefly a subject of scrutiny when intelligence officials intercepted a drug trafficker's telephone call for a „General Salinas." They described the report as disturbing but unclear.

Most recently, United States officials became concerned again this summer when it emerged that General Salinas Altés and several other senior officers had met with a top lieutenant of Mr. Carrillo Fuentes. According to a military document published in the Mexican magazine Proceso that appears to be notes from the Jan. 14 meeting, the lieutenant, Eduardo González Quirarte, said the trafficker had offered essentially to clean up his business - halting the sale of drugs in Mexico, eschewing violence, helping the economy - if he was allowed to keep half his fortune and continue operating in peace.

General Salinas Altés was interviewed at his Mexico City offices on the condition that he not be questioned about the allegations against him, but only about the cooperative efforts he oversees as the military's representative to an anti-drug group of senior officials from the two countries. But in a separate interview, Gen. Tomás Ángeles Dauahare, a senior aide to Mexico's Defense Minister, Gen. Enrique Cervantes Aguirre, dismissed the allegations against General Salinas Altés vehemently. General Angeles confirmed that Mexican military officials had received an unsigned American report forwarded from the Foreign Ministry. After an extensive investigation, in which United States officials did not answer repeated requests for supplementary information, he said, it was found that the guilty officer was in fact a Gen. Javier Salinas Payares, the commander of a military air base, and that he was eventually imprisoned in the case.

Similarly, General Ángeles said there was no evidence that General Salinas Altés had acted inappropriately in meeting with Mr. González Quirarte, who he said had posed as a young businessman with information about the Carrillo Fuentes mob. „He spoke about Amado Carrillo," General Ángeles said. „He gave information about the drug organization internationally. It was only discovered later that this was Eduardo Gonzalez Quirarte." General Ángeles also strongly denied a claim made by General Gutiérrez Rebollo during his trial that Mr. González Quirarte had two other meetings and that he paid a $6 million down payment on a promised gratuity of $60 million to Government officials.

„You can be fully certain that had he done that, he would have been arrested because that is bribery," General Angeles said. Referring to General Gutiérrez Rebollo, he added, „That is characteristic of his accusations - the lies, the infamy, the slander." One current and one former American official said there was credible information that Mr. González Quirarte had been to see military officials more than once, and they added that a recent assessment of General Gutiérrez Rebollo's testimony concluded that much of it was true.«

2002: AN UNDOCUMENTED BOY RIDES FROM HONDURAS

Don Bartletti, *Los Angeles Times*

The photo jury of 2002 selected the following three finalists: Bradley Clift of the *Hartford Courant*, Don Bartletti of the *Los Angeles Times* and Matt Black, a freelancer, also working for the *L.A. Times*. Black's pictures, in the eyes of the jurors, „documented a little known legacy of the black sharecroppers who migrated from the Depression-era Dust Bowl to the San Joaquin Valley of California ... Black's photographs present their lives in a striking documentary style that borders on art." Don Bartletti had told „the story of a young boy who traveled for 57 days, more than 8,400 miles, from Honduras in search of his immigrant mother somewhere in the U.S.A .... No collection of photos could better illustrate the ambitions of feature photography." Bradley Clift's entry, called „Heroin Town", also had told a big story. „As America struggles with the reemerging problem of domestic heroin abuse," the jury stated, „Bradley Clift's remarkable photographs document the struggle of middle-class victims of a town in denial. His telling photographs show heroin addiction in a way words can't describe and probe the motives of city fathers' attempts to deny accountability."

The Pulitzer Prize went to Don Bartletti of the *Los Angeles Times* „for this memorab-le portrayal of how undocumented Central American youths, often facing deadly danger, travel north to the United States." The photographer had told a personal story of a boy, but also the story of thousands or tens of thousands of Central Americans trying to make new lives it the U.S. Bartletti walked with him, rode on the tops of rail cars through Central American jungles, snuck past Mexican borders guards and waded rivers. As they moved North, Bartletti produced photographs that are artistic and technically perfect in spite of difficult, uncontrolled and often overtly dangerous circumstances. He and writer Sonia Nazario, both authors of the Pulitzer Prize-winning article series „El Norte Bound", took remarkable risks to photograph and report the story.

Don Bartletti, born on December 29, 1947, in Philadelphia, Pa., is a graduate of Palomar College in San Marcos, California. He worked as a photographer at the California newspapers *Vista Press*, *Oceanside Blade-Tribune* and *San Diego Union* before he joined the *Los Angeles Times* in 1992. There he specialized on photo stories of immigrant children, bringing to him the 2003 Pulitzer Prize. His following key photo also earned him the UNICEF Photo of the Year Award:

DANGEROUS JOURNEY FROM HONDURAS TO THE U.S.

Photo shows Enrique, a teenager, who rode a freight train from Honduras through Mexico to the United States in search for his mother, Lourdes. She had left him eleven years ago, moved to the U.S. and never returned to their home in the outskirts of Tegucigalpa, Honduras. Virtually unnoticed, Enrique became one of the estimated 48,000 children who enter the United States from Central America and Mexico each year, illegally and without either of their parents. Roughly two-thirds of them will make it past the U.S. Immigration. Enrique had jumped on the freight train and noticed that there were already about 200 other migrants on board. Finally he found a chance to travel on the roof of a train car. When Enrique had to walk, the photographer walked too, nearly 100 miles. When the boy rode buses or hitchhiked with truckers, the photographer did too, about 800 miles.

Don Bartletti, September 29, 2002

2002: THE CRIMINAL JUSTICE SYSTEM OF MEXICO

Kevin Sullivan / Mary Jordan, *Washington Post*

The two reporters became the *Washington Post*'s correspondents in Mexico City in 2000, according to the newspaper's statement in a letter to the Pulitzer Prize jurors, „started examining rule of law as a key to the challenges facing the Mexican government after seven decades of authoritarian, one-party rule. They were shocked by the depth and breadth of abuses they uncovered. A painter is falsely imprisoned after police knowingly assigned him the name of another suspect. Two deaf, teenage sisters bear pregnancies resulting from rape, but no police investigation ensues. A man serves a long jail term even though police acknowledge that he was tortured to gain a confession. Kidnapers built their lucrative industry with impunity. Local 'bosses' dominate regions where their word is law. Thousands of children are locked away in 'little jails' unregulated and unexamined by the state. One conclusion common to these stories is that Mexico has two justice systems: one for the rich, another for the poor."

Sullivan and Jordan's reporting anticipated the emergence of crime and justice as the most explosive public issues in Mexico, their stories were widely followed in the Mexican press and by officials, and had impact. The Pulitzer Prize jurors of the International Reporting award category also were impressed by the two journalists and stated in their report of March 7, 2003: „Mary Jordan and Kevin Sullivan exposed and explored the medieval criminal justice system of Mexico and brought to life horrific injustices that have destroyed lives and warped the values of a country ever more important to the U.S. economic and strategic well being. They took readers to lawless places they would have never visited, told the story of victims, and showed how those in power have not only benefited but perpetuated a system that yet shows little sign of change." For the Board it was no question that Jordan and Sullivan earned the Pulitzer recognition.

Kevin Sullivan, born on November 5, 1959, in Framingham, Ma., was raised in Brunswick, Maine, and graduated from the University of New Hampshire in 1981. After working for the *Providence Journal* in Rhode Island and the *Gloucester Daily-Times* in Massachusetts, Sullivan joined the *Washington Post* in 1991. On the *Post*, Sullivan reported on six continents from more than 75 countries, including Afghanistan, Pakistan, Iraq, Cuba, Burma, Democratic Republic of the Congo, Sierra Leone and Haiti. In 2000, Sullivan and his wife, Mary Jordan, reported from Mexico; they both earned the 2003 Pulitzer Prize for International Reporting. - Mary Jordan, born on November 10, 1960, in Cleveland, Oh., graduated from Georgetown University in 1983 and earned a master's degree from Columbia University in 1984. Jordan began her career at the *Washington Post* as an intern and moved up to higher positions at the newspaper and finally she became foreign correspondent and reported from nearly 40 countries. With her husband, Kevin Sullivan, Jordan ran the newspaper's bureaus in Tokio, London and Mexico City. In 2003 she became the co-winner of the Pulitzer Prize for International Reporting. Following are several of their award-winning articles:

February 3, 2002: »ISLA MARIA MADRE, Mexico. Lorena Avila Suarez was 8 years old when she arrived by boat on this tiny Pacific island, coming ashore to be with her father, a convicted murderer. She grew up among the other innmates and their children in one of the world's most unusual prisons, an island with a church, a bakery and a dance hall where convicts are allowed to serve sentences alongside their family members.

Then she fell in love with a convicted cocaine trafficker. So when her father was released a few years ago, and her mother and three sisters left with him, Avila Suarez stayed behind with her new husband. She still lives here in the prison where she has spent most of her life. „Sometimes I would rather be on the outside. It is always the same here," said Avila Suarez, 25, nuzzling up to her husband, Jesus Lopez, 33, who has 18 years left to serve. „But when I leave, I would like it to be with him."

Isla Maria is a Mexican government prison experiment in the Pacific Ocean 95 miles south of Mazatlan. Started at the turn of the century as a Mexican version of Alcatraz, where the worst of the worst were condemned to a life of hard labor, it has been transformed into a relative paradise for inmates who have shown a willingness to reform. Rehabilitation is a bedrock principle of the Mexican judicial system, so much so that neither the death penalty nor life imprisonment is allowed under law. Proponents say Isla Maria is a logical extension of that idea: If prisoners are going to have to return to life in a normal community one day, why not keep them in a prison that simulates a normal community?

There are no cells or bars here. The inmates are called „colonists." They wear no uniforms and live in ordinary housing on streets that look like those in any Mexican town. While navy officers on the perimeter of the 54- square-mile island carry machine guns, the prison guards carry no guns. About 600 children of inmates live in little houses with their parents and attend public schools on pretty, palm-lined streets.

„This prison used to be almost hell. The inmates were treated savagely and humiliated," said the warden, Raul Soto Calderon. Now, he said, „If you didn't know this was a prison, you wouldn't realize it. There is nothing like this in the world." For one thing, it would be expensive to duplicate. With an annual budget of $4 million for 1,600 inmates, the government pays about three times as much to handle each prisoner here as it does for those at any other prison. Transportation costs for supplies and people are high. The warden, for instance, recently had to rent a small plane to airlift a prisoner with a severe kidney problem.

Public Security Minister Alejandro Gertz Manero, whose department runs the prison, questions the wisdom of a cash-strapped government running what he calls a „paradise." He would like all Mexican prisons to focus on making criminals pay restitution for their crimes. Some also question the wisdom of allowing children to grow up in prisson. In several other Mexican prisons, children also live alongside their parents, usually their mothers. Although this practice is lauded for keeping families intact, it is also criticized because it means children are raised in a community of criminals, where everything from freedom to food is limited.

„For some children it can be a little damaging,“ said Oliva Suarez Ilago, Avila Suarez's mother, who now lives on a peach farm in central Mexico. „They see things they shouldn't. They become aggressive and badly spoken.“ Avila Suarez, who does not have children, says other parents worry about having to wait for medicine that

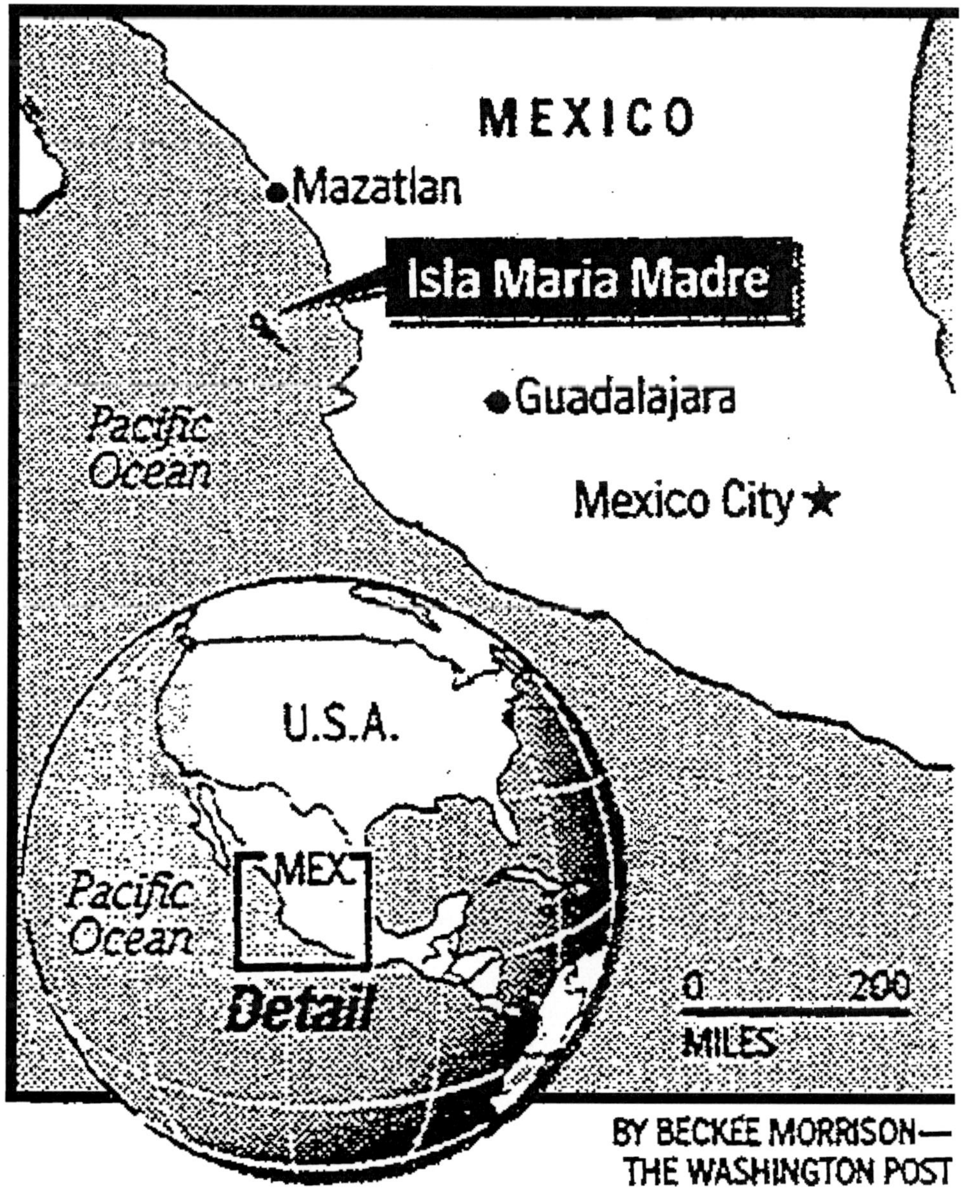

BY BECKEE MORRISON—
THE WASHINGTON POST

arrives on a weekly ship. „Some children are exposed to good people on the island who say to them, 'See where I am. Learn from me, „she said. But other children live among „people who don't want to change."

Yet for some children, living here is far safer than it is in the rough neighborhoods they left behind, and the government white-washed housing is often better, too. „I like it here because I am here with my dad," Maribel Cisneros, 13, said recently as she sat at her desk in a history class. „My dad is here because of drugs." The inmates clearly like it here. „When I got here I cried. What beauty!" said Guadalupe Rodriquez Quiroz, a convicted heroin-seller who spent four years in a crowded, violent Tijuana prison before arriving here. There, she said, guards made inmates pay for everything, including use of the bathroom.

A key element of the Isla Maria experiment is to take power away from guards, who have often turned Mexican prisons into sewers of bribery and illegal punish- ments. Here there are only 36 guards. Most of the inmates are at Isla Maria on drug convictions; the typical sentence here is 10 years for marijuana trafficking. But there are a few who committed robbery, assault or even murder. And the sight of Luis Oscar Mendez Juarez, who killed a man during a robbery in Mexico City, swinging on a hammock by the ocean can be a bit jarring. The new warden said he is still weeding out the prison population. He said some of the inmates who have been sent here do not meet the island's current standards. He is in the midst of a major expansion, nearly doubling the inmate population this year to 3,000. He is also planning to order off the island any children over the age of 12.

All inmates have the option of bringing their families, but many spouses and children do not want to forfeit their jobs and routines on the mainland. For some, it is. prohibitively expensive to get to Mazatlan, where a navy ship shuttles families to the island. Isla Maria has also been unable to completely shed its reputation for harsh treatment, so it has not been much in demand among the main prison population in Mexico. But word is getting out.

Avila Suarez and her husband share a one-bedroom home with a concrete floor and sparse furnishings a double bed, a tiny television and a radio. They eat red snapper and other fresh fish caught by inmates. Their two lime-green parrots, Lino and Gustavo, fly freely about the house.

„They have never been caged," Lopez said. Before being moved here, Lopez spent several years in a Guadalajara jail, where, he said, „you are obliged to be aggressive to stay alive." „I would be a different person if I had to stay in Guadalajara," Lopez said. There he learned that „you rob or are robbed, you defend yourself or you are beaten. Here, it is so safe you can leave your bike outside for three days and nobody would take it. Now the chatty Lopez is host of the island radio show, „Window by the Sea." He said people here „are afraid to make mistakes because they will be forced to leave the island."

Warden Soto Calderon said that in the nine months that he has been here, he has transferred 93 troublemaking inmates to mainland prisons. A few people have been punished for trying to ferment corn or rice to make moonshine or for smoking marijuana. Punishment is banishment to a camp on the far side of the island where there is no music, television or family life. In the old days, it used to be splitting rocks in the hot sun. Suarez Ilago, Avila Suarez's mother, said there were many good things about Isla Maria. Her husband, who killed a man in a street brawl, had no formal schooling when he arrived, but spent his years on the island finishinng primary school and learning to work a farm. She said he now works hard on their little peach farm no longer drinks and has had no more troubles with the law.

Despite the rehabilitative effect Isla Maria had on her husband, Suarez Ilago said, „I never forgot for a moment that I was in jail." During the decade she spent on the island with her four daughters, she would look out at the endless ocean and see it as invisible bars. „I feel bad that I brought her to the island and then left her there," she said about her one daughter still in the penal colony. „It was like leaving half of my heart there." But Avila Suarez said she does not feel like someone left behind. She has a job as a telephone operator, takes occasional vacations and lives what she considers a normal life. She said she misses the little comforts that the mainland provides, like variety of food, the sight of a mountain or a highway, the latest magazines.

But more important to her are the good times, and the lifetime of memories here. Nearly everyone on the issland came to her wedding ceremony seven years ago. She was just 18, stepping lightly into marriage and adulthood in a prison dining hall with an inmate band playing salsa.«

March 15, 2002: »DOS RIOS, Mexico. Teofilo Gonzales Cano stabbed his cousin to death with two quick jabs to the heart. They had been the best of friends, growing up together in the same mud-brick house in this tiny village in southern Mexico. But one night they drank themselves nearly blind on homemade grain alcohol. An argument about nothing got out of hand, and soon Vicente Gonzalez Santiago lay dead in the dirt.

Teofilo ran. They found him at dawn, sitting in a forest clutching his empty bottle. The local farmer who served as village constable, another cousin of Teofilo's, bound his hands behind his back and brought him in.

The whole village was waiting, more than 300 people. They forced Teofilo to lie facedown next to Vicente's corpse. They shouted at him, called him a murderer. His mother sat in the dirt next to her son, pleading for mercy. The nearest police were more than two hours' drive away and there was no telephone in Dos Rios, hidden in rugged mountains 180 miles southwest of Mexico City. Justice in this backwater belongs to a half-dozen town elders, who stood over the two cousins in their early thirties, one dead and one accused, and debated the punishment that day in 1999. Finally they agreed. "They said the two of them should be buried, together," said Catarina Cano Santiago, Teofilo's mother.

According to Cano, other Dos Rios residents and human rights investigators, the elders enlisted villagers to carry out the sentence. Some of the men hacked a grave in the rocky soil of the village cemetery. Someone banged together a flimsy wooden coffin, and the villagers put Vicente's body in it. They hoisted the box and began a procession down a narrow cow path to the graveyard. Others dragged Teofilo by the arms. Women and children followed, marching under a hot sun past fields of dead corn. They placed Vicente's coffin in the hole, then threw Teofilo in on top, with his arms and legs tied together. He screamed and begged for his life, calling out to his mother, „Please don't let them do this to me!" She tried to help him, but her neighbors and friends held her back. The law had spoken, and no one would stand in its way.

Twenty men started throwing dirt into the hole with shovels and sticks. Teofilo, screaming, tried to climb out. His 14-year-old son, Felipe, ran to him and tried to hug him and pull him up. Someone tossed a lasso around Teofilo's neck and jerked him back into the grave, ripping him from his boy's embrace. They pulled the crying youth away from his father as the dirt piled higher and higher on top of him, until he disappeared into the ground. „When they finished," said his mother, „you could still hear him screaming under the ground."

Dos Rios is a dusty wisp of a village clinging to a mountainside in Guerrero state. It takes 12 hours to drive there from the capital, down a road that turns from pavement to dirt to a harrrowing path that drops thousands of feet on either side. Fewer than 400 people live in Dos Rios, in a cluster of soft-brick huts baked by a close, heavy sun. There is no electricity, not a light bulb in town. The only vehicle is an old Ford pickup truck. A priest comes once a year to say Mass in the crumbling Roman Catholic church. It has been months since a police patrol passed through. As Mexico seeks to modernize, setting up a formal justice system in places like this is one of its most difficult challenges.

Mexico has more than 148,000 communities with fewer than 100 residents, many of them isolated in the vast stretches of mountains and deserts that cover much of this country. By comparison, the United States, which has five times more land area, has fewer than 2,000 towns with populations under 100. More than 25 million Mexicans - a quarter of the population - live in communities of 2,500 people or fewer. Government officials say it is simply too expensive to run roads and electric lines to many of them, let alone provide police, prosecutors and judges. As a result, millions of Mexicans live in places that remain largely beyond the law. „The rule of law is absent in these towns. The level of impunity is extremely high," said Adolfo Aguilar Zinser, Mexico's new ambassador to the United Nations, who served until recently as national security adviser.

He said the administration of President Vicente Fox is working to equip rural police with satellite communication systems and create more uniform police coverage around the country. But he said many state and local government officials have resisted that idea because they still operate under the practices that dominated during seven decades of rule by the Institutional Revolutionary Party. For years, he said, the PRI encouraged powerful local bosses to handle justice in their own way. Abel Barrera, a human rights activist based in Tlapa, near Dos Rios, called justice in Mexico „unbalanced." „Things have changed in the cities, but in parts of the country like this, here in the countryside, violence is still the accepted mechanism of justice," said Barrera, who investigated the Teofilo Gonzalez Cano case. „It's still the law of the jungle."

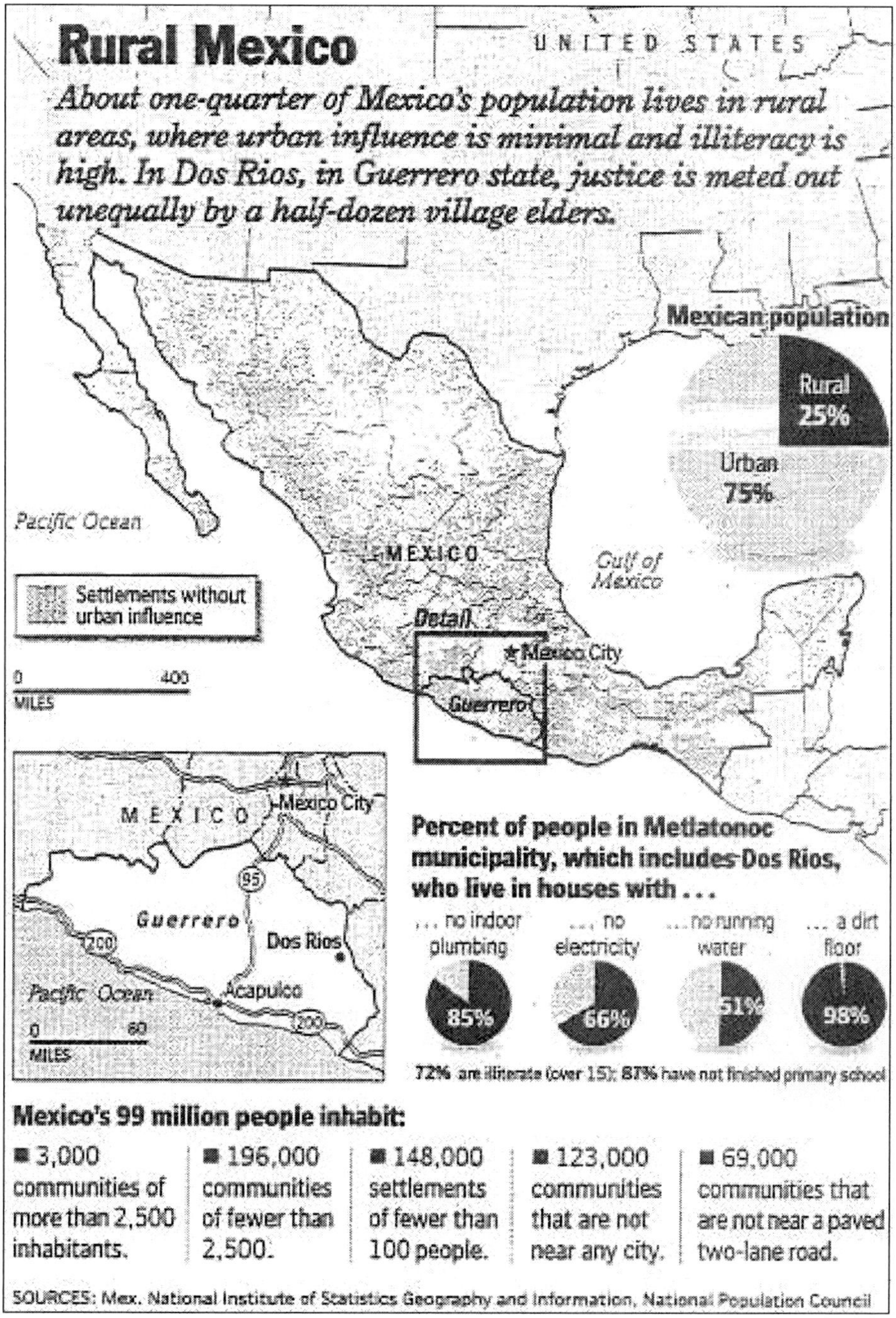
Rural Mexico
About one-quarter of Mexico's population lives in rural areas, where urban influence is minimal and illiteracy is high. In Dos Rios, in Guerrero state, justice is meted out unequally by a half-dozen village elders.
UNITED STATES
Mexican population
Rural 25%
Urban 75%
Pacific Ocean
MEXICO
Gulf of Mexico
Settlements without urban influence
0 400 MILES
Detail
Mexico City
Guerrero
MEXICO
Mexico City
95
Guerrero
200
Dos Rios
Pacific Ocean
Acapulco
200
0 60 MILES
Percent of people in Metlatonoc municipality, which includes Dos Rios, who live in houses with . . .
. . . no indoor plumbing
85%
. . . no electricity
66%
. . . no running water
51%
. . . a dirt floor
98%
72% are illiterate (over 15); 87% have not finished primary school
Mexico's 99 million people inhabit:
3,000 communities of more than 2,500 inhabitants.
196,000 communities of fewer than 2,500.
148,000 settlements of fewer than 100 people.
123,000 communities that are not near any city.
69,000 communities that are not near a paved two-lane road.
SOURCES: Mex. National Institute of Statistics Geography and Information, National Population Council

There is no formal accounting of how many people are killed in Mexico's rough rural justice every year. But human rights groups estimate that hundreds have been killed and hundreds more beaten over the years in punishments meted out beyond official scrutiny. Barrera said at least 10 people a year are killed in the region around Dos Rios in a form of local justice. „People here have not yet taken notice that Mexico is changing," Barrera said. Equal protection under the law does not exist. Sentences are given out on the judgment of a few men, who often have little education and no legal training. Their decisions are effectively beyond the oversight of federal, state and municipal governments. In some cases, their punishment is far more harsh than the formal legal system requires. For example, Mexico has no death penalty or life sentences, but the Dos Rios villagers buried Teofilo alive.

In other cases, local elders are far more lenient than judges. Town elders in Dos Rios said they would punish a rapist with „a few hours" in the town's small jail cell, plus a restitution payment of perhaps $100 to the victim's family. They recalled one case in which the rapist was forced to pay for a party that the victim's family was planning. Dos Rios is a Mixtec Indian community, governed by traditional practices. Mexico has long debated how far to go in allowing its 10 million Indians to run their own judicial systems. Critics argue that all Mexicans should be governed by the same legal system. But Dos Rios remains one of many places - Indian and non-Indian - set apart from mainstream justice in Mexico.

With each passing decade, roads and other public services creep closer to these self-ruled villages. Ten years ago, the road into Dos Rios was little more than a donkey path used largely by farmers hauling their opium poppies to market. Today, trucks hauling beer and Pepsi lumber down the roads, supplying villages with the syrupy smack of globalization. But the rule of law cannot be loaded onto a delivery truck, and the protection of police and courts still barely exists. „We can't get everywhere," said Isidro Basurto Mendoz, the official in charge of police in Metlatonoc, the municipal seat, which is three hours from Dos Rios by car and l0 on foot. „The distances are too great, and we have no communications. The problem is that when we can't get there, people take justice into their own hands."

Basurto said he has 18 police officers and one pickup truck to cover 30,000 people in 156 small communities spread over an area about the size of Montgomery County. Most are reachable only by four-wheel-drive vehicles. In the rainy season they are cut off by impasssable roads. As Basurto spoke, word filtered in that two men had been killed the night before in a village a couple of hours' drive into the mountains. A dozen of Basurto's officers grabbed their shotguns and hopped into the back of the police pickup. Despite the display of firepower, Basurto said he and his men would almost certainly not solve the crime. „I'm going to get the information, give the bodies to the families for burial, then I'll come back to do the paperwork," he said. Basurto said it was unlikely that any suspect would ever be convicted. He said his officers are not trained to gather or handle evidence. Witnesses would need to drive for hours or walk for days to give testimony before a judge. He said people have no money to make such a trip, and would fear retaliation.

Two suspects were recently arrested and charged with murder in a nearby village. Basurto turned them over to regional prosecutors, but they were free within three months. He suspects they paid a bribe to get the charges dropped. Now, he said, they are back in their village, threatening to kill those who identified them. Basurto said that case is unusual because the suspects were charged and turned over to prosecutors. „Usually by the time we find out about a case, it's already been resolved," he said. „Or we don't find out about it at all." Teofilo and Vicente grew up the way all children do here: poorly nourished, without shoes and with little knowledge of the outside world. They played among the chickens and mango trees, and they were lucky to survive. Elders here say that until a state government doctor began making regular visits a few years ago, many children died for lack of medicine and basic care.

The two boys were reared in one of the village's small red-brown cubes of mud. Together, working the fields of corn and beans, they grew into men. There are no known photos of either cousin in this village, where cameras are rare. Their families describe them as typical in every way, two sturdy farmhands. They both married and had the same kind of families: three sons and a daughter. Then things went sour for Teofilo. His wife died in childbirth. He remarried, but his second wife died of a fever about five years ago. He was raising his children alone. Vicente was building his own house, next to a shady grove of banana trees where he was raised. His uncle lived there, too. It was in his house that Vicente and Teofilo started drinking one afternoon in March 1999. They drank all night. Some here say that Vicente began making jokes about Teofilo's two dead wives. All that is known for sure is that sometime after midnight, Teofilo pulled out a small knife and stabbed Vicente twice in the chest.

By 8 a.m. Teofilo had been brought in and the two men lay side by side on the dirt floor of Vicente's house, with the six elders standing over them, discussing their fate. Vicente's brother, who declined to give his name in an effort to avoid drawing more attention to the case, said the elders made the decision to bury Teofilo alive. The town elders also wish to avoid attention. Asked about the case one recent morning, Juan Gonzalez Ruiz, the comisario, or head of the local government, switched out of Spanish and consulted with the five other elders, all men in their forties and fifties sitting outside the village hall. They debated for 20 minutes in their Indian language. According to a local schoolteacher who speaks both languages, Gonzalez wanted to tell the truth but the elders instructed him to lie. They said they did not want any more trouble. Following their orders, Gonzalez told a reporter that Vicente had died in an accident and that Teofilo had run away. The elders nodded in agreement.

The comisario is elected by village residents, and the elders are former comisarios. They said their main goal was to find negotiated solutions to crimes and disputes. They have 10 unpaid „community police" officers, whose duties include helping to keep the peace at festivals and tracking down stolen animals. Justice varies greatly by community. In some villages, stealing an animal has led to hanging. But here, Gonzalez said, the penalty for stealing a cow is a few hours in jail. He said he or the elders go to the cell and ask the thief why he stole. They try to impress on him that stealing is bad.

Education is sorely lacking. Sixty-seven children study in the village school, which goes to the sixth grade. Only a few children finish all six years. If they wanted to continue their schooling, they would have to drive three hours to Metlatonoc. No one can remember anyone ever doing that. The people are accustomed to accepting the punishments meted out by the elders. But Teofilo's case shocked many residents. Guadalupe Martinez Castillo, who said she is about 40, said she still cannot believe what her town did. „It frightens me because I think the same could happen to me, my children, my family," she said. „Everyone lives in fear because they didn't do that to an animal, they killed a person."

Cano, Teofilo's mother, said she lives with fear and regret. From her horne, she can just about see the village's hilltop cemetery, where the two cousins are buried in a grave marked by a single anonymous slab of wood jammed into the rocky ground. Sitting in the red dirt at her house, Cano said she wished she had filed some kind of commplaint about her son's death. But she is afraid to challenge the men who run Dos Rios. „I don't have the courage to confront them," she said. „If I were a man, it might be different. But people here don't know who to go to for justice." Francisco Estrada Rojas, who teaches at the elementary school, said the elders ordered Teofilo to be buried alive to „teach a big lesson." He said there had been several murders in Dos Rios in the years leading up to Teofilo's execution. He said that, in the absence of police, disputes over land, family matters, a few cattle or other minor issues often ended in bloodshed. He said few of those killers were caught, and when they were, they almost always seemed to be able to bribe police or prosecutors to let them off.

„That's why people take justice into their own hands," Estrada said. „This happened because the community had been beaten down by so many crimes without punishment. Estrada said that when the police arrived a day after the murders, they wanted to dig up the men to see for themselves what had happened, and to put the two men in separate graves. But local officials told the police that no one in town would help them. Estrada said they told the police: „You'll have to pay for the food and drink of the laborers, and no one wants to do that kind of work." Several people in the community said the police stayed only a few minutes longer. There is a widespread belief here that the officers were paid a bribe to forget about the whole thing. They didn't arrest anybody," Estrada said. „Because they would have had to arrest the whole community."«

June 2, 2002: »PACHUCA, Mexico. Alfonso Martin del Campo Dodd stood naked in the basement of a Mexico City police station, where he said cops took turns punching him and slapping him, kicking him in the groin and screaming at him. His sister and her husband had just been murdered in their sleep, stabbed a total of 64 times, and the police wanted Martin del Campo to confess. They waved a typewritten statement in his face and ordered him to sign it. He told them he didn't kill anybody and wasn't going to sign anything.

Then came the plastic bag. According to Martin del Campo, whose story was corroborated under oath by an officer who was suspended for torturing him, two cops held him by the arms while another put the bag over his head. „That's one'minute," he remembers the officer saying."Next we will do it for two minutes, then three, until you confess." They put the bag over his head again and again. „I was sure they were going to kill me," Martin del Campo said.

So naked, bleeding and gasping for breath, he scratched his name at the bottom of a confession he did not write and had never read, admitting to a crime he said he did not commit. Based on that document and no direct physical evidence - no witnesses, fingerprints, bloodstains, hairs or clothing fibers - a judge convicted him of the double murder and sentenced him to 50 years in prison. That was 10 years ago.

Martin del Campo, a U.S. citizen born in Chicago, now sits in prison in this city 40 miles north of Mexico City. His appeals are exhausted. Four different judges ruled that his allegations of torture were irrelevant. Confessions obtained by torture are not necessarily false, they ruled, repeating a conclusion, reached frequently by Mexican judges. The principle that someone charged with a crime is innocent until proven guilty does not exist in Mexico. Until 1984, federal law explicitly said a defendant was guilty until proven innocent. Although the presumption of guilt was later removed, it remains the practice defendants must still prove their innocence. Martin del Campo could not.

He is 37 now, and his hair is tinged with gray. His father moved to this small city to be near him, and he visits every day; his mother, who lives in Mexico City, comes on weekends. They said losing a daughter was devastating enough, and they want their son back. „I have been legally kidnapped here, and I want to be free," Martin del Campo said, sitting in his tiny cell. „The worst of this is losing my sister. But I am dead, too. I am dead in life."

Martin del Campo is a ghost in Mexico's closet, haunting this country as it tries to move beyond a history of authoritarian abuses. Even now, Mexico's record on torture is one of the worst in the world, according to the United Nations, Amnesty International and other groups. It is a legacy that built up over generations. For much of the 20th century, Mexico was run by the Institutional Revolutionary Party, or PRI. Under its rigid system, from the president's gilded office to thousands of rural villages run by strongarm political bosses, official power was wielded as a blunt and often brutal tool of control

In a rule-of-law state, the law is a higher authority than the arbitrary action of any individual, whether a police officer or president But throughout recent Mexican history, it was the other way around: Party bosses were above the law. Police departments, especially in the countryside, were developed largely as political security forces to support local bosses, and not as investigative law enforcement units to solve crimes.

Fists and kicks and plastic bags have long been standard practice for solving cases. The innocent and the guilty have confessed simply to stop the pain. Prosecutors have been neglected. There has been little need to professionalize them when their chief function has been to present confessions to judges. „They just look for a quick, easy solution to a crime, rather than the truth," said Emma Maza of the Miguel Agustin Pro Juarez Human Rights Center in Mexico City.

Mexican judges have also been part of the system that ruled above the law. The goal has been to keep the political bosses satisfied, resolving cases by whatever means necesssary. To keep their jobs, they have to do what they are told," said human rights lawyer Pilar Noriega. Defense lawyers also have seen little chance to buck the system. Public defenders have been even more poorly trained and less likely to serve their clients well.

The PRI era ended in December 2000 with the swearing-in of President Vicente Fox, who was elected by voters fed up with the abuses and corruption of the PRI system. Fox has promised to clean up Mexico's human rights record, but Amnesty International and even Fox's top human rights adviser, Mariclaire Acossta, ack-nowledge that torture continues. Acosta said Fox's government was trying to pass new anti-torture laws, train police and soldiers not to beat confessions out of suspects, and enact reforms to prevent judges from accepting torture-induced confession. But, she said: „Those are still common practices. Its an abomination."

Theoretically, torture is illegal in Mexico. The constitution prohibits „all incommunicado detention, intimidation or torture" and states that confessions made before anyyone other than a prosecutor or a judge are not admissible in court. In 1986, Mexico began enacting laws to punish torture, and to make torture-induced confessions inadmisssible in court.In addition, in 1987, Mexico ratified a U.N. convention against torture. Fox has invited U.N. human rights officials to set up an office in Mexico.

But Mexico is slow to change, and torture is still a common tool of the authorities. Last month, in Nuevo Leon state, a man suspected of robbing an ATM died of asphyxiation while in police custody. The state attorney general's office said it believed he died as the result of torture, and the case is under investigation. On Wednesday, the Durango state human rights commission concluded that five state police officers had tortured three murder suspects in March. Two weeks ago, the national human rights commission concluded that a suspected kidnapper who died in custody of federal police in March was beaten to death.

The challenge facing Mexico today is not only to enforce the ban on torture but to change the mind-set of a generation of police, prosecutors and judges, whose practices and beliefs were set in an earlier era. Acosta said the government faces enormous obstacles, including decades of official indifference to torture and other abuses. Just as important as preventing torture in the future, she added, is redressing wrongs of the past-including victims of torture locked away in prisons.

Sitting in his cell, next to a dirt field where other inmates played soccer, Martin del Campo, who has a round face and a soft voice, recounted the story he has told many times, about the early morning hours of May 30, 1992: He woke to the sound of his sister, Patricia, screaming his name. She and her husband, Gerardo Zamudio Aldaba, slept in another bedroom in the Mexico City apartment they shared. The two men were partners in two businesses: importing carpets, and operating buses for the city. Patricia, 33, worked as a waitress and took care of the couple's three daughters, then 6, 4 and 2, who were sleeping in the next room.

Martin del Campo ran toward the screams. He was met at his bedroom door by two men with stockings over their heads. They called him by his nickname, Chacho, then, he remembers, they beat him. They forced him downstairs and threw him into the trunk of a car. They drove for about 30 minutes, until the car came to a crashing stop. Martin del Campo heard the two men get out and run. He said he found a tire iron, smashed out a brake light and saw that he was on a highway, where the car had crashed into the concrete barrier dividing the road. He fiddled with a lock until the trunk popped open.

He flagged down a passing bus and rode it to the first tollbooth, where he ran to some police officers and told them what happened. The police drove him to the crashed car, where they found a bloody knife and started asking questions. They drove him back to his apartment, now surrounded by police cars and ambulances. A neighbor's teenage son told him that his sister and Zamudio were dead. Police drove Martin del Campo to the station, where, he said, he was taken to a basement room and surrounded by a dozen police officers. The officer in charge, later identified to him as Sotero Galvan Gutierrez, asked him to tell his story. Martin del Campo said he told them everything. They made him tell the same story at least four times. Nobody wrote anything down, he recalled, and there was no tape recorder.

Finally, he said,one officer started hitting him swore at him and said, „Tell us how you did it - how did you kill them?" Martin del Campo said he was shocked. Then all the officers started taking turns hitting and kicking him. They made him strip naked and kept hitting him, some with wet towels wrapped around their fists to leave fewer marks. Eventually, he said, Galvan came to him with a typed statement and demanded he sign. He still refused. Then came the plastic bag. And he finally signed.

„That made them very happy," he said.

The case against Martin del Campo, who had no previous criminal record, was made largely by Galvan, according to the court file. In Galvan's version, described in his investigative report, Martin del Campo was drunk and killed his sister and her husband because he was angry with his brother-in-law over a $70 car repair bill. He waited until the two were asleep, then stabbed them with kitchen knives. He smashed his own head and face, hard enough to cause deep cuts, and staged a phony kidnapping to cover up his crime, Galvan said in the report.

But hundreds of pages of court documents contain no evidence to support Galvan's version. They don't prove Martin del Campo's innocence either. But the record shows blood tests indicate he was not drunk. Lab tests showed that hairs found in the clenched fist of his sister when she died, presumably from her killer, were not Martin del Campo's. There were no witnesses, no blood-soaked clothes. There was no motive offered for why he would kill his sister.

Galvan offered as evidence a reconstruction of the events, based on his theory. Officers brought Martin del Campo back to the apartment, over his objections, and took 85 photos as they made him reach for knives in the kitchen, and forced him to pretend to stab the victims, played by two police officers posing in the bloody bed.

Reenactments are a common technique in Mexican criminal investigations and are often accepted as evidence in trials, although they are based on nothing more than a prosecutor's version of events. The trial judge, and several judges who considered Martin del Campo's appeals, cited the reenactment photos as evidence of his guilt, and an appeals judge called it „convincing“ evidence, according to court documents.

Galvan said Martin del Campo was represented by a public defender during the reenactment. But the person listed by Galvan as defender was a police department computer specialist, court documents subsequently showed. The record also shows that a public defender eventually assigned to his case never argued that the confession should be excluded because of torture. An appeals court judge called the confession „the only relevant piece of evidence“ against him.

During the trial, Martin del Campo was given the opportunity to question Galvan directly. He asked him if he and other officers had stripped him, beaten him, suffocated him with a plastic bag. The court record shows that, under oath, Galvan acknowledged that he had done it. But the judge accepted the confession anyway, noting, as the appellate judges also did, that in Mexico, confessions obtained by torture are often still considered as evidence, despite the laws that say confessions obtained by torture are inadmissible.

In April 1993, Galvan shot and killed an unarmed man while on duty. He was convicted of murder, fired from the police force and sentenced to 10 years in prison. After serving five years, he was released for „health reasons.“ In October 1994, acting as a result of Galvan's admission in the trial, the Mexico City attorney general's office punished Galvan for violating Martin del Campo's human rights. Although he had already been fired, his punishment was a three-year suspension from the police force. The notice was delivered to him in prison.

Galvan, in response to a message sent through an intermediary, said he would not comment on the case. Martin del Campo also filed a complaint seeking criminal torture charges against Galvan. But prosecutors closed the case in 2000, saying there wasn't enough evidence, despite Galvan's admission that he bad tortured Martin del Campo. Enrique Plota, a top official in the prosecutor's office, was asked why Galvan didn't face criminal prosecution. „That question has no answer,“ he said. „It's something that we are going to look into. We are very worried that there were irregularities.“

In one sign of the potential for change, the leadership of the city attorney general's office has changed hands since 2000, when a new mayor was elected. In an office that had long been suspected of covering up abuses, several former private sector human rights activists have been hired to high positions. Flota, for example, was previously a private defense lawyer who specialized in human rights cases. Flota, who started his job in January, said he and others in his office were just now beginning to confront abuses from the past. They plan a complete review of Martin del Campo's case. „There was a frequent practice of torture and irregularities by the police, we all know that,“Flota said. „In this case, we have to find out exactly what happened. We have many doubts about this case.“

Flota also said he planned to review why his predecessors never investigated a 1998 complaint filed by Martin del Campo's relatives in which they offered another version of the case. The complaint alleged that Zamudio's family arranged the murders to collect his inheritance. It also alleged that Patricia was killed to prevent her from inheriting her husband's assets, and Martin del Campo was spared so he would be blamed.

The complaint includes documents showing that Zamudio's brother and his mother ended up with all of his assets, as well as Martin del Campo's share of two small businesses in which he and Zamudio were partners.

Martin del Campo, speaking in the fluent English he picked up as a child in Chicago, said no one has ever investigated what he said was the obvious line of inquiry: „In murder cases, the first question you ask is, 'Who benefited?'" he said. „Look at me. Did I benefit?"

With no legal appeals left, Martin del Campo has thrown his fate to the Inter-American Commission on Human Rights in Washington, an arm of the Organization of American States, which is reviewing his case to determine if the Mexican judicial system violated his rights. The commission's report is due by the end of the year. If it recommends his release, Acosta said, Fox would find a way to comply.

Martin del Campo has asked the U.S. government for help, but so far it has given him only vitamins and copies of Sports illustrated, delivered every three months by an embassy official who checks on all U.S. citizens in Mexican prisons. With 40 years left in his sentence, Martin del Campo passes his days working at a little snack shop in the prison. His father, 68, works alongside him during his daily visits. His mother, 67, spends much of her time trying to find her orphaned granddaughters, who are now 16, 14 and 12. A court awarded her custody of the girls in 1995, but she said Zamudio's family has them and she does not know where they are. „This has all been the worst thing anyone could imagine," she said. „It has been hell."

Earlier last month, Martin del Campo married his longtime girlfriend, Janeth, in the prison. They had been dating at the time of the murders. At the ceremony, they stood in a bare prison room before a priest, nuzzling and giggling and pledging to spend their lives together. It was almost normal, except that the photographer was a convicted drug dealer and the honeymoon trip was a walk past the guard tower to a prison cell. „It's not how 'd like it to be," Martin del Campo said. „But time is passing. I've had a lot of years of bad news. Now I want to have children, and a life."«

June 30, 2002: »REYESHOGPAN, Mexico - These gorgeous mountain slopes in central Mexico, blooming with black pepper plants and golden cornstalks, camouflage the sorrow of the two silent sisters. Antonia and Isabel Francisco Melendez, who were born deaf, are nine months pregnant and, according to the doctors treating them, were raped.

The sisters, who cannot speak, cry and crumple, and literally fold up, when asked how they got pregnant. Their babies are due at the same time, within a week or so. Do they know the man? Did it happen in the fields on their way home from school? Isabel seemed to try to reply once, to her grandmother, by pointing to a spot high on a mountainside before tears streamed down her face and she turned away again.

Antonia is 13 years old, and Isabel 16. Perhaps if they were older, the pregnancies would have been easier to keep secret, the way rapes and beatings of women are usually dealt within Mexico. But in this little town of fewer than 500 people, a place where the church bells toll every afternoon at 5 to call everyone to say the rosary, the reality is hard to hide. The girls' tiny frames swell more each day. Their backs and legs are sore - not from playing tag with schoolmates, but because their bodies are telling them they will soon be mothers. „This is a crime and there should be an investigation," said Juana Maria Diego Victor, a community leader in this village 85 miles northeast of Puebla city. „Someone should protect these girls."

Mexico is struggling to modernize its justice system, but when it comes to punishing sexual violence against women, surprisingly little has changed in a century. In many parts of Mexico, the penalty for stealing a cow is harsher than the punishment for rape. Although the law calls for tough penalties for rape - up to 20 years in prison - only rarely is there an investigation into even the most barbaric of sexual violence. Women's groups estimate that perhaps 1 percent of rapes are ever punished. Although the two girls' medical charts say their pregnancies were the „product of rape," no police authority has looked into the case.

In recent decades, Mexico has made strides in improving women's rights and opportunities. Mexican women still have much higher illiteracy rates than men, but that is slowly changing as young girls are staying in school longer. During the 19OOs, laws that trampled women's rights were abolished, such as those that said a married woman needed her husband's permission to hold a job outside the home. But in the country that made the term „machismo" famous, where women were given the right to vote only in 1953, women's rights advocates said rape and other acts of violence against women are still not treated as serious crimes. And they said police, prosecutors and judges often show indifference or hostility toward women who claim rape - such as in the case of Yessica Yadira Diaz Cazares.

Diaz testified that three police officers raped her in 1997, when she was 16, as she was on her way home from school in the northern city of Durango. She then did a rare thing: She tried to punish her attackers. When she went to the police station with her mother, she was jeered and then jailed overnight. The police forced her, as is mandatory in Mexico, to have a physical vaginal exam by a government doctor. They made her submit to eight separate blood tests, telling her, falsely, that the tests would determine whether she had been raped. But no one ever told her what the lab results were. When the teenager did not back off, even after her family received death threats, a prosecutor told her that to identify the officers who attacked her, she must physically lay her hand on them. It was not good enough to point out her attackers. She needed to touch them, she was instructed. When she reached out and touched an officer, he taunted her and told her she was crazy.

Finally she gave up. She told her sister she was tired of seeking justice. Three months later, the young girl with big brown eyes and long, wavy hair killed herself with an overdose of prescription drugs. After her burial, the national human rights commission took up her case and helped convict two officers of rape. „They make the few women who dare to report rape give up," said Yessica's mother, Maria Eugenia Cazares, who said her daughter's rape and death shattered the family's life. After her daughter's suicide, she moved her family to Canada, where, she said, there are more enlightened laws to protect women. „In 90 percent of the cases of rape, the Mexican police blame the women," she said in an interview. „In the few cases where they know the man is guilty, they let him 'fix' it with money."

She said she believes that a „machismo culture," instilled through what is learned in the home, school and church, has allowed many men to „believe they are superior and dominant, and that women are an object." She said that mind-set has contributed to making many men - including policemen, prosecutors, judges and others in posiitions of authority - believe that sexual violence against women is no big deal. „The thinking is 'she's a woman, so she deserved it,' or 'he's a man, so what do you expect?" said Cazares.

Rape in Mexico is prosecuted at the state level, and state laws vary. A review of criminal laws in all 31 Mexican states showed that many states require that if a 12-year-old girl wants to accuse an adult man of statutory rape, she must first prove she is „chaste and pure." Nineteen of the states require that statutory rape charges be dropped if the rapist agrees to marry his victim. „What message is this? That the crime is not serious," said Elena Azaola, author of „The Crime of Beeing a Woman," a book about how the Mexican justice system discriminates against women.

In order for a woman to file a criminal complaint alleging rape, she must submit to a medical exam by a doctor assigned by the prosecutor's office. Patricia Duarte, president of the Mexican Association Against Violence Against Women, said these exams, routinely conducted in the prosecutor's office, are often carried out with little sensitivity or privacy. The exams, she said, are an obstacle to reporting rape that contributes to „impunity of rapists" in Mexico. Whatever problems women face in the cities and towns, they are compounded in small villages where old customs are still the only true law. Ten million Mexicans are indigenous, as are most of the people in these highlands of the Sierra Madre. In Mexico's march toward modernity, there is great tension here between protecting women from violence and honoring indigenous customs.

In many of the thousands of indigenous communities, by longstanding custom, women are essentially servants of their fathers, brothers and husbands. In many villages around Reyeshogpan, a woman is forbidden to go out after dusk without her husband or her husband's permission. After 7 p.m., streets in village after village are populated by men only, many of them drunk. Alcoholism is another problem that contributes to violence against women. Town elders who act as judges in local criminal matters are invariably men. In one village in Guerrero state, elders were recently asked how they punish rape. The six men looked confused, as if they did not know what the term meant. When it was explained to them, they all laughed and said it sounded more like a courting ritual than a crime. When they stopped laughing, they said a rapist would probably get a few hours in the local jail, or he might have to pay the victim's family a $10 or $20 fine, but that all would be forgotten if he and the victim got married.

In the case of a cow thief, they said, the robber would be jailed. And unlike the rapist, a cow thief would be brought before the elders for a lecture about the severity of the crime. In the southern state of Oaxaca last summer, the one-year-old government-funded Oaxacan Women's Institute persuaded the legislature to pass heavy criminal penalties against a practice known as „rapto." Laws in most Mexican states define rapto as a case where a man kidnaps a woman not for ransom, but with the intent of marrying her or to satisfy his „erotic sexual desire." The new law championed by the women's group established penalties of at least 10 years in prison. But in March, the state legislature reversed itself and again made the practice a minor infraction. A key legislator - a man - argued for the reduction, calling the practice harmless and „romantic."

Human rights groups disagree. They say it is not charming for a man to spot a woman he fancies sitting in a park, pick her up and carry her away to have sex with her. Yet to this day, that is still how some women meet their husbands. The attorney general's office said there have been 137 criminal complaints of rapto in the state of Puebla since January 2000. Complete statistics are imposssible to find, because most cases are settled between the two fumilies involved and never reported. Because rapto implies that the girl was taken away for sex, her parents want to avoid the shame associated with making a public complaint to police.

In some cases, the girls voluntarily go with the man as a way to elope to avoid wedding expenses. But Gabriela Gutierrez Klerilan, a lawyer with the Oaxacan Women's Instiitute, said in many cases the women are taken against their will. Gutierrez said it is hard to ask girls to complain about rapto, to buck a system that has changed litttle since their great-grandmothers' time. If they do, she said, the family or the community often „treats them as outcasts." The regional maternity hospital in Za-capoaxtla caters to women and children from scores of villages in the highlands here in the northeast corner of Puebla state. White-coated doctors and nurses scurry about among the crying children, past brightly painted walls decorated with basic information about nutrition, breast-feeding and sanitation.

About 220 babies are born there each month, many of them to mothers who are children themselves. Hospital officials said babies are born there frequently to girls as young as 12, many of whom do not understand that intercourse caused their pregnancy. The pregnancy of a child that age implies a crime: In Puebla, it is illegal to have sex with a person younger than 18. But only rarely are rape charges filed in these cases. Teresa Arrieta Martinez, 13, petite and hugely pregnant, cringed as a nurse took a blood sample as part of her prenatal care. Her boyfriend, Eliazar Hernandez Martinez, a 20-year-old grocery store manager, stood outside in the waiting room.

About seven months ago, when Teresa was 12, Hernandez had sex with her and she became pregnant. Because of her age, the law says that Hernandez committed statutory rape. But it was not the police who came after him; it was Teresa's mother, Maria Juana Martinez. „He could go to jail. If he doesn't carry through on his promise to marry her, I'll have to report him," she said. „I'll sue him if he fails her." In most states marriage is a legal remedy for statutory rape. Women's groups say if the penalties were harsher, statutory rape cases would not be so common. As it is now, a man can agree to a wedding to avoid going to jail, and then abandon the woman. Social workers say many unhappy, abusive marriages begin with statutory rape.

Any day, Antonia and Isabel., the two deaf sisters, are due to deliver their babies at the same hospital. Antonia, the 13-year-old, lives with her mother in a small house near the main road of Reyeshogpan, a tiny village with little more than a church, basketball court and general store. Antonia is carrying her baby in the breech position, so her doctors expect a difficult delivery.

Isabel, 16, lives with her 95-year-old grandfather in a small wooden house nearby. It is at the bottom of a ravine lined with cornstalks, a challenging 50-minute climb straight down from where her mother, stepfather and sister live. No one seems quite sure how Isabel will be able to make the climb up to get to the hospital once she is in labor. Isabel passes her days sitting on a log at her front door, staring off into the cornfields or embroidering. She wears her silky brown hair neatly tied up, her white dress and apron are impeccably clean and she folds her hands nervously over her huge belly.

The girls' mother, Ventura Melendez, 35, communicates with them using rudimentary sign language and drawings. When she asked Isabel if she had any pain, the

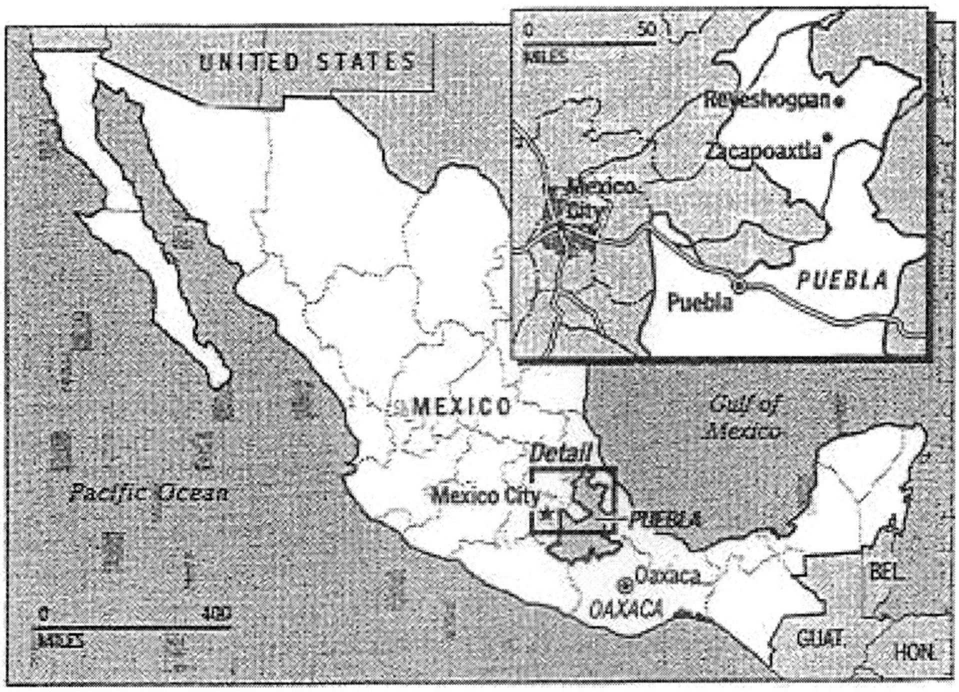

girl put her arm against her lower back. She nodded when asked if she is scared about being such a young mother. Melendez said she prefers not to dwell on how they got pregnant. „What happened to them happens to a lot of girls," she said. „We don't want justice. We don't want trouble." But Diego Victor, the neighbor who has known the girls since they were born, said she is angry that what happened to the girls will never be punished. „They deserve better," she said.«

July 6, 2002: »MEXICO CITY - Giovanni Hurtado Aviles was hurrying to his engineering class when he realized he didn't have the two pesos - about 20 cents - for the subway. When be tried to use some body's elses pass to get on, he was caught and hauled to jail. „I made a mistake. I am really sorry. I won't do it again," Hurtado, 20, said he told the guard who nabbed him that January morning. But the Mexican justice system which often fails to punish serious criminals, zealously prosecutes the most minor of offenders. So the college student with no criminal record was denied bail and forced to mop floors for 12 hours a day for two months while he awaited trial. „Our justice system is not just," said the Rev. Jose Luis Tellez, a Roman Catholic priest and lawyer who tries to get such prisoners freed. "The real criminals are at home in their houses while these people are in jail."

Mexico's courts and jails are clogged with people like Hurtado, people who stole a bicycle, bread, shampoo, subway fare. More than half of the 22,000 prisoners in Mexico City's jails are there for offenses so slight that human rights advocates - and increasingly, city officials - say they never should have been jailed in the first place. According to recent testimony to the Mexican Congress by top law enforcement officials, well over 90 percent of serious crime goes unpunished. In a nation with one of the world's highest kidnapping rates, much drug-related bloodshed and a chilling level or violence on the streets of the capital, the prisons are choked with people who stole to eat. Tellez said a man who stole a Gansito, similar to a Twinkie, was released in November after spending three years in jail. He said another man who stole bread worth about $4 was sentenced to six years.

Public opinion polls show that Mexicans are fed up with their justice system. One of the key complaints is that it thunders down so hard on petty criminals. At every turn, the system is consumed with the smallest crimes: Poorly trained police. focus on the easiest crimes to solve; corrupt officers, often paid to look the other way when there is more serious crime, have no such incentive to let small-time offenders go. Legislators under political pressure to combat rising crime rates have set tough minimum sentences for the smallest of robberies. The result is that in many cases, as with Hurtado, the subway cheater, judges are forced by the law to hand down sentences they believe are unfair. Judges in Mexico have almost no discretionary authority. The Mexican legal system, based in 19th century Napoleonic Code, deliberately limits the role of judges. The theory is that legislators should craft penalties and judges should simply impose them.

The judge in Hurtado's case wanted to be lenient but said the law would not let him. He convicted Hurtado of „using a false document" - showing a subway worker's pass that Hurtado said he had found on the floor. That is the equivalent of a felony, a crime considered too grave to warrant bail, punishable by a minimum of four years in prison. Behind bars, Hurtado vomited from nervousness. He fell far behind on his class work and lost wages from an after-school job. „What my son did wasn't a crime; it was a mistake," said his mother, Laura Aviles Rodriguez. „Who would call this justice?" Behind the high brick walls of a Mexico City development called Poinsettia, amid gardens of purple bougainvillea and expensive SUVs parked in a row on the cobblestones,Oscar Espinosa Villareal lives the life of an accused embezzler with means.

Espinosa, Mexico City's mayor from 1994 to 1997, is accused of illegaly diverting $45 million that was never accounted for during his term. When a judge issued a warrant for his arrest in August 2000, he did what many wealthy Mexicans do in the same situation: He bought a plane ticket and fled the country. His top aide is still a fugitive. Espinosa flew to Canada and then Nicaragua, where he was caught. He maintains he has done nothing illegal and that he is the victim of a revenge campaign by his political enemies. He fought extradition on grounds that the case against him amounted to political persecution, but the Nicaraguans sent him home.

Espinosa is part of the well-connected old guard of the Institutional Revoluutionary Party, or PRI, which ran Mexico from 1929 to 2000. He served as campaign finance manager for his old friend, Ernesto Zedillo, who became president and rewarded Espinosa with the mayor's job, a presidentially appointed position until 1997. When Espinosa's term expired, Zedillo appointed him to serve as national tourism minister from 1997 to 2000. When Espinosa arrived back in Mexico on a federal police jet from Nicaragua, his wealth and connections kicked in. He hired one of Mexico's leading lawyers, who persuaded a federal judge to issue an order forbidding his arrest and detention, allowing him to remain free pending trial. Espinosa was ordered to post bail of about $400,000. He paid about $12,000 in cash, put up his house to cover the balance, and then went home.

Based on Mexico's long history of elites beating criminal charges, few here believe Espinosa will ever be convicted. It is a story Mexicans know well. Accused of stealing $45 million, Espinosa sleeps in his own bed at night, while Hurtado, who sneaked a 2o-cent subway ride, was forced to sleep on a jailhouse cot for months awaiting trial. Francisco Garduno, the former head of prisons for Mexico City, has given speeches to inmates citing Espinosa as an example of how those accused of major crimes get better treatment than minor offenders, who are invariably poor. „The road to justice opens up wide for them," Garduno said. „But for the poor it is very narrow."

Far from Espinosa's hillside retreat, in a rough neighborhood in the southeast side of the city, Tellez, the Catholic priest, runs a church program to get minor offenders out of jail. Frustrated with the government's approach to petty criminals, the church has quietly begun its own effort to help. The church pays fines and bailfor thousands of nonviolent petty criminals, most of them first offenders. People convicted of a crime are often allowed to choose jail time or a fine. Tellez said he has handled cases of many who could have avoided jail or served less time by paying a fine of as little as $25. „It absolutely is unfair that money determines freedom," Tellez said. Church lawyers last year reviewed the files of 11,000 prisoners in Mexico City jails, half the city's inmates. They concluded that at least 4,000 were minor offenders stuck behind bars because they could not afford to pay fines or bail. In all, the church has arranged for the release of 4,100 people.

A private foundation, supported by Telefonos de Mexico, or Telmex, the country's largest telephone company, has paid for the release of 20,000 minor offenders in the last five years. The foundation spokesman, Mario Cobo Trujillo, said cases have included a man, charged with injuring another man in a fight, who spent eight months in jail awaiting trial until the foundation paid his $25 bail. Cobo said another man spent more than 18 months awaiting trial for want of $100 for bail. Mexico's culture of official secrecy has kept the extent of the problem hidden. Until recently all prison records in Mexico were considered confidential, and they are still difficult to obtain. That has made it hard to document how the system has been primarily focused on the least significant crimes. But now that church lawyers and human rights workers are being given access, members of the public are getting their first glimpses at the make-up of the prison population. What they are finding has sparked a drive to substitute restitution and community service for prison time for minor offenders.

Hurtado's case was handled by Judge Eduardo Mata, a chain-smoking former prosecutor. „Ever since I got this case, I thought it was a shame," Mata said in an interview in his glass-walled courthouse office. „He just did something stupid. But there was nothing I could do."Mata, who has been a judge for nine years, said the case was a frustrating reminder of the strict limits on his authority and how minor offenders end up behind bars. „I think we need reforms that give judges more freedom", he said. „We don't have the flexibility we need." A Mexican judge's main task is to read files and issue a sentence that falls between the minimum and maximum penalty established in the criminal codes. In Mexico there are no jury trials. And in many cases, the judge never even sees the defendant, issuing his decision based on the written record. Limiting the judge's authority is meant to limit bribery and other corruption on the bench. „Our hands are tied by the law," Mata said. „We can't do anything if we think the minimum sentence is unfair."

Mata recalled a case in which a young man stole a bag of bread from a woman in a Mexico City market. Police grabbed him immediately, and they and the thief discovered that the woman had also stuffed 40,000 pesos - about $4,500 - into the bag after a trip to the bank. Mata said he wanted to sentence the man based on his intention, which he said was to steal a loaf of bread. But because the man had committed a major robbery, even unwittingly, Mata said, the law required him to sentence him to several years in prison. In Hurtado's case, Mata said the best he could do was issue the minimum sentence for his crime: four years in prison and a fine of about $950. Mata said he then used the only wiggle room the law allowed him: letting Hurtado substitute an additional fine of about $560 for his prison time. „He didn't damage society in any way," Mata said. „I didn't like the sentence I had to give him. Our laws aren't that fair."

Gaunt and defeated, Hurtado walked out of jail on March 13 after 63 days behind bars. A former employer lent him more than $1,500 to pay his fines, allowing him to avoid a prison sentence that would have kept him locked up until 2006. That makes him luckier than most. But it will take every peso of his earnings - and his mother's-for more than a year to pay back his debt. Former prison chief Garduno, who now runs the city's transportation department, is outraged at how the system treated Hurtado and how it punishes the wrong people. So he gave him a city job to help him pay off his debts. „I am trying to repair the damage done to our society," Garduno said. „I am trying to rectify something that has happened to thousands of people in Mexico."«

September 17, 2002: »MEXICO CITY - The videotapes and photos arrived every few days. They showed a young woman, bound and scared, crying out as her kidnappers slapped her face and beat her. The pictures, the sounds of pain, tore at her uncle Gerardo like a dull razor. „When do you want us to stop?" the kidnappers asked on the tapes, and in phone calls that always came between 2 and 4 in the morning. They threatened that the next time they would send her tongue, her eye, her ears, her fingers. They wanted $5 million in ransom, and they offered specific suggestions about which of Gerardo's properties and businesses he could sell to raise it.

He didn't call the police. The kidnappers said they would kill his niece, his mother, his children if he did. From the extent of the kidnappers' information about him, he suspected that the police were involved anyway, as they are in so many cases here. Police cars parked outside his office and his mother's house seemed like a warning he didn't dare ignore. Gerardo said he considers himself brave, a steel-spined businessman, tough as his Lebanese grandparents who moved to Mexico at the turn of the last century. But the cries of his 19-year-old niece, kidnapped at the point of a machine gun as she walked to school, were more than he could take. And, he said, the words - "When do you want us to stop?" - haunted him. „They get one of your kids and they finish you," he said.

At least once a day in Mexico, someone is kidnapped for ransom, ruining lives and extracting a punishing economic cost from the victims and their companies. It has become so common here that being abducted at gunpoint and held for weeks or months has become part of the fabric of life, an accepted risk, a simple cost of doing business.

Mexican businessmen are overwhelmingly the victims, largely because Mexico has developed a culture in which ransoms are quickly paid and the police are rarely notified. According to court records and interviews with victims and security specialists, police are often involved in kidnappings, and a weak and corrupt judicial system often means they won't be caught.

This article is another in an occasional series, about how Mexico remains a nation lacking rule of law. President Vicente Fox took office almost two years ago promising to tackle the legacy of corruption that developed during seven decades of authoritarian one-party rule. But as he struggles against these deeply entrenched forces, Mexico is still a place where criminals carry but the cruelest of acts knowing they are safely beyond the law. „Criminals do risk analysis," said Jorge Septien, a private security specialist. „They know that less than 1 percent of criminals end up in jail because there's so much corruption and impunity. The government is giving the message to criminals that crime is a good business." Fifteen years ago, kidnapping barely existed here. But crime began increasing here in the 1980s and an economic crash in 1994-95 seemed to make fundamental changes in Mexico, turning kidnapping - and crime generaliy - into a growth industry. Kidnappings decreased some in the late 1990s, but analysts said they are again increasing in a society where people feel the authorities do not protect them.

Last Year, businessman Eduardo Gall conducted his own investigation into the kidnapping and murder of his 25-year-old daughter, Paola. Furious with police inaction, Gallo began a private probe that eventually nabbed the killers. He recently published a book on his travails called: „Paola: Denunciation of a Kidnapping and of a Corrupt Society." Officials at Coparmex, the country's largest and most influential employers' association, said they know of at least 360 kidnappings last year; they already know of 331 in the first eight months of this year. There are no reliable and complete statistics available. But security firms say the actual numbers are many times higher than what Coparmex has recorded, leaving Mexico and Colombia in a league of their own in Latin American kidnappings. Kidnapping has become such an industry in Mexico that no one is immune: Maids are held for $500 in ransom; a 12-year-old Tijuana girl was kidnapped this year by college students trying to raise money for school; people fake their own kidnappings to collect from their own families or businesses.

Executives are still the most lucrative target, including foreigners. The daughter of the local head of a Japanese tire manufacturer was kidnapped in 2000, and the company paid more than $1 million in ransom. The chief of a German car manufacturer's Mexican operation left the country about 18 months ago after his wife was kidnapped and a $1 million ransom was paid. A Spanish banker left this summer after he was kidnapped and released. „It's not unusual for people to take their whole families and leave the country," said the president of Coparmex, Jorge Espina Reyes. „Once someone suffers a kidnapping in their family, it affects them for the rest of their lives. They're willing to do anything, leave their country and their business, so that they won't ever have to live through that experience again." Six months after the kidnapping, Gerardo said he is still too frightened of the kidnappers to allow his last name to be used in this article. He said his niece, an architecture student, was held for more than a month in a small, dark room with the television turned up loud day and night. She told him four of her captors slept in the room with her. They never sexually assaulted her, but their presence in the flickering light of the TV everynight , added to her terror.

Another kidnapping victim, a teenage boy, was being held in the same house. The niece told Gerardo that she never saw him, but she could hear him, listening through the wall as the kidnappers stripped him and beat him until he cried, and videotaped it all for his parents. As they hit the boy, over and over, she heard them say the words her own family hail come to dread: „When do you want us to stop?" As the patriarch of an extended family, and as the clear target of the kidnappers' demands, it fell to Gerardo to negotiate. He said he eventually paid hundreds of thouusands of dollars in ransom, but he would not say exactly how much. He got his niece back in March, but the ordeal didn't end. He said the kidnappers kept calling him, threatening to kill his children if he made trouble for them, if he called the police. Once, he said, they called to let him know they were sitting outside his mother's house. They described the place to him, told him what his mother was doing just then. And they said they were going to kill her. You go crazy," Gerardo said. He said he bought a gun.

Then a few weeks ago he sold his Mercedes, put his house on the market and moved his family permanently to Boca Raton, Fla, unable to endure the insecurity he felt constantly in the country where he was born. His niece is now studying architecture in Florida and his children are in school there. „I can't live here anymore," said Gerardo, 45, a fit and trim marathon runner, as he sat among boxes in his Mexico City office on the day before he left. „We have to change our lives. I have a 5-year-old boy. I can't risk. him." He said the businesses he built over a lifetime, manufacturing and selling auto parts and selling real estate, will surely go bankrupt and his 35 employees will lose their jobs. He said he would try to manage his businesses from Florida and with discreet return trips every few months. But he said they require more hands-on management than that, and that the kidnappers have forced him into ruin. He said he spent $150,000 to hire two private investigators to look into his case, and they told him his niece was abducted by a well-organized gang led by state and local police officers. They were too well-connected and too organized to fight, he concluded. „You can buy anyone with the money they are making," he said.

They have taunted him on the phone, telling him, „You will never catch us, we know too much," he recalled. And they did know a lot. „They taped our phone conversations about two or three months before the kidnapping and replayed them for us. They-checked our property records, they knew about our cars and houses. They did an inventory. They said, „Tell your mother to sell her condo to pay the ransom.'" Gerardo said he was angry, that he would like to kill someone. But he said the forces against him were too strong to fight, so his only option was to run. He has never reported the case to the police. „You work, you study, you get married, have kids, a life, stability," he said. „I was going to stay here always. But now we and our money are leaving Mexico."

Pedro Fletes Renteria, director of a private school in Mexico City, was kidnapped as he arrived for work at 6 a.m. on March 1, 2001. Masked men with pistols forced him into a car and put him facedown on the floor with a gun to his neck. He was held for 59 days. Fletes said he was kept for most of that time in a five-foot-square closet, with a bucket to use as a toilet. He was allowed to bathe every three days. Outside, he could hear children playing, families having parties - the sounds of Mexico City's warm springtime. Fletes, 54, said the kidnappers knew everything about him, including his children's names and his schedule. He said the only thing they didn't seem to understand was his business: Their $5 million ransom demand was more than the school's total worth.

„I felt every emotion you can imagine, in cycles: anguish, desperation, thinking badly of my family, thinking I would die, crying," said Fletes, whose face is soft and round beneath asalt-and-pepper beard. „It was so inhumane."

After almost two months, after his family paid a ransom he won't disclose, the kidnappers drove him to a busy downtown intersection and let him out. They gave him back the suit he was wearing on the day he was taken. It had been cleaned and pressed. Fletes said the kidnapping nearly broke him financially. He said his wife, five daughters and a son spent thousands of dollars for bodyguards and armored cars after he was kidnapped. After he was released, he hired a team of bodyguards to protect him for several months. „But I got rid of all that," he said, tapping the desk with his hands, which flutter around him constantly like nervous birds. „It was too expensive, and I didn't want to live that way." The costs to his school which runs from elementary grades through high school continue. Since his kidnapping, he has paid more than $18,000 to install a closed-circuit television security system and motionsensing alarms. He pays more than $5,500 a month for security measures he never took before, including new guards at the doors and new identification cards and seecurity procedures for his 1,200 students. He said he'd rather spend that money for a new language laboratory, paint for the school's cracked yellow walls and upgrades to the school's 40 outdated computers. „If we didn't have to spend so much for security now," he said, „we could make everything here better."

Companies in Mexico pay dearly to protect themselves because the government doesn't. Analysts said big companies typically spend between 5 percent and 15 percent of their annual budgets on security - sometimes $2 million or more. In a country where more than 54 million people - more than half the population - live on less than $4.50 a day, business leaders said their heavy spending on security represents lost jobs and lost opportunities. „Instead of investing in security, they could be investing in new factories or new lines of products," said Javier Prieto de la Fuente, president of Concamin, Mexico's Industrial Chamber of Commerce. „When you are dealing with global markets, even 1 percent is important. We are losing our competitive edge because of these concerns."

While many parts of Mexico are relatively safe from the kidnapping epidemic, problems are severe in Mexico City, Guadalajara, Puebla and U.S. border areas where much of the nation's manufacturing is located. Many Japanese executives at factories near the border are forbidden by their companies to drive in private cars. Buses with armed guards carry Japanese executives between their homes in the San Diego suburbs and their factories around Tijuana. Foreign companies pay premiums - the equivalent of hazard pay - to lure top executives to Mexico. Foreign and Mexican firms often must buy kidnapping insurance for their top corporate officers. The problem is severe enough that a company here has begun offering surgical implants of devices that could help locate people using satellite technology, although as of recently it had no takers. Few, if any, companies have left the country strictly over security concerns, as Mexico is simply too big and attractive a market to abandon. Foreign direct investment continues to grow, but many here say kidnappings and other crimes are a key reason Mexico's economy has not grown faster.

Kidnapping has become so common that Fox mentioned it prominently in his annual state of the nation address this month. Crime analysts say the federal government's new elite anti-kidnapping unit is an important step. But even Fox conceded that wiping out the „scourge“ of insecurity was still „an outstanding debt to our citizens.“ Fletes said he never wanted the police involved in his case. „We don't trust the police, and we want to protect our families,“ he said. „I know of two other kidnapping cases right now, and neither of them has been reported.“ But he said that at the moment he was kidnapped, one of the kidnappers fired shots, perhaps as a warning. That caused so much commotion that police came, and an investigation was started. Fletes said the Federal Preventative Police was the lead agency in the investigation. But Fletes said his brother negotiated directly with the kidnappers, without any police involvement, and eventually paid the ransom himself. Once Fletes was returned, the search for the kidnappers was turned over to the Mexico City attorney general's office, which has a special unit dedicated to kidnapping investigations. „I can say they are very friendly, but not very effective,“ Fletes said. „I think their attitude is that once the victim is returned, the case is solved.“

His own private investigators turned up evidence that top Mexico City police officers might have been involved in the case. Fletes's attorney, Jose Antonio Ortega, a prominent lawyer who heads the security committee of Coparmex, said telephone records show that the cell phone used by the kidnappers was also used to make calls to the home of a top official from the department's anti-kidnapping unit. Jesus Jimenez Granados, head of the attorney general's anti-kidnapping unit, said he investigated the claims and found no evidence that the police had been involved. But he said the officers suspected of involvement had been transferred to another unit anyway. He said that on a matter as delicate as kidnapping investigations, police and investigators had to be totally beyond suspicion. „People have to trust us,“ said Jimenez, a stocky bull of a man in a suit made for someone taller. „We think we're giving citizens results and earning their trust.“

Jimenez said his office received 149 complaints of kidnappings last year and solved 70 percent of them. Jimenez also said police had a suspect in custody who may have been involved in Fletes's kidnapping. „It's about to be resolved completely,“ he said. But Fletes remained skeptical, and scared. Sitting in his office, just a few feet from the street where he was kidnapped, Fletes said the police officers he suspects were involved in his kidnapping could „come back at any time.“ Fletes said Fox's election two years ago was a positive sign, and that some things are beginning to change. But he said Mexico is still a land too often governed more by force and intimidation than by laws. He said his nephew had been „express kidnapped“ this month by abductors who held him for a few hours and forced him to withdraw money with his ATM card - a common crime in Mexico City that is almost never solved. „We've had a political transition,“ Fletes said. „But Mexico still needs a transition of justice.“«

November 4, 2002: »MERIDA" Mexico - The walls are 15 feet high and topped with jagged glass and barbed wire, ugly keepers of ugly secrets. For years they stood sentry over abuses of scores of children in state care, who were forced to eat pig food, beaten, even tied to trees for days at a time. Beto, a homeless boy, was 10 years old when the police brought him here after they caught him stealing two shiny gold buttons from a store bin. He thought he might be going somewhere better than the street. Instead, Betulio Chi Tzec spent the next five years behind the walls of the Yucatan state juvenile correctional facility, a little boy locked in a dormitory room with two teenagers convicted of rape. Beto, as well as a teacher and a physician who worked there, said the woman who ran the youth detention home regularly beat the 50 children in her care. They said she kicked the children in the genitals, slapped them and sheared off their hair in fits of rage. Beto said she told the children, „You are all going to rot here," and he came to believe she was right.

According to youths who have spent time inside the system, as well as parents, government officials and many experts here, children are frequently mistreated, abused and forgotten in Mexico's „little jails," as the youth lockups are known. 0fficially called „schools for young offenders," many of these places are nothing more than cold prisons where classroom teaching is rare. There are 4,200 children living in dozens of detention centers across Mexico. Conditions vary, and some centers are well run. But many operate the same way they did a century ago: out of public view and with little or no internal regulation or outside supervision. Parents are often barred from entering, though they are encouraged to slip money to guards to prevent harsher treatment of their children. The Mexican government, battered by crime, has displayed little concern or tolerance for children who break the law. That indifference, as well as the secrecy that shrouds the detention centers, has perpetuated shoddy and often cruel practices, according to those with firsthand experience in the troubled system. „These institutions are horrible," said Elena Azaola, a criminal justice specialist who has conducted studies of the juvenile centers. „The children live in misery."

Mexico relies on an informal and largely unregulated system of juvenile justice that has existed for decades. Children who break the law often have no access to an attorney. Administrative judges who handle juvenile cases set sentences, but there is often no judicial follow-up once children are sent to detention homes. The real power is held by the directors of the centers. They effectively decide how long a child will be held and under what conditions. The directors are appointed by governors or other top officials in each of Mexico's 31 states. „For children there is no system of justice. They are the victims of arbitrary decisions by those in charge," said Guillermo Alonso Angulo, a consultant for UNICEF in Yucatan state.

A system that abuses children and fails to punish the abusers is a legacy of the one-party rule that dominated Mexico for most of the 20th century. From 1929 until 2000, Mexico's presidents, and most of its governors, mayors, police and local officials -including those in charge of youth programs - belonged to the Institutional Revolutionary Party. During that era, government jobs were dispensed more out of political loyalty than expertise. People running programs intended to benefit society often did little other than steal agency funds. Because of the party's hammerlock on power, they rarely had to answer to the public.

President Vicente Fox, who took office in 2000, has promised to create a new day for justice in Mexico. He has vowed that the law, not the personal or political whims of officials, will reign. Now, the children locked away in detention centers are trying to hold him to his word. Nearly every week recently, youths have climbed onto the roofs of their detention homes, setting fires and starting small riots to draw attention to their living conditions. When reporters arrive, the children yell over the wall that they have been beaten with brooms and belts. On Oct. 2, in the western state of Nayarit, 37 children took over a detention center, throwing stones and screaming that they were „tired of the beatings." The day before, in the northern state of Sonora, 40 children brawled with their keepers, complaining about brutality. Similar uprisings have occurred in six other states and Mexico City this year, as angry children demand better treatment in their little jails.

Mexico is struggling to transform itself into a nation where people feel protected - not menaced - by the law. Yet old ways prevail, as seen in the horrors of the Yucatan detention center. The director, Maria del Rodo Martel Lopez, was a physician who had superb local political connections. Some who knew her recalled that she was tall, thin, blond and impeccably dressed. Dozens of children under her care have now come forward to say she brutalized them. According to the findings of an investigation by the National Human Rights Commission, which issued a report in April, Martel presided for four years over an institution with „cruel and degrading treatment" of children, which included „denigrating punishments, humiliations, beatings and mistreat-ment." Allegations of cruelty by Martel were reported to the governor's office as early as 1999. But the powerful, longtime governor who appointed her, Victor Cervera Pacheco, did nothing. Many here attribute his inaction to Martel's social and political standing; she is the widow of a former powerful party boss in the state.

A Merida radio station aired a report in 1999 about the allegations against Martel, but the reporter, Jose Luis Preciado, said he was pressured by state officials to drop the matter. „Sometimes she would tell boys to pull down their pants and she would kick them in their private parts until they cried," Beto said of Martel, echoing testimony given to human rights investigators by people who worked at the center. Psychologists and teachers, in interviews and in their statements to investigators and police, said that Martel beat children until they bled. Several recalled how she forced one homosexual boy to dress like a girl. Many of Martel's accusers cited the case of a teenage orphan, Catalina Gijon Granados. She was held in the center for four years, often in windowless isolation, even though she had committed no crime. Dulce Maria Alavez Soberanes, who taught crafts at the detention center, called Martel's treatment of Catalina „unforgivable." She said that Catalina was beautiful, sweet and relatively well-adjusted until she landed on Martel's bad side. After months of mistreatment, Alavez said Catalina appeared lost and disoriented and became a chronic bedwetter, a skinny girl with sickly yellow hollow eyes. „She was locked up for almost two months in a room without a window, given just one meal a day," Alavez said. „When she was let out, it was as if she was drugged."

For two years, Yucatan human rights lawyers complained without success to the governor and other officials. Then they called the human rights commission in Mexico City. On an August day in 2001, the commission arrived at the center to investigate. That day Martel quit her job and walked out the door. A criminal investigation was later opened, but no charges have been filed. Martel's answer to the allegations against her is unknown. Efforts to locate her were unsuccessful. Several months ago, neighbors said they saw a moving van pull up to her house, and they haven't seen her since. 0fficials at the state attorney general's office said they did·not know where she was, and that she was being sought for questioning. Rights workers here in Merida said the government allowed Martel to slip away to avoid the embarrassment of a messy trial with potentially nasty political implications. Mexico has a long history of looking the other way at official misconduct. „They would rather bury this part," said Angulo, the UNICEF consultant. „I think there should be a criminal trial. But I don't think there ever will be."

When Isis Maria Velazquez was 13, she recalled, her mother became exasperated with her misbehavior and turned her over to state care. She spent the next two years in Martel's facility. The dates of her mistreatment remain etched in her memory. On July 27, 1999, she entered the center, and Martel chopped off most of her long, shiny brown hair, leaving it a short-cropped ugly nest. On May 9, 2000, she said, Martel forced her into a muddy, filthy pen where she spent the next three nights sleeping with 15 pigs. „She shoved pig food in my face," Isis said. „She was crazy." Her father, Lucio Jesus Velazquez, a retired night watchman, said poor people in Mexico are accustomed to being powerless. He said he paid staff at the center so he could visit Isis and tried to buy better treatment for her. He said Mexicans know they have to pay bribes to get service from the government, and that complaining often gets them nothing but more abuse. „I don't know the laws," Velazquez said. „I'm not educated in them." He said that until a human rights lawyer told him the state had no right to treat his daughter as it did, he did not realize that what happened to her might have been illegal.

Isis said she watched as other children were beaten with rubber tubes and wooden sticks. She said some boys were tied to trees,blasted with cold water from a hose and left to sleep standing up. Those allegations have been backed up by others who have complained to police and human rights officials, including Sylvia Zenteno Ruano, a physician hired by the state to make weekly visits to the center. She said she is still haunted by what she found one day; four boys tied to trees, rope wound around them from their necks to their knees. „There was urine and excrement in their clothes so they must have been there for a while," she said. Zenteno filed a complaint with the police and waited. They did not return her call for nine months. Isis has now been out of the center for several months. She works as a stripper in a bar called Atlantico. There, at night, she dances under a mirror ball that throws the glinting colors of the rainbow on zebra wallpaper. She said dancing helps her forget her hatred, which she described as the only thing she learned during her time in the state's hands. They have punished no one," Isis, now 16, said of the authorities. She now supports her father and they live in a tiny home in Merida with almost no furniture. „Some of the people who beat us are still working there. They just don't care." „I used to have dreams," she said. „But I don't anymore."

A sad failure of juvenile detention centers in Mexico is that some of the imprisoned children have committed no crime. They are held because they had no home and the governnment could find no other bed for them. The government operates few shelters for street children, ceding most of the responsibility to churches and other private groups. Thousands of children live in private shelters without any government supervision. The risks of this unregulated system were recently highlighted in Puerto VaIlarta, according to children's advocates, who said an American, Thomas White, started building a shelter for street children in 2000. He was allowed to do so with almost no scrutiny or investigation of his background or qualifications, they said. „It is easier to open a shelter for children than a restaurant," Angulo said.

Police said they are looking for White, who has been charged with offering money· and food to street children in exchange for their posing for pornographic photos and videos. He fled after a state judge issued an arrest warrant last year, and his whereabouts are unknown. Juan Diaz Gonzalez, a Mexico City legislator, said such abuse is common. He said some shelter operators in the capital have forced children into prostitution rings or illegal adoptions. Many of the shelters are so poorly run and funded that he called them „trash cans where kids are thrown away. The government is investing nothing in these children," he said. „They are throwing away thousands of lives." There are new efforts to clean up the system. Since Fox came to power, top officials have been replaced, but· many middle- and lower-level officials have not, particularly in the ranks of prosecutors and police. The government has little money to pay good salaries for difficult jobs, such as dealing with delinquents.

Under a new governor from Fox's National Action Party, Yucatan state officials said they plan to build a $lmillion detention center. They said that only children who have committed crimes would be sent there. They promised better record-keeping to ensure that children serve their sentences and no more. They promised that lawyers and human rights observers would be allowed access. But Yucatan, like most Mexican states, has plans and promises bigger than its pocketbook. So far, the officials have had little success in recruiting people willing to take such difficult jobs for as little as $50 a week. Beto had been abandoned by his parents. Living on the street was tough, he recalled, but it was nothing compared to the years of misery he suffered at the hands of the government. „I lost a lot of my life," said Beto, who is now 16 and was recently released from the facility.

Beto wonders what his life would have been like had he not been forced into the state system. His manner is withdrawn and unsmiling. He seems like a serious man in a child's body. He lives with his ailing grandmother, earning a few pesos a day pedaling a bicycle taxi in a town 45 miles from here. He doesn't like to talk about his years in Merida. Interviewed at a taco stand in a colorful town square, Beto paused for a long time after each question, sipping on a soda. He said he was not angry, but the what-ifs nagged at him. „If I hadn't taken those two buttons, the police wouldn't have picked me up," he said. „I could have found a job and a place to live. You can't do that when you're in jail."«

December 26, 2002: »NANCHITAL, Mexico - The pilgrims began arriving before dawn, with hope in their hearts and folders in their hands. They wanted jobs, pensions, favors, loans. They stood in line for hours, even when the rain came slashing down sideways, waiting outside a fancy stone house to plead their case to the man with the power: Ramon Hernandez Toledo. „Uncle Ramon," as he is known to all here, is the local union boss of Petroleos Mexicanos, or Pemex, the national oil monopoly and one of the world's largest producers of crude oil. With annual sales of nearly $50 billion, Pemex accounts for about a third of government revenue in Mexico. That makes its 117,000-member union the most powerful in the country. And as boss of the union's largest chapter, Hernandez's word is law in this town built on oil. „If he doesn't say so, we don't get it," said Alfredo Canepa Martinez, 63, a retired union worker. „If he says the wind shouldn't blow, the wind doesn't blow." In Nanchital, 400 miles east of Mexico City near the Gulf of Mexico, Hernandez directly controls the lives of more than 13,000 union workers, from chemists to truck drivers. They cannot hold their jobs, get a promotion, take a vacation or earn retirement benefits without his blessing.

His influence is everywhere. Children in this town of 28,000 grow up studying in schools and playing in parks paid for by the union and worshiping in a church built by the union. They eat food bought at union-owned grocery stores, take medicine bought at the union-owned pharmacy and, more often than not, eventually become union workers themselves. When people need a loan, they often turn not to banks but to the union. When they die, the union-owned funeral home sends them on their way. But the few people here who dare criticize Hernandez say his power is corrupt, and describe him as a sort of shadow emperor. Angry oil workers allege that he has stolen millions of dollars, draining union coffers to become wealthy and fund political campaigns. They say he benefits from Mexico's weak system of justice, under which those with the right political connections are accountable to no one. Critics say Hernandez is the true power in town hall, which the union built. Many people interviewed here said the mayor, a union member, could not have been elected without Hernandez's say-so and could not govern without his largesse. When the mayor needs a new road or school or garbage truck, he said he often asks Hernandez for the money or the land.

Alberto Olvera, a professor at the University of Veracruz who studies the union, said Hernandez's influence extends to the justice system. Oil workers angry at Hernandez said they don't bother complaining to local prosecutors and judges, because justice officials work in a building owned by the union and aren't about to rule against their landlord. „He has the power to influence the decisions of judges, so the judicial power is unable to have autonomy," Olvera said. „You are looking at a place where the past is still alive."

There are hundreds of local strongmen like Hernandez across Mexico, according to human rights groups and academics. Some are union leaders, some own large amounts of land, some are simply well-connected thugs. „What they have in common is that they are the de facto government and law for tens of thousands of people. They pass

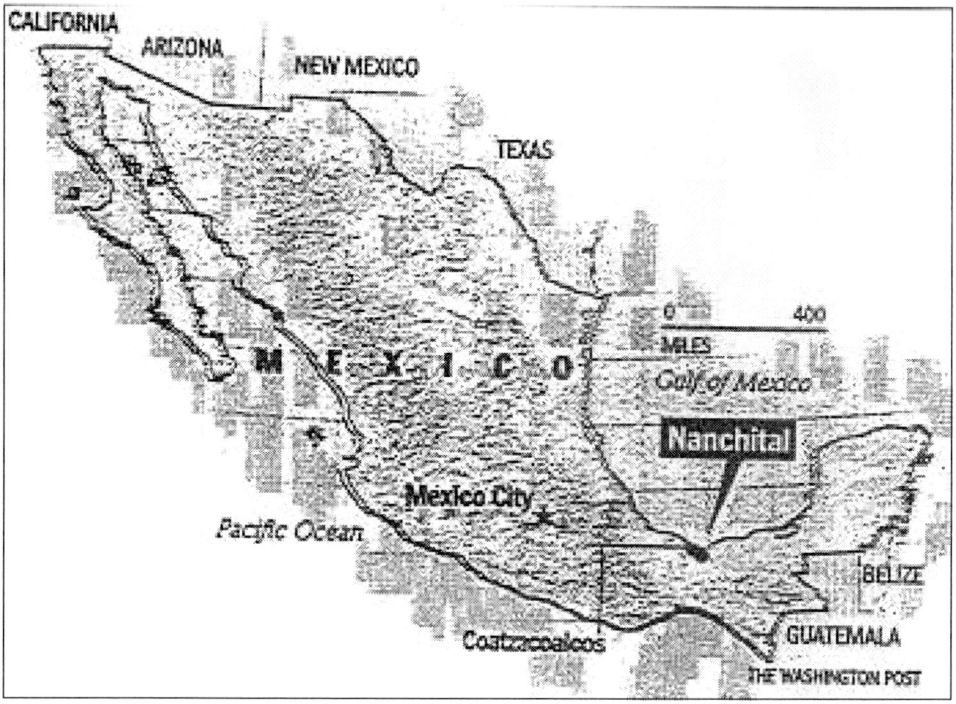

out favors to friends and punish enemies, protected by a system that thrived during seven decades of authoritarian, one-party rule in Mexico. „It's like a medieval royal court where the king sits there, people line up to see him, and he makes all the decisions," said historian Lorenzo Meyer of the Colegio de Mexico in Mexico City. President Vicente Fox, elected two years ago after campaigning against corruption, is trying to establish a justice system based on laws, not on the arbitrary decisions of powerful individuals. But local bosses remain a powerful obstacle to those efforts. As federal authorities try to tear down old castles of corruption, the most explosive scandal is known as Pemexgate. The government alleges that $170 million in Pemex money was illegally diverted to political purposes. They are investigating Pemex and union leaders, including Hernandez, for allegedly shoveling money to Institutional Revolutionary Party, or PRI, for its unsuccessful 2000 presidential campaign.

During the PRI's 71-year rule of Mexico, which ended with Fox's election, it used Pemex as its not-so-secret piggy bank, Meyer said. He said it skimmed off vast amounts of oil money for campaigns and favors, and the looting of Pemex became part of the political culture. Many here say that is a key reason a country with such vast oil resources can't adequately feed and educate its people, more than half of whom live in poverty. Oil workers have also filed federal complaints alleging that Hernandez has siphoned off money from a union bus transportation business. They claim he has bought houses and cars and enriched himself with funds that should have gone to workers' housing, loans and pensions. Hernandez declined repeated requests for an interview for this article. A local union spokesman said Hernandez ordered the union to provide „no help" to reporters. A spokesman for the national union said Hernandez and the other union leaders accused in Pemexgate have done nothhing illegal, and he accused Fox of conductting a „political witch hunt." Officials from Pemex, Mexico's largest company, declined to comment.

On the streets of Nanchital, many people interviewed said they were only vaguely aware of the allegations against Hernandez, which have gone mostly unreported in the local press. „He buys reporters," said Jorge Caceres, who covers the union for a local newspaper. Caceres said the union helps pay reporters' long-distance phone bills at a union-run press room, and Hernandez has handed checks for as much as $600 to reporters who earn as little as $2 a story. Caceres said he had never taken Hernandez's money but knows many reporters who have. „You don't have freedom of expression," he said, „if you cannot criticize the person who is giving you money." Workers here who have created a dissident wing of the union to protest what they see as its abuses say that Hernandez laughs at efforts to hold him accountable while, they say, looting the union for himself and the PRI.

„He does whatever he wants with the money, and nobody can touch him," Canepa, the retired oil worker, said. „People tolerate it and don't demand their rights because they are afraid. If they did, they would get no loans, no raises, no jobs. We're in a circle that we can't get out of." The union's local chapter receives millions of dollars in annual dues, as well as fees paid by Pemex and profits from union-owned businesses. Hernandez has no legal obligation to tell rank-and-file members how he spends it. By tradition, powerful union bosses have no check on their authority to spend union funds as they please. „You simply cannot imagine how much money he has," said Elda Luz Palma Martinez, who worked with Hernandez in the union's leadership for five years in the 1990s. Speaking in her small home here, with a concrete floor and few furnishings, Palma said Hernandez forced her out for questioning his financial dealings. Palma said she saw Hernandez regularly hand union money to PRI candidates. She said other money simply went missing. „He lives totally above the law," she said. Federal Authorities investigating Hernandez have not filed any charges against him. PRI officials are openly discussing plans to place him in the national Congress next year, where he would be immune from prosecution.

Many here say Hernandez is one of Mexico's many „untouchables." Martin Aguilar, a researcher at the University of Veracruz, said most workers are afraid to criticize him. Others, he said, are so accustomed his power that they see nothing wrong with it.

„Corruption is tolerated as long as the union provides them with jobs, schools, health care and other benefits," Aguilar said. It's a balance that has long existed here. Hernandez's predecessor, Francisco „Chico" Balderas, spent millions of dollars on the town. People here say he too was corrupt, but that he was also beloved because of his generosity. Union leaders used to be even more powerful, said Arturo Alcalde, a labor lawyer in Mexico City. After major oil deposits were discovered in Mexico in the 1970s, union bosses were so strong that they controlled even the most intimate corners of everyday life: They arranged marriages, named babies and decided on punish-ments for cheating husbands.

Old-style bosses silenced dissent by bashing heads, Alcalde. said: Today, he said: they are just as nefarious, but more subtle: They keep people loyal by providing jobs and benefits, smiling to their faces while stealing behind their backs. „They are just like the Mafia," he said. „They offer people protection, and they are corrupt." When Balderas died in 1991, Hernandez won a power struggle and was elected to lead the union. Analysts said it has been under his control since, despite his stints in other positions, including Congress, when one of his loyalists nominally served as union head. Julio Cesar Rodriguez, a leader of dissidents who claim 500 workers locally and 9,000 nationwide, said workers are suffering. He said corruption within the union had robbed workers of money that should be used for loans for homes or to send their children to college. And he said it should have been used to improve the town where they live.

Rodriguez said Nanchital was once a „model city," but that since Hernandez took over, it has steadily deteriorated. The postcard-pretty town square is filled with teenagers eating tacos from a stand in the red-tile-roofed gazebo or using computers at the „American Internet" cafe. But just a few blocks away, the roads are poorly paved, and many houses are crumbling. Workers complain that their salaries have not kept up with inflation, and Hernandez is stingy with home loans that were once plentiful. Rodriguez said many workers can't afford to buy houses that the union built for them. Mayor Ricardo Castelo Castillo said Hernandez has spent less on the town than his predecessor did, but only because the union has less money now. But even Castelo, one of Hernandez's closest allies, paused when asked if Hernandez had stolen workers' money. „I don't want to say that he steals or he doesn't steal money," he said. „I don't know about that."

Rodriguez said oil workers see the obvious when they look around their worndown town. „If the benefits that Pemex gives to the union for the workers actually reached them, the workers would live better," he said. „But the benefits don't arrive. The only one who benefits is Hernandez. If there were an honest use of the money, the streets of Nanchital would be paved with gold." The system of local bosses, who are known as caciques, was introduced by the Spanish conquistadors 500 years ago as a way for a relatively small number of Spaniards to control many Mexicans. When the PRI was created after the Mexican Revolution, in the early 20th century, its leaders realized that the local strongmen could be as useful to them as they had been to the Spanish,said Meyer, the historian.

These people helped build the PRI into the 20th century's longest-running political machine. The PRI gave caciques government money, and they handed out milk for babies, seed for corn fields, cash for school pencils. In exchange, recipients were counted as automatic votes for the PRI. The disloyal were cut off from perks and jobs, and, in some cases, punished violently. Although the party was defeated by Fox, the PRI system survives in many areas. The PRI still controls half the nation's governorships and mayors and the leadership of many unions. The long-standing connections between the former ruling party, the oil monopoly and the union endure. Hernandez is president of the PRI in Coatzacoalcos, the nearby oil town where he lives. He also sits on Pemex's 11-member board, a group that includes four of Fox's cabinet members. Despite the investigations, Hernandez moves about as he always has. He rides in his chauffeur-driven Chevrolet Suburban to the popular restaurant his family owns, to the PRI offices and to union headquarters.

And every morning, crowds looking for favors line up at his home in his expensive neighborhood. One recent morning, Adela Hernandez waited like a sad statue beneath her umbrella, her bright blue dress and thin shoes soaked through. Her husband, an oil worker, died five years ago, and his pension payments suddenly stopped. With her money running out, she said she is desperate. So the 62-year-old widow, who is no relation to the union boss, has come here twice a week for two years, lining up with the others to plead her case to Hernandez as he leaves his house in the morning. „I know he is going to help me," she said. If Hernandez didn't restore her only source of income, however, she said she had nowhere else to turn - no one else has the power to help her.

At about 8 a.m., a guard told her and a dozen others waiting in the rain that the boss would be out soon. One young woman, who declined to give her name, said her father was retiring from Pemex, and she wanted to inherit his union job and become a Pemex accountant. Under union rules, jobs can be passed to a relative - but only if Hernandez approves. „It's so hard to see him at the union office," she said, as the sun rose over Hernanndez's house, outfitted with Christmas lights and surveillance cameras. „He's so busy with all the things he's in charge of. It's easier to come here. But now we just have to wait until he wakes up." Asked if she was bothered by allegations against Hernandez, she looked surprised. „No," she said. „The senor helps us a lot. If we need something he gives it to us."

Hernandez's chauffeur pulled up. He ran past the waiting workers through the puddles, carrying a package of soft, hot tortillas for his boss's breakfast. That was a good sign, everyone agreed, because Hernandez usually comes out right after he eats. They know his every move, like well-informed students of the local monarchy. An hour later, however, Hernandez's wife appeared with a bodyguard holding her umbrella. As she stepped into her car, she told the crowd that her husband wouldn't be granting any audiences that moming.«

2008: HURRICANE KILLED MANY PEOPLE ON HAITI

Patrick Farrell, *Miami Herald*

The photographer visited Haiti four times during the 2008 hurricane season, capturing scenes of the dead and the survivors of a series of storms that generated devastating flooding across the impoverished nation. He was in Haiti the night Hurricane Ike - the fourth storm to hit there in a month - washed across the already overwhelmed countryside, drowning even more homes and people. Farrell's published photographs, along with stories by *Miami Herald* Caribbean correspondent Jacqueline Charles and *Herald* reporter Trenton Daniel, were credited with helping raise international awareness of the storms' toll on Haiti and its people's struggle to survive in the aftermath. In all, more than 800 Haitians died and more than 1 million were left homeless by the unrelenting series of storms.

„Patrick's photography is the most provocative and at times disturbing storytelling work that I have seen or edited", the *Miami Herald*'s director of photography said, and he added: „It is exceptional documentary photography with a purpose - to chronicle the misery and headache of the Haitian people." He sent a package of 19 black-and-white photographs to the Pulittzer Prize jurors, entitled „A People in Despair: Haiti's Year without Mercy." The images range from the flooded streets of Gonaives, to the aftermath of a storm-related school collapse in Port-au-Prince. The jurors, in their report of March 3, 2009, stated: „This is a remarkable, heartbraking body of work that is all too real... Every frame is beautifully shot and impeccably composed, full of movement... These photos reach the level of art, again and again... His photographs are unforgettable." The Board agreed and gave the Pulitzer Prize for Breaking News Photography to Patrick Farrell of the *Miami Herald*.

Patrick Farrell was born on July 1, 1959, near South Miami. In 1981 he graduated with a BA degree in television and film production from the University of Miami. He started his career working for several small community papers in Florida before he became a staff photographer for the *Miami Herald* in 1987. His assignments took him to Turkey, Haiti, Cuba and several Latin American countries. After winning the Pulitzer Prize in 2009, Farrell returned to Haiti and covered the 2010 earthquake. Following now are several of his award-winning photos:

EVERYTHING LOST

A Haitian young boy struggles to rescue a stroller from the wreck of his family home after Tropical Storm Hanna struck the town of Gonaives where people lost most of their personal belongings.

Patrick Farrell: September 5, 2008

KILLED CHILD

Haitian father Frantz Samedi holds his lifeless 5-years-old daughter, Tamasha Jean, who died when Hurricane Ike's flood waters swept children and the elderly from their homes in the small town of Cabaret.

Patrick Farrell: September 8, 2008

MEDICAL CATASTROPHE

Pregnant Haitian women experience contradictions and labor pains in the driveway of a Doctors Without Borders maternity clinic, waiting for a bed inside while friends and family peer through the fence.

Patrick Farrell: September 8, 2008

2010: FACETS OF A TERRIBLE EARTHQUAKE ON HAITI

Carol Guzy, Nikki Kahn und Ricky Carioti, *Washington Post*

The disaster was a catastrophic magnitude 7.0 earthquake, with an epicenter near the town of Leogane, approximately 25 kilometres west of Haiti's capital Port-au-Prince. The earthquake occured on January 12, 2010, and within the next two weeks at least 52 aftershocks measuring 4.5 or greater had been recorded. An estimated three million people were affected by the quake. Death toll estimates range from 100.000 to about 160.000,to Haitian government figures from 220.000 to 316.000. The government also estimated that 250.000 residences and 30.000 commercial buildings had collapsed or were severely damaged. The nation's history of national debt, prejudicial trade policies by other countries and foreign intervention into national affairs, contributed to the existing poverty and poor housing conditions that increased the death toll from the disaster. On January 22 the United Nations noted that the emergency phase was drawing to close and on the following day, the Haitian government officially called off the search for survivors.

Journalists from all over the world rushed to Haiti to cover the diaster and its aftermath. Among the many reporters, three photographers of the *Washington Post* tried to do an outstanding job, led by three-times Pulitzer Prize winner Carol Guzy, born on March 7, 1956, in Bethlehem, Pennsylvania. She became graduated from the Northampton County Area Community College. After having served an internship at the *Miami Herald* she was engaged by the newspaper as a staff photographer and earned several prizes. In 1988 she moved to the *Washington Post*. Guzy was accompanied in Haiti by Nikki Kahn, born in Guayana. She earned an M.A. degree in 2004 and became a photographer at the *Washington Post* in 2005. Third member of the photographer team was Ricky Carioti, born in 1968 in Washington, D.C. After having worked as a free-lance photographer, in 2005 he became a full-time member of the *Washington Post*. When the Haiti pictures of the three photographers came to the attention of the Pulitzer Prize jurors, they praised in their report of March 9, 2011: „The team overcame the challenges of horrific conditions to produce this coverage.“ All three earned the Pulitzer award. Following are samples of their work:

CHAOTIC SITUATION

Desperate Haitian survivors take goods from stores in the market area of Port-au-Prince as chaos erupts in the streets. The price of what few staples remain in the city had soared. fuel supplies had dwindled, and thousand of Haitians had abandoned listing homes for squalid tent cities springing up in even the smallest public spaces. Public parks and tennis courts filled with families carrying what possessions they had left.

Carol Guzy, January 16, 2010

CHOLERA EPIDEMIC

Sylvia Frederic tries in vain to rush her son Johnny Frederic, 26, to the hospital before he dies in her arms. Cholera can sause vomiting and diarrhea so severe that it kill from dehydration in hours. The disease had not been seen in Haiti for decades, and many people did not know about it.

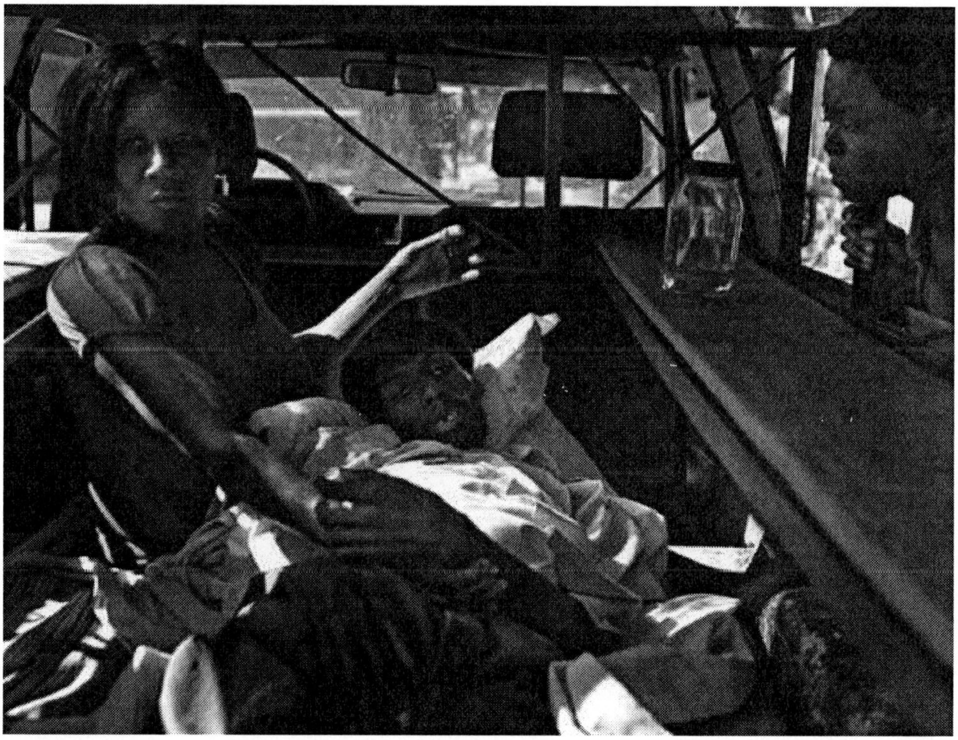

Nikki Kahn, November 25, 2010

SQUALID CONDITIONS

Months after the earthquake, a young boy washes in contaminated water at a tent camp near the severely damaged presidential place looms of Porto-au-Prince in the background. The delays in reconstruction reflect bureaucratic red tape in donor nations and the complexity of rebuilding the Western Hemispere's poorest country, which had little infrastructure, a snarled land-title system and a barely functioning government before the disaster.

Ricky Carioti, August 22, 2010

BIBLIOGRAPHY

Unpublished Materials

Media Exhibits

Brooklyn Daily Eagle Entry for Nelson Harding, 1928
Chicago Daily News Entry for Paul Scott Mowrer, 1929
New York Times Entry for John W. White et al., 1941
New York Times Entry for Arnaldo Cortesi, 1946
New York Daily News Entry for J. Martin/Philip Santora, 1959
United Press International Entry for Andrew Lopez, 1960
Miami News Entry for Harold V. Hendrix, 1963
Miami Herald Entry for Shirley Christian, 1981
Dallas Times-Herald Entry for James B. Dickman, 1983
Boston Globe Entry for Stan Grossfeld, 1985
Philadelphia Inquirer Entry for Larry C. Price, 1985
Miami Herald Entry for Carol Guzy/Michel du Cille, 1986
Miami Herald Entry for Liz Balmaseda, 1993
Washington Post Entry for Carol Guzy, 1995
New York Times Entry for Sam Dillon et al., 1998
Los Angeles Times Entry for Don Bartletti, 2003
Washington Post Entry for Kevin Sullivan/Mary Jordan, 2003
Miami Herald Entry for Patrick Farrel, 2009
Washington Post Entry for C. Guzy/N. Kahn/R. Carioti, 2010

Jury Statements

„Editorial Cartoon“ Jury Report, March 20, 1928
„Correspondence“ Jury Report, March 16, 1929
„Meri torious Public Service“ Jury Report, May 1, 1941
„Correspondence“ Jury Report, April 1, 1946
„International Reporting“ Jury Report, March 12, 1959
„Photography“ Jury Report, March 1, 1960
„International Reporting“ Jury Report, March 8, 1963
„International Reporting“ Jury Report, March 4, 1981
„Feature Photography“ Jury Report, March 8, 1983
„Feature Photography“ Jury Report, March 5, 1985
„Spot News Photography“ Jury Report, March 5, 1985
„Spot News Photography“ Jury Report, March 4, 1986
„Commentary“ Jury Report, March 3, 1993

„Spot News Photography" Jury Report, March 7, 1995
„International Reporting" Jury Report, March 4, 1998
„Feature Photography" Jury Report, March 5, 2003
„International Reporting" Jury Report, March 7, 2003
„Breaking News Photography" Jury Report, March 3, 2009
„Breaking News Photography" Jury Report, March 9, 2011

Published Materials

Allison, Graham: Conceptual models and the Cuban Missile Crisis, Santa Monica, Calif., 1968.

Armstrong, Robert/Shenk, Janet: El Salvador - TheFace of Revolution, Boston, Mas., 1982.

Barry, Tom/Browne, Harry/Sims, Beth: Crossing the line. Immigrants, economic integration, and drug enforcement on the U.S.-Mexico border, Albuquerque, N.M., 1994.

Bonachea, Rolando E./Valdes, Nelson P. (Eds.): Cuba in revolution, Garden City, N.Y., 1972.

Bushnell, David: The Making of Modern Colombia, Los Angeles 1993.

Fischer, Heinz-D.: Outstanding International Press Reporting. Pulitzer Prize Winning Articles in Foreign Correspondence, 5 vols., Berlin - New York 1984-2000.

Fischer, Heinz-D.: Picture Coverage of the World - Pulitzer Prize Winning Photos, Berlin 2011.

Fischer, Heinz-D./Fischer, Erika J.: Der Pulitzer-Preis - Konkurrenten, Kämpfe, Kontroversen, Berlin 2007.

Fischer, Heinz-D./Fischer, Erika J.: The Pulitzer Prize Archive, vol. 4: International Reporting 1928-1985, Munich - London - New York - Oxford - Paris, 1987.

Fernandez, Damian J.: Cuban Studies since the Revolution, Gainesville, Fl., 2005.

Girard, Philippe: Haiti - The Tumuluous History, New York 2010.

Goldenberg, Boris: The Cuban revolution and Latin America, New York 1965.

Hamnett, Brian R.: A Concise History of Mexico, London 1999.

Hohenberg, John: Foreign Correspondence - The Great Reporters and Their Times, New York - London 1964.

Hohenberg, John: The Pulitzer Prizes - A History of the Awards in Books, Drama, Music, and Journalism, New York - London 1974.

Hohenberg, John: The Pulitzer Prize Story - News Stories, Editorials, Cartoons and Pictures, New York - London 1959.

Hohenberg, John: The Pulitzer Prize Story II - Award-Winning News Stories, Columns, Editorials, Cartoons and News Pictures, 1959-1980, New York 1980.

Jackson D. Bruce: Castro, the Kremlin and communism in Latin America, Baltimore, Md., 1969.

Karol, Kewes S.: Guerillas in power - the course of the Cuban revolution, New York 1970.

Lupsha, Peter A./Schlegel, Kip: The political economy of drug trafficking. The Herrera organization (Mexico & the United States), Albuquerque, N.M., 1980.

Mallin, Jay: Fortress Cuba. Russia`s American base, Chicago 1965.

Montgomery, Tommie Sue: Revolution in El Salvador - Origins and Evolution , Bolder, Col., 1982.

Pachter, Henry Macimilian: Collision course - the Cuban Missile Crisis and coexistence, New York 1963.

Rennie, Ysabel F.: The Argentine Republic, New York 1945.

Ruiz, Ramón Eduardo: Cuba - the making of a revolution, Amherst., Mass., 1968.

Salazar-Carrillo: Oil and Development in Venezuela, New York 2004.

Solomon, Joel A.: Implausible deniability. State responsibility for rural violence in Mexico, New York 1997.

Street, John: Artigas and the Emancipation of Uruguay, Cambridge 1959.

Toro, María Celia: Mexico`s „war“ on drugs. Causes and consequences, Boulder 1995.

Villalobos, Joaquin: The War in El Salvador. The Current Situation and Outlook for the Future, San Francisco 1986.

White, Christopher M.: The History of El Salvador, Westport, Conn., 2009.